CW01572833

Becoming Diasporically Moroccan

ENCOUNTERS

Series Editors: **Jan Blommaert**, *Tilburg University, The Netherlands*, **Ben Rampton**, *Kings College London, UK*, **Anna De Fina**, *Georgetown University, USA*, **Sirpa Leppänen**, *University of Jyväskylä, Finland* and **James Collins**, *University at Albany/SUNY, USA*

The Encounters series sets out to explore diversity in language from a theoretical and an applied perspective. So the focus is both on the linguistic encounters, inequalities and struggles that characterize post-modern societies and on the development, within sociocultural linguistics, of theoretical instruments to explain them. The series welcomes work dealing with such topics as heterogeneity, mixing, creolization, bricolage, cross-over phenomena, and polylingual and polycultural practices. Another high-priority area of study is the investigation of processes through which linguistic resources are negotiated, appropriated and controlled, and the mechanisms leading to the creation and maintenance of sociocultural differences. The series welcomes ethnographically oriented work in which contexts of communication are investigated rather than assumed, as well as research that shows a clear commitment to close analysis of local meaning making processes and the semiotic organization of texts.

Full details of all the books in this series and of all our other publications can be found on http://www.multilingual-matters.com, or by writing to Multilingual Matters, St Nicholas House, 31–34 High Street, Bristol BS1 2AW, UK.

ENCOUNTERS: 8

Becoming Diasporically Moroccan

Linguistic and Embodied Practices for Negotiating Belonging

Lauren Wagner

MULTILINGUAL MATTERS
Bristol • Blue Ridge Summit

DOI 10.21832/WAGNER8354

Library of Congress Cataloging in Publication Data
A catalog record for this book is available from the Library of Congress.
Names: Wagner, Lauren (Social Scientist) author.
Title: Becoming Diasporically Moroccan: Linguistic and Embodied Practices
   for Negotiating Belonging/Lauren Wagner.
Description: Bristol, UK; Blue Ridge Summit, PA: Multilingual Matters,
   2017. | Series: Encounters: 8 |
Includes bibliographical references and index.
Identifiers: LCCN 2017010343| ISBN 9781783098354 (hbk : alk. paper) | ISBN
   9781783098378 (epub) | ISBN 9781783098385 (kindle)
Subjects: LCSH: Moroccans—Europe—Ethnic identity. |
   Moroccans—Europe—Cultural assimilation. | Europe—Ethnic relations. |
   Moroccans—Europe—Languages. | Arabic language—Social aspects—Europe.
Classification: LCC D1056.2.M67 W35 2017 | DDC 305.892/764—dc23 LC record
available at https://lccn.loc.gov/2017010343

British Library Cataloguing in Publication Data
A catalogue entry for this book is available from the British Library.

ISBN-13: 978-1-78309-835-4 (hbk)

Multilingual Matters
UK: St Nicholas House, 31–34 High Street, Bristol BS1 2AW, UK.
USA: NBN, Blue Ridge Summit, PA, USA.

Website: www.multilingual-matters.com
Twitter: Multi_Ling_Mat
Facebook: https://www.facebook.com/multilingualmatters
Blog: www.channelviewpublications.wordpress.com

The policy of Multilingual Matters/Channel View Publications is to use papers that are natural, renewable and recyclable products, made from wood grown in sustainable forests. In the manufacturing process of our books, and to further support our policy, preference is given to printers that have FSC and PEFC Chain of Custody certification. The FSC and/or PEFC logos will appear on those books where full certification has been granted to the printer concerned.

Typeset by Nova Techset Private Limited, Bengaluru and Chennai, India.
Printed and bound in the UK by the CPI Books Group Ltd.
Printed and bound in the US by Edwards Brothers Malloy, Inc.

Contents

Acknowledgments

This book is the product of two decades of thinking about, moving within and becoming diasporic. Over that time, innumerable people have contributed to the printed result here in ways that may never be fully appreciated. The following individuals have generously given of their time, attention, feedback and support:

Abdelali Gala and family
Ahlame Rahmi
Alexandrine Barontini
Anonymous participant families A, B and C
Christine Deprez
James Collins
Jan Blommaert
Piia Varis

Transcription Conventions

xx	Inaudible
?	Intense rising intonation
,	Slight rising intonation
.	Intense falling intonation
/	Slight falling intonation
:	Elongated vowel or geminated consonant
bold	Emphasis
[	Overlap
(), (1.2)	Less than 0.2 s pause, pause timed in seconds
.hhh / hhh	Outbreath/inbreath
(( ))	Explanatory or descriptive remark
<___>	Uncertain transcription
normal	Main (matrix) language of conversation
<u>underline</u>	Secondary Moroccan language
italic	Secondary European language
___*	Usage error

In data transcripts of recorded talk, Moroccan Arabic speech is transcribed in Roman letters, following ISO 233 conventions. The sole exception is the letter jīm, ج, which is transcribed as 'j' instead of 'g' in reflection of Moroccan pronunciation. /g/ is a separate phoneme in Moroccan Arabic, reflecting velarization of the Arabic letter qaf, ق, or alternately the phonemic influence of Amazigh languages. Other letters not common in English are listed in the following table:

Character	Arabic letter	IPA symbol
ṯ	ث	θ
j	ج	d͡ʒ
ḥ	ح	ħ
ḫ	خ	x
ḏ	ذ	ð
š	ش	ʃ
ṣ	ص	sˤ
ḍ	ض	dˤ
ṭ	ط	tˤ
ẓ	ظ	ðˤ
ʿ	ع	ʕ
ġ	غ	ɣ
ʾ	ء	ʔ
ə	(short vowel)	ə

The remaining consonants follow English pronunciation. Long vowels and diphthongs have been simplified and standardized for ease of reading. Arabic words appearing in the text have been transcribed as they are most commonly written in Morocco. Within quoted fieldnotes, added text for clarification is enclosed in square brackets.

Introduction

> Not all those at the borders, such as tourists, migrants, or foreign nationals, are recognized as strangers; some will seem more 'at home' than others, some will pass through, with their passports extending physical motility into social mobility. There is no question posed about their origin. The stranger's genealogy in contrast is always suspect. The stranger becomes a stranger because of some trace of a dubious origin. Having the 'right' passport makes no difference if you have the wrong body or name: and indeed, the stranger with the 'right' passport might cause particular trouble, as the one who risks passing through. The discourse of 'stranger danger' reminds us that danger is often posited as originating from what is outside the community, or as coming from outsiders, those people who are not 'at home', and who themselves have come from 'somewhere elsewhere' (where the 'where' of this 'elsewhere' always makes a difference). The politics of mobility, of who gets to move with ease across the lines that divide spaces, can be re-described as the politics of who gets to be at home, who gets to inhabit spaces, as spaces that are inhabitable for some bodies and not others, insofar as they extend the surfaces of some bodies and not others. (Ahmed, 2007: 162)

Instead of flowing easily from one side of the border to the other and back, the bodies Ahmed describes above encounter friction. These bodies hesitate in interaction with borders, which frame them as strange when crossing, but strange in a specific way – the body does not match an assumed categorization made by the passport. Their genealogy, their locality, their place of home becomes suspect – a facet of simply being that they must negotiate in order to pass through.

As people migrate from place to place around the globe, more and more 'next generations' are born into a place where they both belong and do not belong – they are 'from' there, but also 'from' somewhere else. Increased access to modes of travel mean that we can be 'from' somewhere and regularly visit another place where we are 'from'. But sometimes, as Ahmed describes, those visits mean passing through borders where we are categorized: we become 'strangers', even if the passport says we are not.

I first encountered this phenomenon on a ferry boat between Algeciras, Spain and Tangier, Morocco, in July 1999. I was a person who precisely fit into a well-known category: an American college student, spending a summer backpacking through Europe. I was by myself for this leg of the trip, but found that I quickly met people on this boat: other European travelers, looking for adventure in Morocco, as well as Moroccan families living in Europe who were going 'home' for their summer holidays.

I was bowled over by the cacophony of voices I heard on that boat, speaking all varieties of European and Moroccan languages. I was surprised that there were so many people making this journey, since I had not known about the massive flow of Moroccan guestworker migration into Europe during the 1960s and 1970s. People who seemed to be like me – the budget travelers, at a time when there were no budget flights to Morocco – were a minority. The ferry was overflowingly full with Moroccans who seemed to be 'going home', yet who were definitely coming from homes in Europe. Although I was not yet an anthropologist, I wondered who these people were, where they were coming from, and how they found themselves on that boat.

Since then, I have crossed over on that ferry route several times: as a student of Arabic, as a researcher travelling independently for my Masters project, and along with a participating family in my PhD project. The boat is still a microcosm of Moroccan migration in Europe, where original migrants, now grandparents and great-grandparents, travel with their children and grandchildren between homes. It is a place where Moroccans from all different parts of Europe might meet each other, since many still travel by car overland from their European homes in order to spend their summer

Figure 1 Families on the ferry from Algeciras to Tangier, July 2008

holidays in Morocco. It is also a place where they encounter the border: when travelling by ferry to and from Morocco, passport control often takes place during the three-hour ride. Moroccans from all over must present their passports and national identity cards, and negotiate the type of encounter Ahmed describes above. They have to show that they are both strangers and not strangers – that they enter the country as Moroccans but leave the country as Europeans, with the right to live elsewhere.

Becoming Categorized

As much as the homeland is imagined as a place to reunite with one's 'roots' or imagined origins, for many visiting 'home' on vacation gives meaning to the sayings I hear repeated about this group: *'ni d'ici ni de là-bas'* (neither from here nor there), *'entre deux chaises'* (between two chairs), or even from Morocco as *'sahab el-kharij'* (friends from outside). All of these epithets embody some kind of dualistic paradox untenable over time. There is a feeling of being perpetually 'between' places, and never at rest anywhere.

That feeling is so common, and so recognizable to many North Africans in France, that it is the core subject of the song 'Entre Deux' quoted in Extract 1.1. This French-Arabic rap was written and performed by Bachir Baccour, a.k.a. Tunisiano, a French citizen of Tunisian origin. The lyrics evoke many of the themes of dislocation and instability that surface for post-migrant generation individuals visiting their ancestral homeland.

Extract 1.1 Lyrics from 'Entre Deux' by Sniper et al. (2003), translated by the author

Tunisiano, mon blasé	Tunisiano my handle
J'ai pour pays d'origine: la	I have for country of origin
France là où j'crèche	France, there where I was coddled
Où on m'reproche mes origins	where they reproach my origins
J'ai grandi loin de mon pays, on	I grew up far from my country
me l'a trop souvent reproché	and they have too often reproached me
On a trop souvent prétendu que	they have too often pretended
j'les avais trahis	that I betrayed them, "hey my ass
"Eh ma couille, ici c'est pas	here is not the homeland
l'bled où ça pue l'embrouille"	where it stinks of intrigue"
Et en scred même là-bas j'suis	and secrets even there I'm in shit
dans la merde	

C'est comme chaque été, dès que tu m'vois tu dis "<u>chkoune</u>"	it's like every summer when you see me you say <u>who</u>
Regard froid sifflotement, v'la l'etranger dans le saloon	cold looks shivers, there's the stranger in the salon
Monsieur Tounsi <u>smaht manich ji3ane</u>	Mr Tunisian <u>you understand I'm not hungry</u>
<u>Tek el hata ou chabhte bel 3ine tah l'jiraine</u>	<u>and you're eating till you're full with the eyes of the neighbors</u>
Ici un danger, la bas j'suis un intrus	here a danger, there I'm an intruder
Et là où j'aimerai m'ranger	and there where I'd like to put myself
J'suis vu comme un étranger	I'm seen as a stranger
Donc j'suis perdu, en plus j'suis pas le bienvenu	so I'm lost, and more I'm not welcome
Où on s'méfie des barbus d'Oussama à Robert Hue	where they are afraid of beards from Osama to Robert Hue
Toi aussi t'es dans mon cas؟ Un blême de pedigree	you too you're like me؟ a fault of pedigree
Vu que j'ai du mal à m'intégrer, que se soit ici ou là-bas	I can't integrate myself neither here nor over there

This verse excerpted from the song lyrics[1] establishes some of the ways in which negative frameworks of belonging are practiced: the protagonist is questioned by the French, reproached by Tunisians, and feels himself unable to integrate in either place. The remainder of the song elaborates on these themes, with one verse in Tunisian Arabic and another in French, finally identifying all like migrant groups in France – Tunisian, Algerian, Moroccan, and others – who share in this affect of dislocation.

As an artistic depiction of the experience of going 'home' for the summer holidays, 'Entre Deux' illustrates two points that are key discussions I seek to open in this book.

First, the fact of visiting the diasporic home is not a simple 'return to origins'; it involves negotiations that refract on senses of belonging in both the diasporic home and the country of residence. The holidays are imbued with a sense of attachment to the diasporic home, in this case Morocco, and a troubling of that attachment through the sense of being rejected by those living there.

Secondly, this depiction connotes how negotiations of belonging take place along visually perceived dimensions, like visually perceived embodiment, which interlace and interact with other dimensions, like communicative practices. Tunisiano is recognized as a 'stranger' and 'intruder' by his neighbors, eyeing him suspiciously each summer when he arrives. As he expresses, in both Arabic and French, they call him Arab and they call him foreigner – an 'intruder of the same skin color'. He is recognized as Arab by his skin and perhaps by his linguistic abilities, but recognized as foreign by his actions and accent.

This dynamic of negotiating belonging in relation to one's passport, or one's skin and accent among other means of categorization, are familiar to diasporic visitors (DVs) entering Morocco. Coming from Moroccan families, living in diasporic homelands (France, Belgium or The Netherlands in this case), their sense of 'being-Moroccan' is challenged when traveling to Morocco, from crossing the border to other everyday interactions with people and places in their territorial homeland. Even having the 'right' passport, as they nearly all do, they find their sense of belonging as part of Morocco is distanced by their own distance from residing in the homeland.

On the ferry crossing from Algeciras to Tangier, I have observed many times how this negotiation happens as each passenger steps up to the customs officers processing entries. Every visitor to Morocco receives a unique number – I have one stamped in the back of my current passport and my expired passport, and every time I enter Morocco that number is recorded. Moroccan citizens are recorded by their national identity card number; the system assumes that if you are 'Moroccan', then you have a Moroccan national identity card. If you live outside Morocco, then you have to make a trip to your embassy – often a costly and time-consuming affair – in order to maintain your ID card. I have watched over and over again how individuals step up to the desk to have their passport stamped for entry, and must negotiate being 'Moroccan' or not, based on having an ID card, or knowing their national identity card number. One of my research participants, in fact, entered as 'Belgian' because she had lost her ID card. Even while she spoke Moroccan Arabic with the officer, who acknowledged that she is a citizen, he stamped her as a visitor, with the same type of visitor ID number in her Belgian passport as I have in my American passport.

These small instances of classification, or categorization, all contribute to an experience of what it means to be 'Moroccan' or to be 'diasporically Moroccan' for migrant-origin European-Moroccans who took part in this research. During their annual summer visits, 'being-Moroccan' becomes an attractor in assemblage (DeLanda, 2006), a categorial ideal-type, shaped through dimensions and practices of embodiment that emerge in the encounters DVs have with resident Moroccans. I argue that this category exerts considerable force because of the tension between their materially 'Moroccan' bodies – visually categorizable as 'Moroccan' – and their materially and expressively 'non-Moroccan' corporeality. They belong because of their 'Moroccan' bodies, lineages, families and attachments, yet do not belong because of their 'non-Moroccan', 'European' habits, preferences, sensibilities, speech and ways of being in and through their skins.

I do not, however, want to accept this problematic 'betweenness' as the final definition for 'being diasporic'. Instead, this book is concerned with how DVs reconcile this duality in interaction by negotiating the ways in which they are categorized through embodied and linguistic practices of belonging. It is also about how these categories of 'Moroccan' and 'non-Moroccan' are themselves malleable, and are changing in response to the way DVs and others engage with them. So, the subject of this book is not 'being diasporic', but becoming-diasporic: exploring how the practices, interactions, experiences and encounters of people who participated in this research emerge into vibrant categorizations of 'diasporicness' that change what it means to be 'Moroccan' both in Europe and in Morocco, and are becoming more recognizable and more solidified with every return visit.

An Ethnography of the Summer Holidays

In order to explore this intersection of migration, diaspora and practice, the following chapters engage theoretically and methodologically with cultural anthropology, human geography and sociolinguistics. At its core, this is an ethnography of the summer holiday as a timespace of encounter between diasporic and resident Moroccans. I used the anthropological method of ethnography to address how post-migrant generation diasporic visitors negotiate this double sense of attachment and distance to a place – related to both sociolinguistic and geographical discourses of that term – through their linguistic and embodied communicative practices while in Morocco. The ethnographic data, including observed practices as well as recorded interactions, reflect these practices as I observed them taking place during the summers of 2007 and 2008, with additional ethnographic contextual background from before and after these two seasons gathered through interviews and discussions with participants in Europe and in Morocco.

Throughout this book, I frequently use scare quotes, or single quotations around words that relate to categorizational identities. This grammatical form is often discouraged in academic written work, but I am using these purposefully, to remind the reader as frequently as necessary that such things as 'Moroccanness' or 'Europeanness' are always in process, unfixed, and contradictory. As I present this snapshot of becoming-diasporic as I observed it during this project, the 'Moroccanness' I observed will have shifted since then, and the scare quotes should signal that each iteration of 'identity' – as 'local' or 'tourist' or as 'Moroccan' or 'European' – inevitably hinges upon the time and place when it happens. I am never making claims about what it means to be Moroccan; I am only making claims about how becoming 'Moroccan' happened in this moment.

To set the stage for the data, I present in Chapter 1 historical and linguistic contexts related to European presences in Morocco and Moroccan presences in Europe. Next, I argue in Chapter 2 the theoretical bases for my analysis, beginning from theories of nation and diaspora and moving towards assemblage and communicative practice. Included with these, I present the methodological frameworks for this research, based primarily in sociolinguistic and ethnomethodological approaches alongside ethnography.

The three following empirical chapters are incremental and cumulating explorations of how these categories operate through the interactions of participants in and with the homeland. Chapter 3, *Defining the Category*, explores how participants describe themselves and their interactions with others – their metaphorical and discursive ideas about 'Moroccanness' – as well as how I observed their interactions. This chapter addresses some of the specific markers that become identifiable and are discussed as indexing embodied and linguistic belonging in Morocco. Chapter 4, *Negotiating the Category*, turns towards micro-analysis of marketplace interactions. Examples in this chapter show how participants strategically use their embodied communicative resources to negotiate themselves as 'locally-Moroccan' in order to get what is perceived as the right price for goods – whether or not they succeed in ratifying themselves into that category. Finally, Chapter 5, *A New Category?* extends these analyses of embodied and linguistic interactions towards how participants attempt to belong as simply diasporically Moroccan, without reaching towards other categorial definitions.

In combination, these chapters move towards an impression of how this cyclical encounter of diasporic and local Moroccans during the summer holidays becomes one in which the shape of 'being-Moroccan' molds and shifts, incorporating new elements as it sheds old ones, and possibly approaching categorizations whereby diasporic generations can acquire some persistent sense of belonging at 'home'.

Note

(1) This representation incorporates user-produced Latinization of Arabic speech; see http://genius.com/Sniper-entre-deux-lyrics for the complete song. In addition, this site provides user-produced annotations translating Arabic to French and describing some of the pop culture references.

1 Pathways and Backgrounds

As with any story, this one has many paths that were taken and not taken, along with backgrounds that contour the variety of possible paths, leading up to the present day. This chapter presents several of the pathways important for understanding how, when I arrived on that ferry, I found the mass of Moroccan-origin passengers who were born and raised in Europe, traveling 'home' for their summer holidays.

The first layer in this background relates the postwar labor migration history between Morocco and the three European nations under discussion (France, Belgium and The Netherlands). This layer accounts for the presence of Moroccans with similar, comparable migration histories in these countries. Their migration histories created material and social pathways for the annual summer holiday visit to Morocco – now, along with certain other diasporic populations in Europe (Turkish in Germany or Portuguese in France, for example), practically an institutionalized annual exodus.

This annual summer visit sets the stage for the next layer of background: multilingual practices in Morocco. Migration-based multilingual configurations are enabled by intersections of codes that are official, national and regional; written and spoken; local or foreign; and practiced in the home or outside the home by post-migrant Moroccans. All of these configurations are possible in the diasporic population, and can become relevant to practices of diasporic visitors from Europe in interaction with others in public spaces in Morocco.

The last sociolinguistic layer contextualizes how the skills involved in *bargaining* – an everyday activity in Morocco – are also performative utterances that change the state of the world after the speech act has been accomplished. For diasporic visitors, demonstrating bargaining skill has potential material consequences for successful or unsuccessful interactions when they try to purchase goods. These material consequences reflect on how categories of belonging in bargaining become relevant to complex global discourses of value and economic power, which feed back into the first background of migration histories between Morocco and Europe and their contemporary economic impacts in Morocco.

All together, these layers present the driving perspective on the DVs whose practices will be described in the following chapters. They frame both how and why they became participants in this project, and some of the many 'identities' and belongings that shape them as interlocutors with others between Europe and Morocco.

Europe and Morocco

From Europe: Backgrounds from Protectorate to Independence

Morocco experienced a short occupation period compared to other colonized states: it was only under French 'protection' from 1912 to 1956. Yet, the relationship between Morocco and Europe prior to the French Protectorate is long and complex, extending far beyond colonial power (see Cohen & Hahn, 1966; Minca & Wagner, 2016; Pennell, 2000, for more detail).

For Moroccan languages and diaspora, one key ideology that emerged from the Protectorate emphasizes the differences in cultural attitudes and language between Arab and Amazigh people (or Imazighen) in Morocco. Historical evidence indicates that these groups integrated their lives in a different way before colonial intervention and probably would not have taken the same pathway without it (Geertz et al., 1979). Both patterns of linguistic diversity in Morocco and patterns of out-migration from Morocco to Europe reflect how ideological differentiations separate groups within Morocco, so that those separations extend outside Morocco.

Group differentiation and integration between Imazighen and Arabs in Morocco stretch back to Islamic conquest around the 8th century, and travel through different waves of migration from the Arab Middle East to North Africa since then (Barbour, 1965; Cohen & Hahn, 1966). By the time the French arrived in North Africa in the 19th century, both groups were followers of Islam but, according to ideologies reproduced in French colonial research, the Kabyle in Algeria (a specific branch of Imazighen) were descended from Christians and were therefore more amenable to conversion to a French model of life than Arabs (Pennell, 2000: 164–166).

Along with this religio-cultural reputation, these groups also had distinct linguistic practices through their maintenance of the various Amazigh dialects of Morocco. As shown in Figure 1.1, these linguistic group separations stretched along the main mountain ranges of Morocco from north to south. Protectorate leaders in Morocco tried to use these linguistic differences in the same way they had in Algeria. Successive governments, both French and Spanish, attempted to Christianize Amazigh populations and

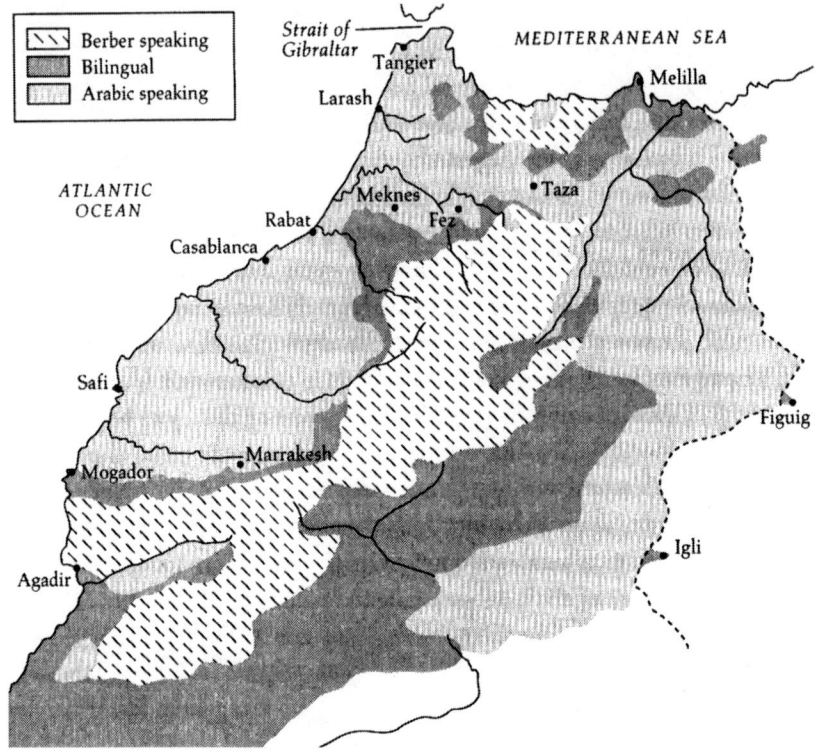

Figure 1.1 Protectorate map of linguistic diversity in Morocco
Source: (Charrad, 2001: 140, adapted from Montagne, 1973: 4).

integrate them into Western power structures (Pennell, 2000: 159). In fact, this attempt to divide and conquer contributed to pathways for political resistance: most revolutionary movements against French protection in Morocco emerged from the areas highlighted as Amazigh, which is still imbued with discursive legacies of resistance and rebellion in contrast to other regions.

Tendencies to rebellion under French rule created pathways differentiating Arab and Amazigh groups, which continued after the Morocco's relatively peaceful revolution in 1956. Post-Independence, predominantly during the reign of King Hassan II (1961–1999), Imazighen regions were again sources of civil unrest that resulted in government suppression. One of the more famous of these was punishing the use of Amazigh languages in public (Dalle, 2004) – symbolically a very violent way to suppress a group difference in order to build a single Arab 'nation' (Bourdieu, 1991).

These pathways, however, have been changing direction in recent years. Since the current king, Mohammed VI, took power in 1999, more democratic and inclusive policies have been instated which symbolically value Amazigh groups as part of the broader nation of Morocco (Howe, 2005). The Institut Royale de la Culture Amazighe (IRCAM) was created in 2001 to promote Amazigh language and culture. There are also now very public and symbolic inclusions of Amazigh identity on state-run television channels. These changes, however, arrived after a disproportionate number of Imazighen were encouraged to leave for Europe during the postwar guestworker migration period, in what was reportedly an effort by Hassan II to control this politically unruly population (de Haas, 2005a: 14).

Towards Europe: Pathways towards migration

Migration has been a nearly constant dynamic between Morocco and Europe, from before the Protectorate and beyond Independence. Throughout the Protectorate periods in the 20th century, traditional circular internal migration routes extended into other newly accessible parts of colonial France, including towards Algeria and to metropolitan France itself (de Haas, 2007). The significant movement of Moroccan populations into Europe did not begin until after Independence, in the context of bilateral labor migration contracts, through which European nations recruited 'guestworkers' to meet the demand of post-World War II industry.

Guestworkers were meant to fulfill short-term contracts and then return to their countries of origin. Beginning with Germany in May 1963, this sanctioned, encouraged and highly monitored migration extended to France, Belgium and The Netherlands over the next decade (Collyer, 2004: 16), finally ceasing officially in 1974. In 1965 there were about 30,000 Moroccans living in Europe; by 1975 the number had increased to an estimated 400,000 (de Haas, 2007: 46). Morocco, like many other newly independent states, looked to 'maximis[e] emigration in order to manage unemployment levels, acquire hard currency through remittances, and raise skill levels through returning migrants' (Baldwin-Edwards, 2005: 4).

Pathways created by migration: Connecting economies, places and generations

This short period of significant emigration has created several pathways and backgrounds which underpin the way diasporic visitors locate themselves in Morocco when they come 'home'. One significant pathway is economic: during the guestworker migration period, while the young independent state of Morocco experienced economic and political crisis, massive recruitment plus equally strong irregular migration meant that in some areas migrant remittances became a principal form of income (de Haas, 2005b) and 'the diaspora' has become part of how Morocco orients towards development (Sefrioui, 2005). Certain communities have since become accustomed to remittance flows of goods and cash from migrants as part of their economic sustenance (Agoumy, 2007).

Another form of this pathway directly connects far distant places through migrants. As recruitment of workers by companies abroad had been regionally focused (de Haas, 2005a), there are now in some places narrow associations between the sending town and the destination town. The Rif Mountains, for example, have a much higher proportion of migrants who left for Belgium or The Netherlands than the Souss area around Agadir and the Anti-Atlas mountains, where France is more prominent (de Haas, 2009). Despite the linguistic and cultural connection between the former Morocco and its former 'protector', just as many migrating Moroccans chose Belgium, The Netherlands or Germany as their destination as chose France. As a result, there are significant numbers of Moroccan-origin communities in France, rooted in pre- and post-Protectorate migration, along with significant numbers in communities in Belgium, The Netherlands and Germany, whose inception usually dates from the guestworker migration period.

These pathways also influence a background layer about the political, economic and cultural significance of this particular flow of migration in present-day Morocco. In 1973–1974, when this legitimate means of migration was discontinued by the European nations who had invited workers, the lockdown on movement had the effect of making the trajectory permanent (de Haas, 2006: 46–47). Instead of risking returning to unemployment in Morocco without the possibility of coming back to a job in Europe, migrants began to bring their families from Morocco to settle permanently.

This transition from guestworker to economic migrant with a family – or from a temporary to a permanent diaspora – prompted new forms of interaction between then King Hassan II and his subjects. Until the 1990s, migrants were viewed by the Moroccan government as an external population that would return, and associations were set up in Europe to monitor and influence their political adherence (Belguendouz, 1999). Since 1999, Mohammed VI has put in place much broader outreach, through welcoming projects providing aid to travelers, encouraging investment by changing regulations to be more favorable towards Moroccans abroad, and building new bureaucratic outposts in the EU (Brand, 2002, 2006). An intended effect of these projects is to create more facilities for incorporating the financial and human capital of migrants into the national economy (Bekouchi, 2003;

Sorensen, 2004). Although remittances are expected to fall off as migration slows and generations of Moroccan origin become integrated into other homes (Leichtman, 2002), they are nevertheless a major calculation in foreign aid received in Morocco (de Haas & Plug, 2006).

Today, Moroccans continue to migrate, both legally and illegally, into Europe, through shifting channels of entry. Legal migration from Morocco to Europe is still possible, primarily for those with social networks in an EU country, who can arrange marriages or family sponsorships. Yet even those pathways have become increasingly difficult, as EU states make parameters of allowable entry for family members more stringent. For example, in 2004 The Netherlands added a linguistic proficiency test, so that Dutch language education is now required before migration instead of after arrival, creating another barrier for potential migrants.

In recent years, primarily illegal migration through Morocco as a gateway from Africa – of Moroccan nationals as well as other African nationals – has become a major concern in policing EU borders (Alscher, 2005; Belguendouz, 2002). Because of the accessibility by water, more recent waves of illegal Moroccan migrants have arrived in Spain and Italy. Historically, these states have not had official links to Morocco to facilitate legal migration, but nevertheless they have significant Moroccan populations within their borders, often in service and agricultural industries (Bodega et al., 1995; Driessen, 1998). Moroccan migration has become a strongly contested political issue, in parallel with other nations like Turkey and Mexico whose migratory tendencies are labeled and construed as illicit (de Haas & Vezzoli, 2010). These flows and blockages of migratory movement contribute to the affective and discursive environment of negativity towards Moroccan communities in Europe, who struggle to achieve political and social stability as rightful residents in these states.

Backgrounds of diasporic communities: Stigmas of being Moroccan in Europe

Moroccan presence in Europe has evolved enormously since the waves of guestworker migrants. Much like counterpart flows of labor migrants in Europe and in North America, these families face challenges in seeking and settling into productive lives, from stereotyping and stigmatization to barriers to entry into education, housing and labor mobility (Crul & Vermeulen, 2003). A few characteristics are generalized across the political, economic and social backgrounds of Moroccan communities in the different European states where they have settled, whereas other characteristics are unique to particular states or communities.

Broadly, Moroccans are usually counted among stigmatized minority migrant groups, and are commonly subjects of negative effects of that stigmatization, including racialized and ethnicized discrimination (see Lesthaeghe, 2000; Manço, 1999; Ouali, 2004, in relation to Belgium; Césari, 2003; Guénif Souilamas, 2000; Lacoste-Dujardin, 1992; Lepoutre, 1997; Tribalat, 1995, 1996, in relation to France; Bos & Fritschy, 2006; Buitelaar, 2007; van Amersfoort & van Heelsum, 2007, in relation to The Netherlands). As post-migrant generation Moroccans are generally among the lower income residents in these places, their socialization into their communities of residence is not unlike that of other 'working class' groups (Willis, 1977). Place-based or locality-based identifiers are often core attributes for post-migrant generation members of the community (Césari et al., 2001; Melliani & Laroussi, 1998). In fact, as many families were settled in state-funded low-income housing, geographic ghettoization has encouraged the exaggeration of difference between the tightly bordered Moroccan community (or collectively oppressed migrant community) and outsiders to it (Lepoutre, 1997; Silverstein, 2004). Religious difference also plays an increasingly important role in the insulation of the predominantly Muslim community (Bistolfi & Zabbal, 1995; Césari, 1994; Maréchal et al., 2003; Sayyid, 2000) from the predominantly Christian hegemony that crosses national borders in Europe.

Some differences in Moroccan communities from state to state are due to particular structures of governance and political activity in each place. For example, the majority of individuals identifying as 'Moroccan' can also claim Moroccan citizenship, which is passed genealogically, regardless of place of birth. Yet because of variations in systems of nationality and citizenship in different European states, and over successive political movements, there is no uniform model of official national identity for post-migrant generation Moroccans. Some obtained citizenship in the European state at birth, some at age of majority and some not at all, depending on their parents' status, their year of birth and the country into which they were born. This lack of uniformity creates enormous difficulty in making an accurate estimate of the size of the Moroccan population in different states, especially in efforts to sort members by generation (Fondation Hassan II & IOM, 2003; Héran et al., 2002; Simon, 1999; Tribalat, 1995).

Another significant difference is found in debates on religious participation and in national ideologies of the role of religion in public life. Islam in France has received attention in public debate in a formulation very different from that in The Netherlands or Belgium (see chapters in Bistolfi & Zabbal, 1995; Césari & McLoughlin, 2005; Modood et al., 2006, for detailed discussions by country). The mixture of migrant groups in each nation-state is relevant to this dynamic. Whereas Islamic religious subjectivities in France became more prominent in a context of colonial independence and violent involvement with Algeria, their onset in Belgium and The Netherlands is linked with the growth of the Turkish Muslim community alongside the Moroccan one. Adherence to Islam has taken on a different character in each national public debate, depending on attitudes towards and ideologies of the role of religion in the public sphere and shifting with notable events that challenge existing systems. In the years since this research took place, these orientations have turned, for some communities, towards increasingly violent measures, including the recruitment of Moroccan-origin Europeans into jihadist groups (*The Economist*, 2015).

In terms of the pattern of migration and settlement of Moroccans into these three states, Belgium and The Netherlands can be grouped to some extent into a separate set of backgrounds and pathways from that of France. France has famously adopted a republican model that effaces any legal reference to ethnicity among its citizenry. Yet, equally famously, ethnic distinctions are a source of discrimination and dissent, as not all groups assimilate easily into the French model of citizenship (Noiriel, 1988; Tribalat, 1996).

Additionally, historical links between Morocco and France create an atmosphere distinct from the relationship between Morocco and Belgium or The Netherlands. Moroccan communities in significant numbers have existed nearly twice as long in France as elsewhere, and Moroccan histories are embedded in the *métropole* through the aftereffects of colonization. Furthermore, the broader North African community of Algerian and Tunisian migrants creates a *maghrebi* (North African) basis for belonging, which includes shared elements such as similar linguistic, familial and religious practices as well as histories of colonization and independence. In fact, French research often groups the three nationalities together (Bekkar *et al.*, 1999; Lacoste-Dujardin, 1992), treating them as one *maghrebi* community.

Across Belgium and The Netherlands, Moroccans shared prominent parallel flows of migration with each other. These flows were also shared with Turkish communities who arrived simultaneously as labor migrants, but whose incorporation has been characterized as more successful (see special issue of *International Migration Review*, edited by Crul & Vermeulen, 2003). Moroccan communities in Belgium and The Netherlands are also linked by the Dutch language, as the majority of Belgian-Moroccans are from Flemish areas and, like others in Flanders, might consume media flows in Dutch or in Flemish. Moroccans in both of these European states tend to come from the north of Morocco, therefore often sharing a regional 'home' referent as well. Additionally, The Netherlands and Belgium pursued policies that enabled migrant communities to maintain insulated cultural practices (e.g. Bos & Fritschy, 2006; Ouali, 2004) without ostensibly requiring assimilation or conformity to a national model of public identity. Moroccans, like other migrant groups, are counted and monitored in terms of their educational achievement, and their perceived assimilation, integration, or isolation from broader national ideologies.

Each of these national patterns has had effects that are distinct at an individual level, but has also created some similar patterns of diasporic 'Moroccanness' for specific pathways of guestworker migration. In all three cases, national origin might be felt as a stigmatized attribute; in all of them Islamic religious practice created rifts between the Moroccan community and the dominant national community. Moreover, the different models of assimilation and/or integration have achieved mixed results of harmony and division in all three states.

One factor that cuts across these distinctions – an extension of the pathways begun in the Protectorate – is the emergence of Amazigh nationalism. The links between Moroccan and Algerian communities in France are a key background to this pathway, as Kabyle activism emerged with particular force in France as a safe haven in the wake of movements for Arabization in Algeria (Chaker, 1998). As Kabyle nationalism became more prominent, a parallel movement of Moroccan Amazigh activism gained strength, but not necessarily as a 'transnational' movement. The dispersion of Moroccan Amazigh populations of different regional origins into migratory flows towards different nation-states makes an international mass of a Moroccan Amazigh 'nation' less likely. Yet smaller, region-specific groups, encouraged by connectivity through online forums, have developed into a vocal movement. The support recently gained for Amazigh languages and cultures in Morocco adds momentum to these organizations, which are often concerned with the maintenance of language and cultural practice in diaspora (Rachik, 2006).

In summary, a number of intersecting elements become evident in the history of connections between Morocco and Europe. The first is the impact of colonization, which has created enduring links between France and Morocco in language and cultural practices as well as through the legacy of ideologies of governance. The second is the history of migration flows, often concentrated from certain regions in Morocco to certain nation-states in Europe. Communities have developed along trajectories that intertwine the place of origin with elements of the European place so that there is not necessarily one, unified 'Moroccan diaspora' but many 'diasporic Moroccans', from communities that consider Morocco to be a homeland. Distinctions between these communities are influenced by both the region and ethnicity (Arab or Amazigh) of origin as well as the diversity of the European space of home, whether in France, Belgium or The Netherlands. The third is the recognition that, despite the multiple possible trajectories, a 'national' origin can exert influence on diasporic communities in other ways beside the representation of the nation-state. That is, as much as these individuals might identify as Moroccans, they also can engage with belonging in Arab or Amazigh groups, and the many regional designations that go with them, or even their cities or neighborhoods of residence. In short, although this research is seemingly concerned with Moroccan nationals, other distinctions within that construct – besides that of the 'nation' – play an essential role.

Post-migrant Mobilities: Backgrounds and Pathways for Temporary Return

The travel practices of the Moroccan-origin individuals living in Europe who participated in this research are examples of diasporic mobilities (Hannam *et al.*, 2006) between their Moroccan and European homes. While other migrant communities might be hindered by distance, disaster, war or politics from regularly visiting a 'homeland' (Ang, 2001; Cohen, 1997; Gilroy, 1993; Glick Schiller & Fouron, 2001), Moroccans in Europe have had relatively easy physical motility and institutional mobility between homes over most of the 50 years since they were invited into Europe as guestworkers. Although many original guestworking migrants suffered delays in making their legal status permanent, they began with legal status that allowed them to cross borders, their families eventually gained legal status as well, and there have not been major political shifts in Morocco or in Europe that prevented them from traveling home.

This relative ease of mobility has enabled the annual summer vacation to become an informal institution: a pathway that becomes more and more solidified over the years, so that members of Moroccan-origin communities expect and are expected to visit 'home' semi-regularly. As time goes on, however, the original migrants are less and less part of these mobility practices. Now, their children and their children's children transform this pathway following their own interests. As visitors with a proximal familial connection, but who have been distanced by migration, the post-migrant generations of Moroccan-origin individuals who travel to Morocco for vacations are both *returning* to a place in which they are rooted by familial origin and *touring* a place where they are not normally resident.

Comparable contemporary and historical accounts of other migrant groups document that most 'return', or visit their ancestral homelands, infrequently if at all. Until relatively recently, intercontinental migration was predominantly a one-way trajectory, with little possibility for either temporary or permanent 'return' (Berger & Mohr, 1989; Cohen, 1995; Hatton & Williamson, 1994). Along these lines, returns are often characterized as momentous occasions, whether as an expensive long-distance holiday (Ali & Holden, 2006), as tracing a historical, genealogical path (Nash, 2008), as a counter-diasporic project (King & Christou, 2009; Reynolds, 2008), or as extensively organized family reunions (Ramirez *et al.*, 2007). Yet some groups, like Moroccans in Europe, have developed regular, annual pathways of temporary return, which continue to be practiced by younger generations (Cisneros, 2002; Levitt, 2009; Levitt & Waters, 2002).

While the motivations for more permanent returns are often framed through connections to 'home', genealogy, or a search for cultural belonging, the practice of repeatedly, cyclicly returning crosses paths with another flow of mobility: travel and tourism from countries in the Global North towards countries in the Global South. This intersection is not often highlighted in studies on migration, but is a recognized part of tourism studies. Specifically, Visiting Friends and Relatives (VFR) tourism involves exploring the practices and impacts of travelers who are grouped outside the classic 'tourist' prototype, because they travel to visit people who are part of their personal networks as well as the place (Coles & Timothy, 2004; Hollinshead, 2004). Their touristic visitation is sometimes distinct from, and sometimes related to, an enactment of diasporic return (Butler, 2003; Conway *et al.*, 2009; King & Gamage, 1994).

Research on VFR travelers often questions what these tourists do, and why they choose to make these visits, in comparison to previous research about other varieties of tourists. Some authors contend that these visits are a means of cementing family links and increasing social capital with reference to family (Duval, 2004a, 2004b; Nguyen & King, 2004). Family interactions are a focal point of the visit, but many of the activities engaged in are not exclusively family oriented (Feng & Page, 2000). Importantly, these studies recognize that visitors are also consumers, and in specific ways that may differ from other tourists, while adhering to a touristic logic of consumption of leisure spaces and cultural spaces, and shopping for non-essential purchases (Duval, 2003: 273).

Framing these visits through tourism responds to the sense of 'not belonging' that descendants of migrants seem to encounter, across different migratory backgrounds and pathways, when visiting their ancestral homelands. Young French-Moroccan women visiting Morocco, for example, felt themselves accused of being '*filles de France*' (Étiemble, 2003: 37) because of their language use and comportment. Likewise, Caribbean-origin Brits felt themselves categorized as foreigners, and reported being pressured by family members for financial contributions because, having travelled from the UK, they were considered to be wealthy (Stephenson, 2002).

Although the motivations of post-migrant travelers may be related to ideas of home and belonging, they find themselves implicated in much broader political, financial and social dynamics upon arrival that categorize them in unanticipated ways. The impetus to 'return', however, is not necessarily diminished because of feeling of 'not belonging', as groups develop different means and motivations to visit 'home'. The reports of being considered 'foreign' because of their language and comportment, however, have clear links to the sociolinguistic positioning of post-migrant generations in their ancestral homelands and languages.

Sociolinguistic Backgrounds: National and Diasporic Morocco

As an inescapable part of everyday social life, language and linguistic practice are forms of embodiment that are in some ways reliant on geographical location. Ideologies of national unity, exemplified by institutions of arts and literature, illustrate how language ideologically attaches to certain geographical places and actors more than others (Bourdieu, 1991). All actors and places, however, have the potential to link with multiple forms – depending on how backgrounds are configured to enable smooth pathways. The diasporic participants in this study are one example of how different shifting backgrounds – from the Protectorate differentiation between Arab and Amazigh groups, to the context of guestworker migration, to the formation of newly interrelated Moroccan communities in Europe – enable pathways towards new combinations of linguistic competences.

The ability to access multiple codes – specifically, the configuration of linguistic competences in both European and Moroccan languages personified by participants in this study – can be challenging to nation-state constructions of a monolithic, unilingual, mono-literate population. Beyond how Bourdieu theorized state institutional interests in determining a 'linguistic market', a multilingual sociolinguistic landscape based on pathways of international migration is connected to physical and social places beyond the nation-state. To address the conflicting ways in which linguistic codes and practices intersect pathways of migration with national unity, this section outlines an approach to multilingual competency and the languages and codes present in the national and diasporic territory of Morocco.

Political economies of multilingualism in Morocco: Intersections of diasporic multilingual repertoires

Bi- or multilingualism, whether within a single national context (Heller, 2002) or in a migration context (Deprez, 1994; Koven, 2007; Urciuoli, 1996;

Zentella, 1997) is often implicated in power relationships between groups. Gal (1987) remarks that the history of power relations between groups resident in the same place, where one is considered less powerful, can influence forms of codeswitching that emerge along different lines of identification. Following that, codeswitching (Auer, 1998; Gardner-Chloros, 2008; Myers-Scotton, 1998) is not simply speech using two or more languages, but engages with complex and creative code systems, just like other forms of linguistic variation (Blom & Gumperz, 1972). Invoking multiple codes in conversation can be a strategy for voicing (Woolard, 1999) or for distancing (Myers-Scotton, 1990), or can be performed as the unmarked code, the 'normal' mode of speech, with its own set of rules and forms. In short, multilingual interaction practices open a portal on ideologies of language tied to nation-state formations through situated political economies of language (Irvine, 1989).

Morocco is a nation-state community where 'normal' speech in many locales might involve codeswitching between several possible codes. The range of linguistic codes potentially accessible to Moroccans, both within national borders and outside them, illustrates that linguistic practices can be very multilayered indicators of national belonging. The official language of Morocco is Modern Standard Arabic (MSA), a language that is natively spoken by no-one, neither in Morocco nor elsewhere. Rather, it is a standardized language, regarded as a 'high' variety in the diglossic (Ferguson, 1971; Holes, 1995; Walters, 2003) context of Morocco, and is the main language of written education. Spoken languages of Morocco that are considered to originate in the region include Moroccan Arabic or *derija* and three grouped dialects of Amazigh languages. These are officially called Tashelḥit, Tarifit and Tamazight by the new institute of Amazigh language and culture (IRCAM) created to codify them. French is the most commonly spoken foreign language, and Spanish is also common in the northern zone of the former Spanish protectorate (Bentahila, 1983; Ennaji, 1991).

Although all these languages are present and accessible in this diasporic linguistic landscape, their functions and symbolic importance vary significantly according to social factors that orient language use, such as gender, class, education, place of origin and social networks – in essence, power. French and MSA are by far the dominant languages in this political economy. They are the primary languages of education, government and media distribution. Until Arabization reforms in the 1980s and 1990s, French was the primary language of university education in Morocco; although it has been officially replaced now by MSA, there is still a strong Francophone academic presence, especially in elite schools (Ennaji, 2002). Even now, codeswitching between Moroccan Arabic and French is very common; beyond certain 'borrows' from French that have been incorporated into the

Moroccan lexicon (Heath, 1989; Ziamari, 2008), codeswitching between Moroccan Arabic and French is related to class and education (Bentahila, 1983) as well as gender (Walters, 1999), and consequently functions as a status marker along multiple, simultaneous dimensions. Alongside these already dominant codes, IRCAM has recently been charged with creating written and standardized forms of Amazigh languages, in order to introduce an Amazigh curriculum in schools (Ameur *et al.*, 2006). The value of Amazigh as a language outside the narrow field of North Africa is, however, seen as low, unlike MSA and French.

The primary language of Morocco is spoken dialectal Arabic, *derija*. In most contexts, with most Moroccans, this will be the assumed common spoken code. While it can be written with Arabic script, it has no sanctioned or standardized written form. *Derija* (or Darija) broadly refers to dialectal Arabic spoken across North Africa, encompassing regional variation such that speakers can often pinpoint local origins through attributes of speech. Most individuals who identify as Imazighen raised in Morocco will also speak *derija*, except those from particularly disadvantaged backgrounds or isolated areas.

However, *derija* is not always the 'right' Moroccan code for conversation. In certain contexts, an Amazigh dialect, French or Spanish might be the first language used in conversation among Moroccans, depending on the region, the level of education, and the social and family origins of the speakers. MSA, although incorporated into the landscape, is primarily known in written form or through very formalized speech events (and even then there is often codeswitching with French or *derija*), and so is not a 'spoken' language in common social settings. The management of all of these linguistic influences is part of the linguistic repertoire of resident Moroccans, in a broad sense: these languages are recognizable to most Moroccans in their specific uses and status connotations, even if s/he is not capable of speaking, understanding, reading or writing it him/herself.

These dynamics of linguistic repertoire are key differences between non-resident and resident Moroccans. Their repertoires do not necessarily overlap: places of origin, family dynamics, access to education and individual ability all play a role in what linguistic codes and what forms of those codes are accessible to an individual. These differential abilities are embedded in ideologies of 'right' and 'wrong' languages to speak as a Moroccan in Morocco, both in a sense of knowing which code is appropriate to a certain place or situation, and in the embodied ability to actually communicate – to pronounce and perceive phonemes and morphemes in a 'Moroccan' way. The linguistic practices of speaking Moroccan languages in Morocco are really then *communicative* practices. They intersect with political economies of language within the nation, reflect hierarchies between codes within global scales, and encode individuals as successfully or unsuccessfully producing the communicative practices they are expected to produce.

Pathways of languages: Moroccan communicative practices outside Morocco

Extending this landscape outside the frontiers of Morocco, following the trajectories of migrating individuals from different corners of the country to their eventual destinations, diasporic communities present a different picture of a Moroccan linguistic repertoire. Leaving aside the numerous Moroccan populations in North America, Israel and the Gulf countries (de Haas, 2007), this research is limited to communities created through the labor migration of the 1960s–1970s in France, Belgium and The Netherlands. This population is over-represented in Amazigh origin in comparison to the population of Morocco, due to the government encouragement of recruitment in Amazigh areas discussed above. Also, as recruiting agents representing specific companies tended to focus on certain regions or cities, the migrant neighborhoods constructed in Europe can be rooted in the same area in Morocco – meaning that they may share a regional dialect in Arabic or in an Amazigh language. These patterns of displacement of linguistic practice from one neighborhood to another have created interesting and unexpected configurations of Moroccan linguistic communities and competences abroad.

Linguistic repertoires in diasporic communities can be modeled roughly in ordinal sequence by generation (see Fishman, 1985 or Romaine, 1991, for broad discussions of migrant bilingualism; or Li Wei, 2010, for an encyclopedic reader). The migrant generation, defined for these purposes as those who migrated after reaching maturity and leaving their parents' homes, are often in the most challenged position in learning a new language. Their potential for competency in the destination country language(s) generally depends on the availability of education in that new language and on their circuits of interaction in the new community, which may encourage them towards learning the new language or permit them to continue practicing their home language in their daily activities. The post-migrant generation, defined here as those who are born to migrant parents or who migrated before beginning school (around age four), have a higher likelihood of becoming fluently competent in the language(s) of their country of socialization, including often acquiring literacy skills in that language that their parents lack. Post-migrant generation linguistic competences in the ancestral home language also vary depending on similar community factors, such as the presence or absence of the home language in the surrounding community in oral and/or written forms, but also on factors internal to the family, like birth order and the presence or absence of monolingual elders in the home.

Diasporic Moroccan multilingualism fits broadly into the diagram shown in Figure 1.2, which describes repertoires in Morocco and outside based on the patterns of migration and the community settlement in the three countries in question. The figure demonstrates the ways in which many diasporic Moroccans do not intersect with the linguistic 'nation' in Morocco. As residents in nation-states other than Morocco, they acquire oral and written repertoires and communicative practices that are not 'Moroccan' – that is, that do not closely follow patterns of Moroccan multilingualism as practiced in the territorial space of Morocco. Their particular patterns of multilingualism belong specifically to the post-migrant diasporic population and reflect the influences they encounter. This highlights an interesting after-effect of migration: the creation of a population of speakers of 'Moroccan' languages, such as Dutch-Amazigh bilinguals, who do not also have competence in the dominant languages of Morocco – MSA and French. The lack of typically 'Moroccan' language skills by some diasporic visitors, such as the ability to speak Tarifit but not *derija*, can be a key characteristic of their diasporic 'strangeness'.

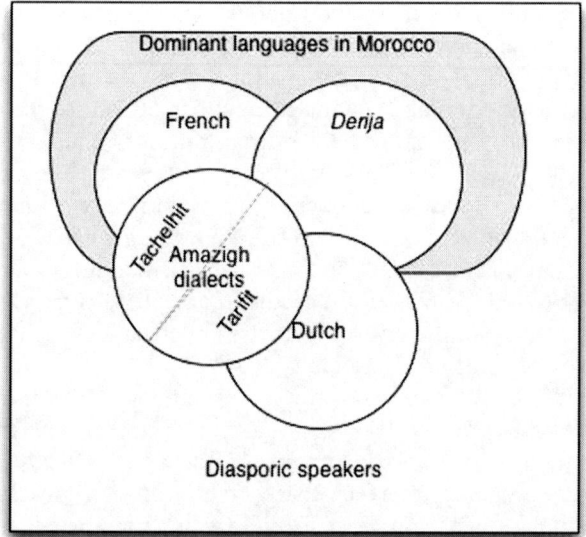

Figure 1.2 Overlap and disparity of spoken language repertoires between resident Moroccans and diasporic Moroccans

Their communicative competences as diasporic Moroccans are grounded in pathways available to them for learning Moroccan languages. Acquiring and being socialized in a diasporic heritage language occurs primarily through four avenues: regular face-to-face interaction with fellow community members, regular interaction at a distance with speakers from the 'homeland', occasional face-to-face interaction with speakers from the 'homeland', and consumption of media available in the diasporic setting (Deprez, 1994). More pathways are always appearing and disappearing: for example, a formal academic system to teach the written form of the heritage language is also available in some nation-states, but the diversity of the Amazigh and Arab diasporic Moroccan communities makes implementation of this on a wide scale challenging and complex (El Aissati & Bos, 1998; Extra & Gorter, 2001; Tilmatine, 1997). As communication increases in speed, availability and frequency across geographical distance, members of diasporic communities have access to more forms of written and spoken communication with homeland communities. Yet it is essential to recognize that interaction at a distance fosters a different kind of linguistic socialization from face-to-face conversation.

Face-to-face interaction with the 'home' community, however, has not often been a subject in the research on migrant multilingualism. Although they may recognize its importance, researchers on migrant multilinguals' language use usually do not include data from visits 'home' (Collins & Slembrouck, 2006; Deprez, 1994; Melliani, 2000; Tetreault, 2004; Zentella, 1997). This site for linguistic practices is often simply outside the scope of the research. One classic study in migrant bilingualism in France focused on the importance of visits home as a means of maintaining linguistic practices in the heritage language (Dabène & Billiez, 1984). That study, like most work in migrant bilingualism, follows the tendency to circumscribe a 'linguistic community' within a spatial community in the country of residence – effectively limiting the physical landscape to the immediate surroundings. More recently, however, Koven (2002, 2004, 2007) studied Portuguese-origin French individuals enacting a more permanent 'return' to Portugal, which will be discussed in more detail in later chapters.

This project follows Koven's example, by putting the focus on interactions in the country of ancestral origin, although not in the same 'return' migration context which she documented. Rather, this study focuses on the importance of mobility between spaces to multilingual practices, and the relevance of emplacement and deterritorialization (Vigouroux, 2005) to the indexicality and polycentricity (Blommaert, 2007, 2013b) of communicative practices. In particular, the ways in which post-migrant generation diasporic visitors discuss their linguistic capacities, and in fact execute communicative practices, address distinctions between the ways in which locally resident Moroccans and post-migrant generation visiting Moroccans perceive of and use *derija* as part of asserting themselves as 'being-Moroccan'. The primary way I observed their practices in face-to-face interaction with others during their trips to Morocco was in the linguistic activity of *bargaining*.

Bargaining: A Linguistic Activity with Tangible Results

Bargaining in the marketplace is a site in which participants actively use sociocultural categorization devices to achieve their material goal of successfully negotiating a sale. As a genre of marketplace interaction (Bauman, 2001; French, 2001), bargaining is talk between vendor and client in the context of a non-fixed price purchase. Because bargaining is common across Morocco (Geertz *et al.*, 1979; Kapchan, 1996) and also a common activity for tourists and locals alike (Desforges, 2001), it sits at an intersection between key pathways in this research: it is a place where post-migrant diasporic visitors repeatedly use their Moroccan communicative practices both to achieve the material goal of purchasing something and to achieve a social goal of being recognized as 'Moroccan' by other locally resident Moroccans.

Bargaining is a highly structured form, with identifiable openings and sequences, including offers, counteroffers, justifications, acceptances or refusals. To set a price for a piece of merchandise, vendors and buyers make judgments about one another based on initial perceived impressions that may have relatively little to do with the cost of the object, but can have an important influence on the final agreed price (if it is achieved). Prices are emergent as a negotiation between potential buyers and potential sellers, as collectives or as individuals, which determine value in terms of what a buyer is willing to pay for a given object. These structures allow the possibility for situated creativity, including using multiple linguistic codes as means of creating interactive proximity to obtain the tangible goal of setting a price (Drivaud & Peretz-Juillard, 1984; Gardner-Chloros, 1985; Lindenfeld, 1990).

The key to effective bargaining, across geographic and cultural locations, is embedded in a sense of 'localness' created between vendor and client through the interaction (Juillard, 1990; Orr, 2007), to the extent that local vernacular may be preferred to other possible codes (Van den Berg, 1986). Likewise, bargaining skill in Morocco involves incorporating specific social and cultural references in the course of conversation that signify 'local' and 'Moroccan', and create a bond between vendor and client (Kapchan, 1996), in order to establish commonalities that encourage mutual understanding on price.

Although marketplace interaction is in public space and therefore a genre accessible to anyone, it is not a verbal art practiced by all. Participants' past experiences and strategies as infrequent bargainers play a part in setting their 'skill level' in this linguistic activity, which is generally lower than the professional vendors with whom they are bargaining. Even resident Moroccans do not necessarily consider themselves 'good bargainers', and may delegate others who are seen as more skilled to help make significant purchases. Yet, marketplace interaction is a part of everyday life in Morocco, practiced to different ends by both men and women (Kharraki, 2001). In Europe, in contrast, the practice of bargaining is commonly limited to either major purchases (car, house) or marginal ones (Crewe & Gregson, 1998), meaning that diasporic Moroccans may not have frequent access to situations where they can refine their skills.

According to post-migrant generation Moroccans, linguistic competence in *derija* is the most significant factor in bargaining, although the analysis in Chapter 4 demonstrates that this ideology is not always substantiated in practice. Competence in *derija* does, however, play a large part in how DVs strategically attempt to bargain. Past research (Wagner, 2006, 2008) indicates that both vendor and diasporic client have preconceptions about the importance of linguistic competence in a local language as a marker of 'localness', where 'local' speech facilitates a 'local' price. These attitudes about 'belonging' are expressed during bargaining through sequential talk, and sometimes afterwards. Vendors and clients often voice opinions about bargaining partners in the aftermath of an exchange that may not be made explicit in other circumstances – assigning them categories as 'local' or 'nonlocal', but also as sympathetic or unsympathetic in other ways that relate to a sense of affiliative 'belonging'.

Above all, bargaining is an economic activity, facilitated by language but implicating broader relationships of economic power. Vendors are attuned to taste preferences and financial capacities based on broad categorizations of their clients (Wagner, 2015a, 2015b, 2015c) – including foreign tourists and Moroccans from abroad that they see on a regular basis – and often tailor their bargaining strategies according to these perceived indicators, in order to get the best possible price. For post-migrant generation clients, issues of trust and distrust often emerge in these interactions in parallel to how tourists perceived their interactions with locals as 'inauthentic' because they involve monetary exchange (Desforges, 2001). Yet, in repeated interactions, they attempt to use *derija* to achieve the 'right' price, and therefore to 'belong' as 'locally-Moroccan'. In short, their language use and communicative competence in bargaining has a cash value (Irvine, 1989), manifest in the success or failure of participants in their bargaining goals.

Conclusion

These layerings of backgrounds and pathways combine to map how forms of belonging and non-belonging become relevant to diasporic Moroccans in Morocco.

Migration histories led their parents and grandparents to specific destinations, where they became part of the resident community. Yet being part of that resident community means they are distanced socially and geographically from Morocco as a homeland, even if it is one that they visit regularly. Those who visit every year, or every few years, may maintain a sense of belonging in Morocco as 'Moroccan', but may also feel themselves at times to be 'foreign'. This 'foreignness' is often characterized through their linguistic skills, their embodiment, and their comparative wealth as normally resident in a richer nation of the Global North. Feeling 'Moroccan' by speaking like a resident Moroccan involves a dense set of *communicative* skills, which many post-migrant generation visitors do not master. But they do encounter unknown others in everyday contexts, such as marketplaces, where they can attempt to speak *derija* and increase their skill in the verbal art of bargaining.

Yet as much as bargaining is a linguistic activity, it is also a site of economic power. When diasporic Moroccans feel themselves categorized as 'foreign' by resident Moroccans, it is not a category that is limited to their communicative practices: it necessarily includes other perceptible markers about them, reflecting their economic status or their embodied living conditions in ways that are significant to a category of 'being-Moroccan'. Using this ethnographic site, where resident and non-resident Moroccans negotiated what it means to 'be-Moroccan-in-Morocco', can elucidate how these categories are shaped.

2   Integrating Theory and Method

[O]ne can be simultaneously college-educated, an engineer, a church-goer, the mother of three young children – one of whom has leukemia – local officer in a political party of the moderate left, child of divorced parents, owner of a Border collie, member of an immigrant minority group, person in their thirties who worked on an assembly line as a young adult, and a woman who is bisexual. These attributes are located on various dimensions of identification. Which particular aspects of identity – or particular combinations of them – will become salient within a given encounter is something that interlocutors point to behaviorally during the course of their interaction together and that others ratify in their reactions to the speaker of the moment. At one moment some attributes may be made relevant and salient and at other moments some others may become salient, but the full multiplicity of aspects of social identity rarely become salient simultaneously in a single social encounter. Rather, specific social identities of the moment are constructed/accomplished through the conjoint actions of interlocutors during the course of interaction, and this kind of contextualization is a basic and continuous aspect of the local practice of discourse. (Erickson, 2004: 149–150)

Like many other migrant communities around the world, Moroccans in Europe often share a conflicted sense of belonging. They may, at certain times and in certain places, feel themselves to be more 'Moroccan' than 'European', or vice versa. This sense of hybridity associated with diaspora is often construed as a problematic – or even impossible – simultaneous attachment to two different spaces of home and belonging (Kalra *et al.*, 2005). In the way Erickson described above, though, it only amounts to being more than one thing, in a complex 'multiplicity of identity' – with a *seemingly* paradoxical 'hybrid' twist on Erickson's 'dimensions of identification'. Being diasporic means belonging in two categories on what many interlocutors interpret as the *same* dimension: that of ethno-national 'identity', which is usually, instinctively, imagined to refer to a community descended from a single group that 'belongs' in a linguistically and geographically unified place. To think about how diasporic belonging works in interaction, I break down these processes of categorization into their component parts – specifically, as *descent* and *place* – in order to think about how 'ethno-national identity' itself can include a multiplicity of sometimes contradictory dimensions.

In this chapter, I argue for an ontological approach that combines perspectives from sociolinguistics and linguistic anthropology on how people are doing 'identity' in their everyday lives and interactions, with perspectives from social theories of assemblage on how the different entities become *something* in relationship with one another in interaction. To me, these two bodies of literature seem natural friends, as they both pay close attention to the ways in which society and the material parts that make it up – including speakers and their bodies – are always in process, involving the complex integrations of many parts. This ontological approach means that I can do away with the idea of 'hybridity' because, implicitly, it depends on a fixed opposition; in an assemblage, a hybrid cannot exist because every relationship (even the unexpected ones) is a neutral combination of entities. This ontology also creates a different imagining of what an 'interlocutor' is in sociolinguistic interaction: instead of the unit of measurement being a speaker and its body, we will have to pay attention to how component parts of bodies are themselves entities in interaction, and how they can connect with components such as clothing, accent and each other. This ontology is still supported by the epistemological framework of ethnomethodology, in that the data here are based on observation of naturally occurring activity and the analysis focuses on how certain categorical distinctions become relevant. The chapter concludes by detailing what sorts of categorical framings – linked, of course, with diasporic belonging in Morocco – I have paid attention to in approaching and formulating this research.

Where Sociolinguistics Meets Assemblage

Many theories of sociolinguistics discuss different ways in which individuals access multiple identities and categorizations, particularly as to how interlocutors are able to manipulate and categorically manoeuver from context to context, and moment to moment. From Goffman's (1971) thoughts about presentation of self as malleable with changing circumstances, to more recent theories of polycentricity and superdiversity as means of understanding migratory complexity (Blommaert, 2013b), this human capacity to draw on many influences in situational performances has been a common thread of sociolinguistic research. I want to build on this tradition here, by building a theoretical basis for thinking about diasporic belonging not as 'hybrid' or 'multiple identity' but, in the spirit of sociolinguistic complexity that Blommaert (2013b: 10–13) outlines, as constantly reshaping and reforming assemblage (DeLanda, 2006).

That is, I am seeking harmonies between assemblage theories that draw attention to how entities ranging from molecules to power grids interact (Bennett, 2010), and the methodological approach to human interactions developed by sociolinguists and linguistic anthropologists. These methodologies include those rooted in Garfinkel (1984) and Sacks (1992), which have developed to interrogate how membership categorization functions in interaction (Hester & Eglin, 1997; Housley & Hester, 2002; Stokoe, 2012). I am also taking into account other sociolinguistic theories about managing interaction that have not used the term 'categorization' explicitly (Giles et al., 1991; Piller, 2002; Rampton, 2006), but do address 'identity'.

The central focus of this combination of theory from one lineage and methodology from another is to think about how categories emerge and take shape through many mechanisms simultaneously. The mechanisms of categorization have become a subject of study in sociolinguistic analysis, but they are also a major topic in related social science fields such as anthropology (Hirschfeld, 1998; Lakoff, 1990), sociology (Brubaker et al., 2004) and social psychology (Semin & Smith, 2008). These other perspectives do not focus on categorization as a linguistic event, but rather as a cognitive or neurological event or as part of social institutions. Although as Erickson suggests above, different dimensions can become salient through discourse, it is not only through linguistic discourse that salience happens. In face-to-face interactions, there is also communication without speaking (Goffman, 1963) which, although it might not be readable in a transcript, is part of the mechanisms of categorization. These elements, I argue, are what become more apparent by basing my exploration on theories of assemblage, where different material and expressive entities – including language, bodies, voices, clothing, histories, etc. – are all potential interactants in mechanisms of categorization.

In order to investigate how these unspoken and spoken, latent and active, explicit and inexplicit elements are part of the linguistic ideologies, practices and interactions that participate in categorization, I follow the ethnomethodological model proposed by Katz (1999) to take participants' metaphors seriously. That is, I look at how the attitudes, stories, opinions and practices of the participants in this research shape categories of diasporic belonging of migration and diaspora, produced as assemblages of multiple, simultaneous, complex interacting parts. So, while I start out by assuming – based on my previous observations on the ferry boats crossing back and forth between Morocco and Spain – that there is such a thing as 'being diasporic' – and such a thing as 'being Moroccan' or 'Moroccanness' – I will explore what shape 'diasporicness' takes through participants' metaphors and practices in interaction. While these terms may appear as if they have an external definition, I will always put them in quotes to remind you, and me, that these category labels only exist and persist in the ways that interactants collectively conceptualize and act upon them. Inasmuch as they are always in motion, they are always also coming together and breaking apart, repeating and differentiating in tiny increments, so that by the time you read this book, 'Moroccanness' may have significantly shifted from how it happened in the summer of 2008.

What Does it Mean to 'Be Diasporic'?

Following on from its original restricted application to certain historically specific cases of population dispersal (Gilroy, 1993; Schnapper, 1999; Shuval, 2000; Tölöyan, 1996), diaspora has been used in reference to various large-scale movements (Cohen, 1997) and to different approaches to attachment to a distant homeland (Anthias, 1998; Mavroudi, 2007; Werbner, 2002). Cohen is particularly concerned with defining diaspora as representing only migrant groups that adhere to a list of qualities related to dispersal, idealization of the homeland and desire to return (Cohen, 1997: 180), which arguably includes the Moroccan diaspora in Europe and elsewhere.

Yet, the application of 'diaspora' as a term to describe all Moroccans outside Morocco, regardless of their conditions of migration, may create an imagination of a coherent group of the 'Moroccan diaspora'. Diasporic practices of post-migrant generation Moroccans living in Europe may be apparent, or indeed absent. Governments and communities may explicitly and implicitly link to Morocco as a geographical, cultural and linguistic reference point of dispersion, or they may be ignorant of, or disregard, Morocco as a place of origin among local residents. In this sense, umbrella definitions of what a diaspora 'is' do not necessarily help in understanding what it feels like to 'be diasporic' – what configurations of experiences, perspectives, structures and senses of belonging to places and groups make up a simultaneous engagement, whether active or latent, with multiple homelands.

Instead, then, I use 'diasporic' here as an adjective, not a defining noun, describing attachments to places and families that some individuals sometimes feel, which can foster multiple belongings to different homespaces

(Bidet & Wagner, 2012). This definition is not necessarily limited to contexts of international migration – anyone might feel the pull of a distant homespace while living in a new one – but international migration often engenders greater distances and broader sociocultural and linguistic differences between diasporic homespaces. Pronounced and noticeable distinctions, no matter what the distance crossed, make international diasporicness more apparent.

Diasporic dispersal and its resultant distancing, following Massey (2005), is both spatial and temporal. That is, 'being diasporic' reflects nostalgic impulses for moments of past experiences, reaching across a spatio-temporal distance created by migration, whether between adjoining regions or across remote borders. By describing what these individuals do as 'diasporic' instead of transnational, ethnic, hybrid or any of the many other terms frequently used in migration research, I orient their connectedness along two specific dimensions: (1) they are 'rooted' in a genetic lineage through perceived origins following a path of *descent*; and (2) that lineage is historically situated in a specific distant *place*.

The relationship of Morocco to Europe is thus one example of a 'diasporicness', in parallel to other examples of groups in Europe – such as those from Turkey, Ghana, Bosnia, Poland, the Caribbean and the Indian subcontinent (Brown, 2006; Bryceson & Vuorela, 2002; Conway & Potter 2009) – as well as groups in North America, like those from Mexico (Stephen, 2007) and elsewhere in Latin America, Southeast Asia and the Caribbean (Rumbaut & Portes, 2001), or even Ireland (Nash, 2008). All of these groups participate in imaginings of connectedness to a distant place of origin, wherein these imaginings result in actions big and small – sometimes in the practice of visiting 'home' regularly or once in a lifetime (Levitt, 2002). Although not all of the practices of members of these groups are purposefully diasporic – nor do these communities necessarily constitute 'diaspora' – the practice of visiting 'home' is one that references attachment to that 'homeland' as a response to dispersal from it. Even if it may serve as simply a 'vacation', it is underpinned by a relationship of *descent*.

Dimensions of diasporic belonging: *Descent* and *place*

In relation to groups that organize around ideas of 'ethnicity' or 'nationality', the metaphor of *descent*, as lineages and relatedness, and the metaphor of *place*, as a sense of geographical location, are key dimensions to understanding how interlocutors draw boundaries of belonging. These dimensions, I argue, are buried inside categorizations that explicitly refer to 'ethnicity' or 'nation', which often involve creating configurations of *descent* and *place* to define who belongs, and who does not. Much like 'race', these metaphors, even if they reference biological attributes like skin color or genetic connection, are not universal or perpetual definitions to apply to any individual. Rather, I use them in italics throughout this book to bring attention to how they work as trajectories and relationships: they are dynamic metaphors, sometimes appearing to have fixed reference points and stable significations, but in fact being constantly in flux.

These metaphors appear in many variations across research in the social sciences. They are reflected in the ways in which states normalize an idea of 'nation' or 'ethnicity' through being from a certain place (Verdery, 1993), and in how cognitive anthropologists argue for the relevance of perceived ethnic similarity and difference through blood relationships (D'Andrade, 1995; Gil-White, 2001, 2005). In migration literature, Brubaker's (1992) analysis of immigration law in France and Germany describes the effects of state classificatory systems privileging *ius soli* (right of soil) versus *ius sanguinis* (right of blood). The same metaphors appear in many other comparative analyses of how states organize migration, keeping some people in and others out (Brubaker, 1989; Castles *et al.*, 2013; Joppke, 1998, 1999; Joppke & Morowska, 2003; Kymlicka, 1995, 2007).

As much as *descent* or *place* play material roles in defining citizens against non-citizens in a state-based 'nation', they also impact who can participate by exercising diasporic connections to it. People who can trace their *descent* back to a *place* may or may not be universally welcomed to seek a sense of belonging among its current occupants. Nash's research (2002, 2004, 2005, 2008) on Irish migration histories and genealogies reflects the significance of perceived genealogical connection for her participants, who travel from far-distant locations to discover themselves through their genetic heritage. Her 'geographies of relatedness' point to the implicitly geographical dimension of forms of kinship and *descent*, in that tracing one's genetic heritage leads to seeking *places* in historical homelands.

Likewise, Smith (2003) describes how *pieds-noir* of Maltese origin, who were forcibly resettled in France after the end of the Algerian war, have complex liminal connectivities between Malta as a *descent* homeland and Algeria as the *place* where they locate their memories and nostalgia. Unable to return Algeria and unsettled in France, they make pilgrimages to Malta. This pattern of 'roots to routes', moving back and forth between links defined by *descent* and those defined by *place*, is as relevant to generationally distant diasporas (Basu, 2004; Clifford, 1997) as to more proximal descendants (Levitt, 2009) who enact pilgrimages 'home'.

Supported by mythology, family, genetics or other explanatory systems (El-Haj, 2007; Franklin, 2003; Glick Schiller, 2005; Nash, 2005), individuals often hold a set of beliefs about bloodline *descent* and its implicit connections to particular *places*. Sometimes, these explanations come dangerously close to being deterministic – to defining individuals by their family histories or circumstances. By evoking the metaphors 'blood' and 'soil' to talk about how some individuals trace their histories through migration, I do not want to suggest in any way that 'being diasporic' is predetermined by *place* and *descent*. Rather, I want to point to how certain conditions of possibility combine to make 'diasporicness' relevant for certain actors, as a material condition in which distance has emerged between their sources of *descent* and location in *place*.

Furthermore, the way combinations of *descent* and *place* emerge is beyond a 'discursive' distinction. In this research, for example, individuals are implicated in lines of *descent* because their birth certificates label them as 'Moroccan', in relation to the *place*-based genetic *descent* they inherited from their parents. But when they are in the *place* of Morocco, they betray 'Europeanness' as a *place* that has shaped their embodiment.

Rather than thinking of these labels as 'discursive' or socially constructed, I think of them as material: these dimensions of belonging are both ways in which physical attributes, as part of one's genetic heritage, might be read as 'Moroccan' and ways in which 'Europeanness' becomes, through embeddedness in a *place*, part of one's embodied physicality. These materialities become relevant in relation to 'diasporicness' because diasporic practices challenge the ways in which *descent* and *place* have normalized into a unified, assumed category of 'ethnicity' or 'nationality', where this hybridity does not fit.

Reframing Hybridity: From Duality to Multiplicity through Assemblage

The problem with framing 'diasporicness' through hybridity is that simply applying the term creates an opposite, 'non-hybrid' category that is assumed to be 'normal'. This assumption runs through many otherwise productive discussions of the problematics of belonging in and to multiple *places*.

For example, in their discussion of migrant and post-migrant Bajans living in Britain – a strikingly similar dynamic to Moroccans living in Europe – Phillips and Potter frame their participants' practical hybridity through Fanon's 'black skin-white mask identity'. They call this hybridity 'a new liminal identity, the state of flux of which is its in-between nature of being neither white nor black, neither English nor West Indian, neither self nor other. This hybrid identity of the Bajan-Brit embodies both white and black characteristics and is constantly in a state of slippage' (Phillips & Potter, 2006: 311). In order to give a voice to Bajan-Brit discourse about diasporic return to Barbados, they are using the concept of racialized liminality, giving agency to what they call 'hybridity'. Yet, by doing so, they assume, define and stabilize either side of the 'hybrid' as fixed points of reference – between white or black. Furthermore, they place their participants in a liminal, precarious, unseated 'state of slippage' between the two. As Kalra *et al.* (2005: 72) put it, 'to what degree does the assertion of hybridity rely on the positing of an anterior "pure" that precedes mixture?'

I also want to give agency to a categorization my participants embodied and enacted that references both 'Moroccanness' and 'Europeanness', but not by reframing that 'identity' as hybridity. Reinforcing this positional liminality only reinforces the idea that 'diasporicness' is something precarious and unseated, a slippage between two other fixed 'identities'. Instead of using the more common vocabulary of hybridity (or bricolage, syncretism or creolization that have been part of anthropological lineage – see Hannerz, 1987; Herskovits, 1990; Lévi-Strauss, 1966) I use a vocabulary and framework of assemblage to frame such evolutionary processes of complex combination and slippage as multiplicity. This vocabulary points more towards the 'space of possibility' created by multiple influences (Hutnyk, 2005; Kapchan & Strong, 1999; Samuels, 1999) – a space which is filled with networks and webs of many interacting parts.

What does assemblage do?

Assemblage, as rooted in the work of Deleuze and Guattari (1987), among others, is a move further away from essentialism than social constructionism, advocating the 'avoidance of the categories of typological thought: resemblance, identity, analogy and contradiction' (DeLanda, 2002: 177). Using terms like 'identity' and 'contradiction' assumes that 'identity' exists in some sort of permanence. An ontology based in assemblage, instead, assumes that everything constantly *becomes*, through complex, multidimensional relations of material and expressive qualities of actualized, unactualized and virtual entities that emerge as multiplicities.

Elizabeth Grosz eloquently frames how multiplicities consist of webs and networks of relationality:

> In Deleuze and Guattari's work, subject and object can no longer be understood as discrete entities or binary opposites. Things, material or psychical, can no longer be seen in terms of rigid boundaries, clear demarcations: nor, on an opposite track, can they be seen as inherently united, singular or holistic. Subject and object are series of flows, energies, movements, strata, segments, organs, intensities – fragments capable of being linked together or severed in potentially infinite ways other than those which congeal

them into identities. Production consists of those processes which create linkages between fragments, fragments of bodies and fragments of objects. Assemblages or machines are heterogeneous, disparate, discontinuous alignments or linkages brought together in conjunctions (x plus y plus z) or severed through disjunctions and breaks. (Grosz, 1994: 167)

This passage describes a parallel, but distinct, way of imagining social individuals to how Erickson described an individual at the beginning of this chapter. What Erickson might call 'discursive identities' through the social constructionist approach to hybridity, in an assemblage approach are material and expressive manifestations of multiplicity, without a 'core' subject underneath them. As Grosz says above, using assemblage to analyze these interactions attends to how interactions between these fragments, or *entities*, leave products and remainders. Many entities of social life – language, culture, spaces, bodies, and all the parts and practices that make them up – can then be explored on a single plane as interacting parts, by analyzing the ways in which these different entities are creatively, productively and sometimes destructively brought together. Assemblage disallows us from imagining pre-existing but inactive *identities*; rather, entities are shaped and shape each other only in interaction with many other entities as *multiplicities*.

I connect the way assemblage works in constant motion, interweaving many elements into new machines or configurations, to the way categories work as constantly creating in-groups and out-groups, and constantly reshaping in response to new influences. Imagining categories through assemblage unites arguments from different sides of categorization: they can be simultaneously conceptualized as a centripetal force, attracted to a central core (DiMaggio, 1997; Edwards, 1991; Haslam *et al.*, 2000; Smith, 2005) and as a differentiating force, repelled by tense boundaries (Barth, 1969; Lamont & Molnar, 2002; Pachuki *et al.*, 2007; Sollors, 1986; Tilly, 2004; Vermeulen & Govers, 1994; Wimmer, 2008, 2009). Instead of categorization as either a process of differentiation *or* a process of affiliation, both vectors become part of a single mechanism, in response to complex influences, creating complex effects (Blommaert, 2013a).

These actions of categorization still work, however, along a primary dimension – like *place* or *descent*. Each dimension changes the shape of multiplicity, both its actualized form and potential forms, through processes that act primarily along that dimension, but are interrelated and inseparable from all other dimensions. That is, although the act of migration can be distilled down to a change in *place*, change in that dimension interacts with trajectories and mechanisms of other dimensions, like *descent*. In other words, all the dimensions of identity Erickson describes can be individually identified, but they cannot be separated: all affect each other as they constantly change. They form a person as a material and expressive entity, with a plethora of moving parts along various dimensions, which cannot be wholly disentangled from one another even though some may be situationally, interactionally more active than others.

Just as different dimensions of categorization become relevant in different ways at different events (but cannot be disentangled in assemblage), social elements are, inseparably, both tangible and intangible – both material and expressive. Accent is an excellent example of this: accents can be *expressive*, simultaneously indexing social class and regional origins in speech; but accents are also *material*, in that they involve the physical apparatus for producing sound in a human body and how this apparatus has been trained, over time, into certain abilities and inabilities. These materialities and expressivities become relevant *together* when discussing how categorizations work in face-to-face interaction: people in these interactions can practice widely varying communicative competences, but they are also embodied presences, neither of which can be completely separated from the other.

Through this model, the so-called 'hybridity' of being both 'Moroccan' and 'European' is reimagined as a single system, with two nodes of attraction ('Moroccanness' and 'Europeanness') that themselves are not fixed in place: they push and pull against one another in every dimension, with every combination of materialities and expressivities. Some of the dimensions that are relevant both to 'Moroccanness' and 'Europeanness' seemingly create exclusivity in membership between them. The way in which the dimension of *descent*, for example, is imagined to lead to one and only one of these contributes to the vernacular perspective on hybridity – that people belong to one or the other, or are hybrids as neither one nor the other. The assemblage perspective brings attention away from the neither/nor dynamic, to emphasize how individuals are multiplicities, with nested, interconnected reference to both 'Moroccanness' and 'Europeanness', among other qualities, but cannot be separated into component parts. Framing this as assemblage rather than hybridity – as many interacting parts rather than two incompatible essences – leads to more productive analysis of how such individuals produce a state of 'Moroccan/Europeanness' through how aspects of each category emerge as relevant in interactions.

Communicative Bodies in Interaction: Doing Multiplicity in Multi-modal Interactions

Assemblage further differs from more common theories in sociolinguistics by reorienting some basic assumptions. First, as stated above, instead of investigating 'hybridity', I assume *multiplicity* – encouraging an imagination of everything and everyone as multiple, rather than singling out certain entities as 'hybrid'. Then, I can methodologically explore how different interacting parts create a categorical idea of 'Moroccanness'.

An assemblage perspective also assumes that this 'Moroccanness' is both material and expressive – that 'doing being Moroccan' involves shaping bodies as much as it shapes verbal and non-verbal language. These material and expressive processes are inextricable from one another: becoming-bodies involves transformations that are physical as much as discursive, although these different trajectories of transformation may not move at the same speed. Thinking about the materiality of bodies in this way means taking into account physical aspects to embodiment that contribute to categorization – from accent, to skin pigmentation, to a way of walking.

It is important, however, to distinguish between interpreting materialities in categorization and determining categories through materialities. While it is inarguable that no attribute of a human body determines any aptitude, perspective or orientation, there remains tension around the propensity for embodied characteristics to become deterministic, or for natural difference to be construed as essential.[1] This distinction has long been a problem for social scientists, and possibly one of the main reasons why it is still politically sensitive to talk about the body as part of categorization.

A great wealth of social research explores how bodies are categorized and performed in normative, silencing or oppressive ways (Back & Solomos, 2000; Hall & Bucholtz, 1995; Mahtani, 2002; McDowell, 1999; Skeggs, 1997, 1999, 2004; Twine, 1998). In corollary, however, it is futile to analyze social interaction without reflecting on the corporeality of the actors who embody them – including race. As Linda Alcoff (2006: 188) writes, '[i]f race is a structure of contemporary perception, then it helps constitute the necessary background from which I know myself. It makes up a part of what appears to me as the natural setting of all my thoughts. It is the field, rather than that which stands out.' While essentialisms that attach to material aspects of bodies are never tenable, they are also learned structures, both by those who apply them and those to whom they are applied, that become part of embodiment. In an assemblage perspective, the part these structures play – including the ways in which 'race' becomes a practiced category, in and through bodies – is part of *becoming*, as processes that are emergent and ongoing, even if they appear stable.

Seeing bodies as multiplicities prompts approaching a process like 'racialization' – as Sara Ahmed (2002: 55) describes it, a 're-negotiation of categories and norms that are never fully fixed into place' – not as a social condition that happens to bodies, but as part of how bodies are assemblages: always involving the material (fleshes, genetics, places, etc.) and expressive (correctness of bodies and places, etc.) as dimensions in multiplicity.

Different categorizations, then, like 'whiteness' and 'blackness' or 'Europeanness' and 'Moroccanness', are recognizable as potent material and expressive influences. They are, however, not discourses *put onto* bodies, but both material and expressive entities interwoven with bodies, and all their parts, in assemblage. Although the end result is not so far from the theoretical perspectives that Alcoff and Ahmed suggest for how to think about bodies and 'race', from an assemblage perspective their claims are part of the initial assumptions rather than arguments for the final conclusions – that is, that materialization of bodies is always in process and categories are not fixed, even though they may be perceived as deterministic.

The task at hand for analysis, then, is to discover what creates a 'body' as a mass of material and expressive entities, and how that assemblage of interacting entities becomes recognizable and categorizable as an entity itself in face-to-face interactions. The majority of work in interactive sociolinguistics, however, has focused on linguistic production in a seemingly disembodied way:

> In an effort to escape biological essentialism, sociolinguists have, I fear, preferred to act as if individuals do not have bodies. We claim to wish to understand the social construction of language, sex, and gender, yet seem embarrassed by the fact that speech is necessarily embodied, ultimately theorizing as if bodies don't and can't matter. (Walters, 1999: 202)

Part of this 'blindness' is purposeful: it is difficult, if not impossible, to keep track of all of the many dimensions of communicative and categorical activity. These can include, to name a few, complex layers of linguistic genres, registers, codes and functionalities alongside spatial proximity, gesture, gaze and facial expression. Limiting communicative analysis to purely audible factors already presents a rich palette, however partial. Bodies have often been incorporated only through ethnographic description, in general terms – gender, age, ethnicity, role in context.

More recently, this focus is shifting more towards communicative embodied activity through its visually empirical layers (Enfield, 2009; Farnell, 2000; Kendon, 2004; van Wolputte, 2004). Many in this vein of research focus on the structures and practices of visually embodied communication in parallel with previous analyses of audibly embodied communication – that is, how interactants produce conversational space as part of their communicative resources (Goodwin, 2000; Mondada, 2009). Less often are they concerned with the bodies as expressivities and materialities themselves – how those particular combinations of parts become categorically recognizable in the analyzed interaction.

So, although I am considering embodiment in this book, I do not focus on gesture, conversational space, or other rich and growing areas for investigation. Rather, I interrogate how material and expressive entities interact to form a categorical body. To do so, I use an assemblage approach in order to think about how bodies are multiple: that they only *become* categorically relevant in interaction.

In order to follow this trajectory, I want to expand beyond the expressive dimensions of language to think about linguistic performance as both material and expressive – as integrated multiplicities (bodies) in assemblage.

Embodimentality: Materiality of communication and habit

Imagining human bodies as multiplicities requires vocabulary to describe bodies as habituated and simultaneously emergent – both *'habitus'* (Bourdieu, 1977) and 'performative' (Butler, 1993), so to speak – but not externally controlled through structures or discourses. These bodies are intensive multiplicities; they *are* structures and discourses, as much as they are flesh and movement. To describe this type of embodiment, I follow Grosz in search of:

> some kind of understanding of *embodied subjectivity*, of *psychical corporeality*, needs to be developed. … The narrow constraints our culture has imposed on the ways in which our materiality can be thought means that altogether new conceptions of corporeality – those, perhaps, which use the hints and suggestions of others but which move beyond the overall context and horizon governed by dualism – need to be developed, notions which see human materiality in continuity with organic and inorganic matter but also at odds with other forms of matter, which see animate materiality and the materiality of language in interaction, which make possible a materialism beyond physicalism. (Grosz, 1994: 22, italics in original)

Grosz describes 'embodied subjectivity' and 'psychical corporeality', both signifying either the latent, material body or the productive, communicative body. Yet, this is one and the same body; it cannot be divided. This intensive combination makes these processes more than the sum of their parts, in the sense that she suggests of reorienting to a 'materialism beyond physicalism'. I use the term embodimentality.

In the way I want to use it, 'embodimentality' describes a recognizable sense of corporeal embodiment that becomes interactionally relevant in an intensive assemblage of material and expressive elements, but is not necessarily divisible into component gestures or movements. Embodimentality refers to the entirety of embodied elements, ranging from the seemingly fixed, like skin or eye color, to the entirely fluid, like speech, all of which contribute to practices of categorization when people meet one another.

This conceptualization relates most closely to Bourdieu's notion of *habitus*, but I choose to introduce a new word in order to ground this idea in multiplicity rather than identity. *Habitus* incorporates bodies with practices (Bourdieu, 1977), consumption habits (Bourdieu, 1984) and communicative habits (Bourdieu, 1991) as a single organism. Most often defined as a set of dispositions that function as an 'organizing mechanism' (Skeggs, 2004: 22), *habitus* reflects the 'internalisation of the social order, which in turn reproduces the social order' (Cresswell, 2002: 380), or Bourdieu's notion of practical sense, 'proposing that an individual's very body schema (the actor's awareness of the topographical structure of their body, its parts, movements and limits ...) is constituted by the class-based conditions of their existence' (Shilling, 2004: 475). Like embodimentality, *habitus* brings attention to the way the social is embodied and habituated, to the point that it is usually unquestioned in social interaction, and can be difficult to perceive and explain.

These definitions reflect the potential as well as the problems of using *habitus* in this analysis. Bourdieu's formulation of habitus reflects primarily how diverse members of a **class** can corporeally produce that class in concert, without premeditation; in fact, he refers to it as 'the class *habitus*' (Bourdieu, 1977: 83), relating it as a singular, universal set of 'material conditions of life' (Bourdieu, 1977: 63) applicable to a classed group. Bourdieu continued to explore this concept in relation to other ways he developed of imagining practice and the social (Bourdieu & Wacquant, 1992), but its usage has concentrated on his main dimension of interest – class. While it may have been intended as a productive encoding of bodily practice counterposing structuring structures, it has been repeated and interpreted as an equally structuring and structured concept in class-specific ways. *Habitus* is often called upon to describe embodiment that is more receptive than interactive, more 'being' than 'becoming'.

In contrast, the holistic perspective on embodiment I propose – as simultaneously physical, habitual and linguistic – creates a platform to discuss how individuals can become many things at once. In order to analyze 'embodimentality' in the chapters below, I will focus on how individuals make different pieces of it explicit in interaction. These pieces fall into two fuzzy realms: *bodily practices*, or *hexis*, which includes physicality, movement, modes of occupying space, and habits that have become so habitual they are difficult to perceive; and *communicative practices*, which include verbal and non-verbal codes. These two are not wholly divisible from each other, as with accent, but identifying them as nodes on a spectrum makes it easier to discuss the ways in which they work together, or they might be perceived to work against each other in diasporic 'hybridity'.

Hexis: Bodily practices beyond communication

> We can understand that, in many respects, the emigrant looks in a way like someone who was colonized at the last moment, like a *colonisé* who has outlived a colonization from which he cannot liberate himself, like a postcolonial *colonisé* and therefore someone who wants to be colonized (because he wants to remain an emigrant). ... And it is significant that the criticisms made of emigration, and, by that very fact, of emigrants, are directed mainly and most violently against the female emigrant population and, more specifically, women's bodies. Criticisms are made of the way they dress, of their corporeal *hexis*, their ways of holding themselves, speaking and behaving, especially in public – in other words, their physical deportment and comportment. (Sayad, 2004: 117)

Sayad's description above demonstrates a key quality of how *hexis* can contribute to being multiple: one can embody 'Algerianness' as a descendant of Algerian families, while also embodying corporeal *hexis* that marks one as *'colonisé'*. The former part is only made relevant by the contradictory, simultaneous presence of the latter – as dimensions of multiplicities with many moving parts. *Hexis* can be identified, but is often vaguely described by a lot of different factors, like 'the way they dress [or] their ways of holding themselves', which makes it difficult to talk about or make explicit. Yet, nevertheless, it plays an important role in how categorization happens, as an interpretation of embodimentality.

'Bodily *hexis*' is in fact another term borrowed from Bourdieu, which he described as 'a political mythology realized, *em-bodied*, turned into a permanent disposition, a durable way of standing, speaking, walking, and thereby of feeling and thinking' (Bourdieu, 1990: 69–70, italics in original). Like my usage of it, Bourdieu considered it as a component part of *habitus*, although it is possibly closer to Mauss's (class-less) definition of *habitus*, as learned 'body techniques' linked to education, generation and sex (Mauss, 1950). Yet, Bourdieu does not implicate *hexis* in class dynamics, but in social circumstances more broadly:

> The child imitates not 'models' but other people's actions. Body *hexis* speaks directly to the motor function, in the form of a pattern of postures that is both individual and systematic, because linked to a whole system of techniques involving the body and tools, and charged with a

host of social meanings and values: in all societies, children are particularly attentive to the gestures and postures which, in their eyes, express everything that goes to make an accomplished adult – a way of walking, a tilt of the head, facial expressions, ways of sitting and using implements, always associated with a tone of voice, a style of speech, and (how could it be otherwise?) a certain subjective experience. (Bourdieu, 1977: 87)

Hexis emphasizes the invisible potency of embodied practices as kinetic, gestural, expressive poses and movements, 'able to pass from practice to practice without going through discourse or consciousness' (Bourdieu, 1977: 87). McDowell (1999: 41) picks up *hexis* in spatial terms as 'different ways individuals and groups have of bearing their bodies, presenting them to others, moving or making space for their bodies'. Following both Bourdieu and McDowell, as well as Noble and Watkins (2003) and Shilling (2003), who invoke *hexis* in the context of sports activity, the term here describes these forms of embodiment as unique to certain groups, encoded, recognizable and significant, but not in any more specific imagination than 'bodily bearing' or mimetic inculcation of movement.

Goffman, on the other hand, incorporates this form as a part of human communicative capacity:

Although an individual can stop talking, he cannot stop communicating through the body idiom; he must say either the right thing or the wrong thing. He cannot say nothing. Paradoxically, the way in which he can give the least amount of information about himself – although this is still appreciable – is to fit in and act as persons of his kind are expected to act. (Goffman, 1966: 35)

This insight encapsulates the rightly labeled paradox of bodies: they communicate with or without any agentive action on the part of their owners. Specifically, they communicate something that is either 'right or wrong' in terms of a 'person of his kind' [sic] – implying succinctly that the material presentation of self is an integral part of the linguistic performance of self, which is both visual and auditory.

In the scope of this project, I do not attempt to catalog and dissect the features or practices of *hexis* into their individual significances. Rather, I want to reintegrate the fact of *hexis* – that these are material bodies consuming and communicating – and incorporate it as part of the embodimentality of participants along with their expressive communicative production. Their basic physical presence in the world, which is learned to be visibly recognized and read as embedded in emergent categories, includes attributes like skin tone, height, 'phenotype' or other elements formerly subsumed into 'race' that are normally linked to genetic inheritance. However, this physical presence is more than that. Their bodies are communicating something, producing *hexis* in interaction with other entities in their environments, but they themselves are not necessarily aware of its activity or in control of its effects.

Hexis, therefore, appears in my analyses through how interlocutors make it relevant in interaction, or how DVs manage to act (or not) like 'persons of their kind' are expected to act. It indicates the ways in which material bodies communicate without intention, as described by Goffman, but also the ways in which expressive forms (like practices of communication) are material, created by and emanating from physical bodies.

Communicative practices: Language use and 'identity'

Communicative practice, in both verbal and non-verbal forms, is an inherently social deployment of learned habits that structure conversation in ways that are usually unrecognized by participants (Erickson, 2004; Goffman, 1971, 1974; Gumperz, 1982; Sacks, 1992). This notion sets apart 'language' as a grammatical structure from 'communication', in a way that is foundational to the field of sociolinguistics (Hymes, 1972). The social properties of language are not restricted to purely communicative goals: linguistic practices have symbolic, affective and tangible impacts that act in ways beyond the scope of the 'message' of an utterance (Austin, 1962).

Yet, languages, as one of the substances with which communicative practices are accomplished, have indexical relationships to places and lineages of practitioners that exceed their quotidian frames of use. They often have legitimated, institutionally codified forms, making certain linguistic or communicative production more valued than others (Bourdieu, 1991; Gal, 1989) with hegemonic force (Woolard, 1985). The synonymity of 'nation' or 'state' with 'language', often traced back to Herder's notion of *volk*, reinforces an image that each communicator-citizen is equally proficient in reading, writing, speaking and hearing the 'native' language of the nation (Doerr, 2009; Héran et al., 2002; Housley & Hester, 2002; Portes & Rumbaut, 2001).

Empirical research demonstrates otherwise: the production of communicative practice in everyday situations involves both legitimated codes and creativity. Many key works in sociolinguistics have documented the fact that speakers vary their practices, where different kinds of variation can signal adherence to or distancing from markers of class, racial, ethnic, gender and any other aspect of 'identity' (Cameron, 1995; Duranti & Goodwin, 1992; Eckert, 2000; Hall & Bucholtz, 1995; Labov, 1966; Milroy, 1980; Schieffelin *et al.*, 1998). More recently, others have focused on how language use is productive of the 'social aggregates' (Muehlmann, 2014) beyond indexing them as entities that somehow exist external to those who use them (Blommaert & Rampton, 2011). In short, communication is usually based on common systems of form, but incorporates innovation and flexibility to associate or disassociate oneself from attributes that linguistic elements can be used to symbolize.

These ideas of language as indexical and fixed, without creativity, were a problematic axiom in early research on bilingualism and codeswitching, when choosing a code was thought to be a much more conscious and purposeful process. Contact between languages was 'interference' (Weinreich, 1953), and parsing how that intermingling was structured became a long field of study in itself (Myers-Scotton, 1993, 1998), with the result that we cannot point to code choice as necessarily indexing categorization. Access to multiple codes is just one more dimension to the way categories might operate in interaction. However, alongside the many dimensions addressed in the research listed above, the inability to practice a code – the inability to speak or understand, read or write – can create an absolute distinction between those who belong and those who do not. This severe distinction, however, is rare; more often individuals can access some part of a range of communicative practices to enable communication, even if they would not be considered 'bilingual'. This conceptualization of multilingualism and codeswitching as a spectrum of possible combinations, rather than distinctive models, is inspired here by the work of Robert Le Page and Andrée Tabouret-Keller.

Addressing multilingual practices as flexible and somewhat unpredictable, Le Page and Tabouret-Keller (1985) based their work in highly multilingual Belize, where they found it very difficult to isolate one model of codes or codeswitching that might correspond to any of the locally more defined ethnic and racial 'identities'. They proposed instead a multidimensional model of linguistic 'acts of identity' to analyze how linguistic variation is 'essentially idiosyncratic' (Le Page & Tabouret-Keller, 1985: 2). All 'acts of identity', for them, are relational and interactional, becoming focused – more regular or habitual – around points of commonality, where linguistic behavior is reinforced, and diffuse – more variable – when modifying behavior in response to others or at the fringe of a group (Le Page & Tabouret-Keller, 1985: 181). Their model is constrained by the centrality of some groups as desirable for identification, accessible, and encouraging of membership. They dispose of labels like 'ethnicity', which in communities of intense mixture tends to have very little meaning in relation to linguistic codes, and consider the way groups become stronger or disband through processes of reinforcement and differentiation.

The question becomes, then, not who is a 'complete bilingual' (as Portes & Rumbaut, 2001, seem to assume in their definition of 'transnational'), but how do individuals manage their abilities in the shifting contexts of interaction? How do different modes of ability in multiple codes connect to sociolinguistic contexts and interlocutor expectations to reinforce (focus) and differentiate (diffuse) groups? These questions relate to how communicative capacities intersect with processes of categorization in interaction.

Analytical approaches to categorization

Processes of categorization are topics for research across the social sciences, in cognitive anthropology (Hirschfeld, 1998; Lakoff, 1990) and sociology (Brubaker et al., 2004; Wimmer, 2009) and in social psychology (Prentice & Miller, 2007; Semin & Smith, 2008). Categorization appears to be inherent to the human ability to interact with the world – to manage enormous quantities of information through breaking it down into subsections. To this framing of the world, communicative studies of categorization provide a means to explore how categories (or attractors, ideal-types or prototypes – all of which act in similar ways in their own theoretical traditions) are shaped and acted upon by individuals in real time, through how categories and their boundaries become relevant to interaction.

Language can ostensibly be a means of categorizing: either an individual demonstrates the ability to communicate in a language or not. But the many variations and gradations of these abilities are negotiable, and become relevant as categorization in interaction only in specific reference to a context. Significant recent work in sociolinguistics and linguistic anthropology, rooted in the suggestions for Membership Categorization Analysis (MCA) in the work of Harvey Sacks (1992), employ linguistic microanalytical methods to address how categories are negotiated in interaction (Fitzgerald & Housley, 2015; Hester & Eglin, 1997; Schegloff, 2007; special issue of *Discourse Studies*, June 2012). There have been divergent strands of development based on Sacks' theories and, like Stokoe (2012), I am not advocating a specific strand as 'correct'. Rather, I want to indicate the commonalities among these and other sociolinguistic research in terms of the theoretical formulation of categories, and suggest expanding these framings to a sociolinguistics that includes embodimentality as well.

Although some researchers explicitly use the term 'categorization' in their work, often examining how participants evoke specific distinctions between in- and out-groups in conversational data, other approaches, such as Communicative Accommodation Theory (CAT) or 'styling', implicitly discuss categories as social objects but approach them with different sociolinguistic methods. Using CAT, researchers interpret the linguistic devices that speakers use in order to 'converge' or 'diverge' with their interlocutors in response to perceived characteristics and the desire to approach or distance oneself from them (Giles *et al.*, 1991; Harwood & Giles, 2005; Ylänne-McEwan & Coupland, 2004). Expanding from this premise of adapting to a speaker, work on communicative 'styling' in variationist paradigms (Bell, 1999; Coupland, 2007; Eckert & Rickford, 2001) also quite often implies the presence of categorical formations, which speakers might 'cross' (Cutler, 1999) or 'pass' (Bucholtz, 1995; Piller, 2002) by *being* one assumed category and *using attributes* of another. While work based on Sacks' MCA is more often focused on how these 'acts of identity' are conversationally achieved, work in accommodation or styling generally considers the 'identities' in play, and what meanings speakers have assigned to their interactional achievements. This distinction is ontologically important – and sometimes epistemologically irreconcilable – but relates to the same basic propensity to negotiate belonging in perceived groups by investigating how these negotiations happen through linguistic verbal and non-verbal communication.

Research beyond sociolinguistics, sometimes also using ethnomethodological epistemologies rooted in Sacks and Garfinkel, engage aspects of embodiment in addition to linguistic production. Katz (1999) provides an example where laughing or crying are considered as multifaceted embodied emotions *and* as conversational actions, in order to explore how conditions create such reactions. His treatment of emotions as multilayered embodiment, beyond conversational or interactional exchange, leads towards including more neurological and systemic aspects of interaction as part of what social scientists (as opposed to medical scientists) can appreciate in analysis. Others along these lines focus on the way bodies can simply be present in public spaces as categorial: Tavory (2010), for example, explores how visible Jewish embodiment becomes part of neighborhood borders as individuals are categorized in mundane incidents between strangers in public. This research, mostly based in sociology that draws on some aspects of social psychology (Lamont & Molnár, 2002), advocates for a focus on 'boundaries' and how they are socially and symbolically enacted by individuals. In other words, it provides an alternate path to a similar goal, that of exploring how categories focus around certain attributes and exempt others at their diffused limit of participation – their boundaries.

The approach to categories I adopt here includes aspects of all of these lines of research, while shifting their ontological assumptions to reflect the fluidity and tenuous stability of the model suggested by Le Page and Tabouret-Keller (1985). That is, I explore how different facets of embodiment – from linguistic ideologies to communicative practice to embodimentality – indicate how categories *focus* around certain attributes and *diffuse* in relation to others. The underlying assumption – as Le Page and Tabouret-Keller came to conclude – is that individuals do not have 'identities', only variance of many entities simultaneously between different categorial nodes: '[t]heir cultural gravitational forces operate in many directions; each of them occupies an individual position, and yet they give evidence of sharing various loyalties and hatreds and alliances and identities within many different spheres' (Le Page & Tabouret-Keller, 1985: 175). Moreover, the 'individual position' they refer to is itself also not perfectly stable. Thinking of this configuration through assemblage, it is a *becoming* and not a *being*. For example, in relation to the concept of passing (see Chapter 3), the person and the categorial boundaries across which he or she attempts to pass are both becomings – they momentarily constitute each other in an interaction, only to be constituted with variations at their next encounter. So, instead of investigating how these individuals are 'doing-being Moroccan' in interaction, this project investigates how 'becoming-Moroccan' happens in this diasporic context.

Jones (2009) remarks that one of the paradoxical aspects of using categories as research tools is that 'when we are trying to think of the boundaries between categories as open and porous – which, intellectually, we know they are – we tend cognitively to understand categories as closed and bounded containers' (Jones, 2009: 179). The struggle in writing down these analyses is to maintain the perspective that these dynamics are not fixed, closed or bounded, and that they will likely have shifted in formation by the time similar research would have been replicated. Some aspects of this becoming are more solidified – like the distinction between speaking or not speaking French – as they are connected to big discourses as well as micro-analysis. Others are more variable and constantly shifting. Still more variable are forms of kinetic embodiment – a way of walking in the sense that Sayad identified above – because they are linguistically ineffable, although instinctively recognizable. All of these, from explicit discourses to inexplicit instinct, play a part in how diasporic visitors are recognized as diasporic Moroccan 'becomings' when in Morocco, through how they struggle to manipulate these embodied aspects in interaction.

Strategies for Analysis: Epistemology and Methods

The methods for data collection and data analysis in this research are designed to integrate the ontological perspective described above – exploring categories in assemblage – using tools from ethnomethodology and sociolinguistics. The central premises for my epistemological approach follow several of Katz's (1999) initial tenets for his exploration in emotion.

First, I treat the *reasoning* and *meanings* individuals assign to their actions (the *why*) as a different form of data from *how* those actions or practices take place (Katz, 1999: 8). While *why* can give one situated interpretation of categorial practice, *how* gives a different interpretation in triangulation, providing an analytical snapshot – just one moment in time – of nonlinear and multifaceted causality leading to the effect of focusing or diffusing categories around particular actions. In other words, investigating how 'Moroccanness' works when thrown into relief by interactions between diasporic and territorially resident communities necessarily means analyzing meta-discourses about 'being Moroccan' as much as individual practice around 'becoming-Moroccan', because the two are inextricable from one another. To perform this analysis, I draw micro-analytical methods primarily from sociolinguistics and linguistic anthropology which are capable of addressing as much the *how* of categorial action in conversation as the *why* of discursive resources in interviews.

The ontology I suggest of interaction and becoming aligns very much with recent suggestions by Blommaert and his colleagues (Blommaert, 2013a, 2013b; Blommaert & Rampton, 2011; Parkin, 2012) towards a paradigmatic shift in sociolinguistics away from 'identities' and towards complexity. Yet, I want to suggest moving slightly further by incorporating embodied materialities – embodimentality – as part of the complex entities that can shift in interaction as much as the communicative matter those bodies produce. I extend micro-analysis of talk beyond transcribed language to embodimentality because, ontologically, I conceptualize linguistic practice and corporeal practice as material formations. To do this, I am using the theoretical distinction between *material* and *expressive* that DeLanda (2002, 2006) makes, but still approaching it with the methodological tools of micro-analysis. As much as speakers can use practices to access different groups or categories (Le Page & Tabouret-Keller, 1985) – through seemingly easy expressive means, like switching from French to *derija* – they are limited by the more stable and tangible materiality of bodies, and how those materialities can also be attached to categories.

In order to explore this expressivity and materiality as embodimentality, I analyze observed and sometimes recorded interactional data, as well as DV narratives about moments of interaction between themselves and resident Moroccans. This analysis touches on elements like dress, flesh and makeup, as well as speech or muteness and presence or absence, by using participants' opinions about embodiment expressed in interviews and analyzing their orientations as they emerge in sequential interactions. This part of the analysis also addresses code choice, to the extent that *derija* language use is again and again cited by participants as an important and stable marker of 'Moroccanness'. Embodimentality combines choosing to speak in a certain code with inculcated habits of *hexis* – from habitual gestures and practices of gaze, to habitual capacities to make certain sounds with one's vocal equipment – as a cohesive process. Through repetition, communicative practices become incorporated into the body in material ways, solidifying *hexis*, or learned habits of the body, that follow certain forms and constrain others. Within embodimentality, I use *hexis* combined with linguistic habits through ways that bodies are 'communicating without intention' – that they are part of interactional encounters, even when they may not be recorded or made explicitly relevant.

Secondly, following Katz (1999: 10), I choose to take metaphors seriously, like the description by resident and non-resident Moroccans alike of 'smelling' diasporic Moroccanness. Obviously, this does not refer to an actual scent of 'diasporicness', but rather, I suggest, a combination of visually perceived (and precognitively interpreted) elements that are instinctively more-than-visual – perceived by 'smell' as much as by sight, and sometimes expressed through silence. My analysis of these perceptions is not, however, based on visual data, for practical, ethical and methodological reasons. First, practical restrictions on recording prevented collection of a suitable video corpus, even though visual cues may be helpful to illustrate the descriptions. Ethically, it was not feasible to guarantee participants' anonymity, and not culturally respectful to operate visual recording equipment on the street in Morocco. Finally, methodologically, visible manifestations of the body are evoked through conversation and analyzable as such, in the ways that categories are emergent, assigned and contested by interactants turn by turn, based on the visual and audible information they interpret. What matters for this interactional analysis is not what the researcher might observe on video, but how participants made use of the visual information available to them – much of which may not have been recordable with the mobile technologies available for fieldwork.

Thus, instead of focusing on the physical practices of embodiment, this analysis incorporates ways in which materialities are made relevant as expressed by participants in interaction. Discourses on these visible markers of categorial belonging are analyzed as metaphors emergent from observational and interview data, through how impressions about embodied presences are re-membered and interpreted after the fact. These metaphors taken seriously, then, relate to how embodied, felt and sensed interactions between DV participants and resident Moroccans have impacts beyond the moment of encounter.

Practicalities

This research is designed as an 'ethnography of the holiday', by following the people in multi-sited ethnography (Falzon, 2009; Hage, 2005; Hannerz, 2003; Marcus, 1995). Following as a method has been advocated in literatures on migration or transnational communities (Collins & Slembrouck, 2005; Levitt & Waters, 2002; Mountz & Wright, 1996) in order to embed the ethnographer in a multilocated community, like his or her participants. Consequently, the research activities did not adhere to a typical ethnographic model of embeddedness in a geographically locatable community. Instead, it was a temporally locatable community: the annual, cyclical collective practice of many Moroccans from Europe to go from dispersed geographical locations in Europe to dispersed geographical locations in Morocco on their summer holidays.

The primary population in this research are post-migrant generation diasporic Moroccans who normally reside in France, Belgium or The Netherlands, and who participate in this annual holiday travel to Morocco. As such, I considered their general characteristics to include:

(1) they identify Morocco as a 'homeland' as children of two parents who emigrated from there, but one in which they themselves have not lived beyond the age of entry into school (generally four years old), if at all;
(2) they have some linguistic competence in a Moroccan language, but have broader competence in French, Dutch or Flemish; and
(3) they, as adults, choose to spend holiday time in Morocco, regularly or sporadically, in their hometown or elsewhere.[2]
(4) Their other social characteristics vary, including gender, educational attainment, religious practice, marital status and professional attainment. They come from different towns in Europe and travel to different hometowns in Morocco. Their central unifying characteristic is participation in the holiday, whether actively or passively.

These parameters make one key assumption: that the notion of belonging to a territorial and imagined nation *diasporically* is applicable to the individuals who participate, in the sense that they choose to travel (Wagner, 2012). Yet, this construction of participants leaves open to investigation *how* that 'diasporicness' might be focused and diffused around myriad potential practices of categorizational belonging.

I found participants through networks, snowball sampling, and the recruitment of flow populations (Ritchie & Lewis, 2003: 94). The initial source for networked and snowball participants was close relationships with three key women, one each from France, Belgium and The Netherlands, hereafter families A, B and C, respectively. Other participants were recruited during fieldwork in Europe and in Morocco by approaching individuals with a survey questionnaire and soliciting them for further participation. Through these combined methods, 76 individuals contributed their time and opinions for interviews, participant observation and recordings, along with approximately 70 others who filled in survey questionnaires. Figure 2.1 shows how the previously discussed known clusters of migration between Morocco and Europe are reflected in my participant pool.

The intensive participation of the three key women is reflective of their statuses and positions within their familial social groups, and my own position as a highly educated, female, American researcher. Yasmine A[3] (France) and Malika B (Belgium) are older than 30 and not married, which is unusual for Moroccan women as pressure to marry is strong in Morocco and in diaspora (Buitelaar, 2007). Mouna C (Netherlands) was still relatively young (21 at the time of the research), but was enrolled in advanced higher education. The two older women are in professional jobs, are both highly multilingual and have many friends and connections outside their immediate communities, along with regular contact with their families. The younger woman had

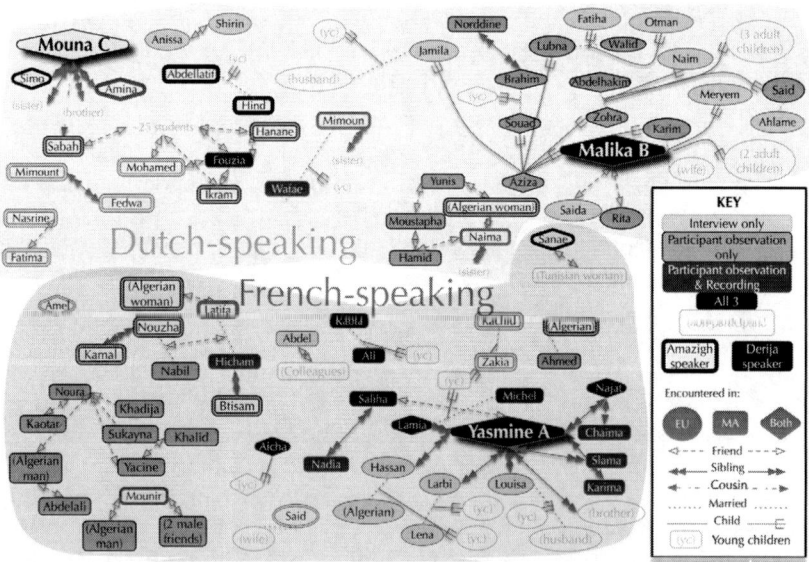

Figure 2.1 Participants coded for Moroccan language, participation type, relationship and place of encounter; grouped by primary EU language spoken

also travelled outside her home community in the context of her education. These levels of education and achievement seem to be more common among Moroccan-origin women in Europe than men, relating to entrenched stigmatization in education (Buitelaar, 2007), yet may not be encouraged in all families.

During fieldwork, I stayed in the family home of each of them – in France and The Netherlands for short visits and in Belgium over the six-week period I spent in Antwerp. All of their family members were made aware of my research aims, and many of them participated in the project through interviews in Europe or through time spent with them on holiday in Morocco.

Biases and Targeted Dimensions

My positioning as a researcher relates intensely to the status of these women as being unusually highly educated or extroverted towards other communities. Their individual interests reflect my own personal interests, to some extent, in that we all enjoy learning languages and interacting with others outside our home communities. Yet, my status as doubly outsider – in that I am neither Moroccan, nor French, Belgian or Dutch – also served a purpose in positioning me to others beyond these women. While my interest in Moroccans was sometimes questioned or thought suspicious – either because I might be an agent of the CIA or because I could be in search of a husband – I was often able to convince potential participants, to the best of my knowledge, that this was not the case. I also invested time, energy and interest in being a reciprocating member of these communities to the best of my abilities.

The unusual status of these three women may make them typical examples of fringe gatekeepers in the broader community, but their families were also generally welcoming to my research. Contact with their families, and sometimes networks of extended families or friends, enabled me to grasp a more average cross-section of potential participants. Given my own relevant recognizable (and categorizable) attributes, as a European-origin American, non-Muslim researcher, entry into this community would be in any case limited by sentiments of distrust for non-Muslims and distrust of researchers among a problematized minority community that has been subjected to successive microscopes.

The most important bias in this research is related to this potential for suspicion, and the political context of conservative Islam in Europe. There is low representation among my participants of individuals who identify themselves as following or who demonstrate more intense religious adherence, which is a growing trend in The Netherlands in particular (Leiken, 2005). Religious orthodoxy, which was growing at the time of research, is undoubtedly linked with increased concerns about security in Europe since the emergence of jihadism: many of the participants in recent acts of violence – most recently in Paris (November 2015) at the time of this writing – would likely be members of the group described here, as Belgian and French citizens of Moroccan origin (*The Economist*, 2015). The dynamics of this trend relate directly to my inability to obtain more contact with this group, as part of the rhetoric of such conservative religious movements is distrust of non-adherents. It is difficult to know, however, to what extent this group is underrepresented, because it is documented by a complicated mixture of religious belief and political discourse, neither of which is easily quantifiable in terms of population. Furthermore, it is important to recognize in the analyses below how frustrations about territorial belonging may influence a young person to choose violence as a method for belonging that circumvents the negative feedback they may interpret from others in both diasporic homes – as well as how others manage that negative feedback without violence.

Participants not associated with these were recruited by approaching individuals in Morocco during the holiday period. This was normally accomplished by spending time in high-traffic pedestrian areas or in certain cafés or restaurants that DVs tended to frequent, introducing myself as a researcher and obtaining a written questionnaire, then pursuing further contact with individuals who indicated willingness to participate. Interactions with these flow population participants ranged from spending an afternoon shopping in the souq, to meeting them over a period of days for various holiday activities. Yet, as Figure 2.1 demonstrates, the variety of forms of participation is fairly balanced, with proportional numbers of individuals who gave their time for interviews, participant observation and recording from each country.

As part of 'following the people' during their vacations, the pool of participants was ephemeral and unpredictable, and therefore unreliable for an ethnographer seeking depth of contact. The composition of diasporic visitors is different each successive summer, in terms of who decides to travel, and where and when they go. While I had initially imagined interviewing many participants in Europe, then participating in the holiday with them in Morocco, in the end very few of those interviewed in Europe made the journey in 2008. Most of those who participated in all three qualitative collection methods, indicated by dark item background as 'all three' on Figure 2.1, did so entirely in Morocco, or across pilot and primary research. I therefore consider each participant's contribution in reference to what I know of his or her personal background, but also as a fragment in comparison with other similarly positioned individuals. Each individual is a multidimensional participant, in relation to an idea of 'Moroccanness' expressed by traveling to and around Morocco and in comparison with other individuals along dimensions of linguistic and geographical belonging.

Given the primacy of linguistic practice to my research, one of my goals in finding participants was to recruit individuals whose linguistic abilities fit dimensions different from the dominant Moroccan Arabic-French model I had previously investigated (see Wagner, 2006). Specifically, I targeted three relevant, non-standard bilingual models: Amazigh-French, Moroccan Arabic-Dutch or, most of all, Amazigh-Dutch as the anti-standard. These linguistic differences are related to emerging geographical dimensions of diasporic Moroccan communities, roughly divided between French-speaking Belgium and France, and Flemish-speaking Belgium and The Netherlands (Figure 2.1), as well as implicit French-Arabic standards discussed above in Morocco. They are also distributed differently in Moroccan geography, as demonstrated by Charrad's map reproduced previously (see Figure 1.1).

Figure 2.1 demonstrates, however, that the participant population is skewed to include an overabundance of French DVs ($n = 35$) in comparison to Belgians ($n = 24$) or Dutch ($n = 17$), and that many more French speakers were contacted in Morocco and participated in recordings than Dutch speakers. Only about one-third of participants are Amazigh-only speakers, the majority of these being from The Netherlands. Mouna C, who was my point of entry into networks of Amazigh-Dutch participants, was unable to go on the holiday during the summer of primary data collection. Her absence no doubt influenced my ability to recruit more Amazigh-Dutch Moroccans because of my positioning as an outsider religiously, geographically, linguistically and nationally. She herself warned me that I would have a hard time finding participants among Amazigh or Rifi-Dutch Moroccans, citing a predominant distrust of outsiders (related, according to her, both in their marginalized history in Morocco and heightened religious conservativism). In the end, I did not have contact with enough individuals along different bilingual models to make any claims about distinctions between subgroups of linguistic practice, but there are some observations that may lead to more research on how minority languages become part of the diasporic community (see above).

Conclusion

The following ethnographic analyses, then, incorporate a revised ontological perspective on familiar epistemological material. With robust and tested methods about interaction, sociolinguistics and linguistic anthropology are uniquely positioned to address the theoretical notion of multiplicity in analysis of how different dimensions become relevant in encounters. Shifting the onto-logical basis of how categories are formed for core concepts like 'ethnicity', 'race' or 'community' renders these dimensions more pliable themselves, and more able to adapt to different ways that what analysts might categorize as 'race' manifests, for example, as discourses about 'class' (Twine, 1998). In these contexts, in the past, we have proposed slightly modified definitions of core concepts to accommodate empirical findings; what I suggest is destroying core concepts in favor of emergent becomings, always interactional and always shaped by how they are made metaphorically relevant. Categorical thinking is a normal human mode of operation, which permits us as researchers to inves-tigate how categories are made.

Thus, by drawing out these categories as ideal-types, attractors or meta-phors which emerge in interactional, discursive and observational data, I hope to demonstrate how an essentialized definition of 'Moroccanness' is proven untrustworthy to interactants who expect certain elements to be linked to the category and discover them absent, or who perform attributes they perceive to be important but lacking.

This -ness does not follow definitions of 'ethnicity' or 'nation', in that it is not necessarily a shared 'culture', language, homeland, politics or religion that make these individuals 'Moroccan'. Instead, I characterize it through assemblage, as an entity emergent through interactions.

Notes

(1) This propensity also applies to the emerging science of genetics (see El Haj, 2007).
(2) With respect for ethical considerations on vulnerable populations, I did not interview or solicit the participation of individuals under the age of 18. Some minors are present in the analysis who were accompanying their parents or older siblings.
(3) All names are pseudonyms.

3 Defining the Category 'Moroccan': Embodied Misrecognitions and Dynamics of Passing

Being (Mis)recognized I: Stopping on the Street

One afternoon (7 August 2008), I accompanied Wafae, her husband, children and sister-in-law while they walked around the Marrakech souq before heading to the airport to return to The Netherlands. At one point they were speaking with each other in Dutch when a vendor seated outside his shop on the street called out in our direction, 'Turkish?' Wafae replied in *derija*, 'bḥalək bḥalna' (you and us are the same), as we continued to walk. Unlike other similar encounters I witnessed, in this one Wafae turned back to ask the vendor why he had called them Turkish. I later asked her what he said.

Interaction Extract 3.1 Assumed they were Turkish

Wafae, Marrakech, 7 August 2008, 15 sec
1 **W:**   I asked him/ because I said I- well- well they're Moroccan just like you (.)
2 **LW:** mm
3 **W:**   and he said, well I heard them talking and I could not understand them/ so I assumed that they were Turkish.

As part of their business practice, vendors use tactics such as guessing the provenance of passersby in order to get their attention and attract them into their shops. Calling out to our group may have been intended as an affiliative conversational opening, but it became a vital (mis)recognition, rendering Wafae and her family as something completely other (Turkish), to the extent that she stopped, returned to him, and elicited his explanation.

Wafae's report on the conversation attributes the burden to language use as what misled him, but that aspect is only part of what a vendor might perceive as they were walking by. Something about this family together on the street – Wafae, her husband, child and sister-in-law (and me) – was ambiguous enough that their embodimentality – including the highlighted linguistic features – was recognized not as 'Moroccan' or even 'Moroccan tourists' but as something in a completely different category. Their bodies and presence on this street became part of how a categorial 'Moroccanness' is continuously shaped in everyday interactions.

Such minor scenes of embodimentality are played out repeatedly as DVs move around Morocco. In this case, simply passing by on the street becomes a moment where 'Moroccanness' is made relevant, without the need for any more elaborate interaction. I witnessed this kind of calling out with other DVs, who occasionally would comment on the parameters of their (mis)recognition, wondering why these vendors would think them to be 'Brazilian' or 'Algerian' as opposed to Moroccan. This instance was significant because Wafae took action to answer that question, by pausing to turn back and ask. Doing this, she also chose to speak to him in *derija*, thereby justifying her 'Moroccan' embodimentality that was misrecognized moments earlier. This encounter reflects how this process is quiet and constant: (mis)recognitions are subtle but unceasing, and to achieve 'Moroccanness' it must be substantiated through embodied acts at unexpected moments. It also reflects one of the ways in which DVs recognize definitions of 'Moroccanness' and react to them – specifically, using an ancestral language to establish their 'local' membership.

This chapter will examine several situations where similar categorial work took place in meta forms, in that DVs are explicitly describing 'Moroccanness' and how it should 'correctly' be done, or they have encounters with others (like Wafae's) where its attributes become a subject of discussion. Talking about the prescribed or discussed ways of 'being-Moroccan' connects directly to how DVs can also seek not to be recognized as 'not-Moroccan' – in other words, how they attempt to pass as 'being-(locally)-Moroccan' using their linguistic and embodied resources.

In other fields and contexts, passing is a means to manage distinctions that create negative experiences or disadvantages for those who experience them. These dynamics of negativity associated with 'Europeanness' are often (but not always) something that DVs seek to avoid. Although many may not attempt to hide their 'Europeanness', many feel pressure to mask what they perceive as characteristic aspects of their embodied assemblage – specifically things like clothing and code choice – as a means of passing towards being accepted as 'becoming-Moroccan'. This discussion frames passing as it can involve both visual and audible embodimentality, but importantly the two cannot be separated from one another: although DVs (and others) discuss how different aspects can be easily manipulable or not, the whole project of passing cannot work without engaging the whole assemblage of body, language and interlocutors together.

As with most categorial boundaries, definitions of 'Moroccanness' become most precise when framed through negation – that is, by identifying what is 'not-Moroccan' or, in the way Sara Ahmed discusses it in the Introduction epigraph, through *strangeness*. To explore how 'Moroccanness' works as a defined category, I approach *strangeness* below as it happens through embodiment, through linguistic practice, and through intersections between the two as embodimentality. Then, I discuss the dynamics of passing in other literatures, followed by some of the visible and audible practices participants describe and use to attempt to pass. Finally, I present an example of misrecognition that inverts Wafae's experience, to conceptualize how becoming-diasporic involves being able to access both 'Moroccanness' and 'Europeanness' when it is situationally possible.

Strangeness: Being Recognized as 'Not-Moroccan'

DVs always know that they are strange in Morocco. Although it is a *place* they are attached to as *descendants*, it is a *place* they are not bound to in the same way as other residents who pass more of their lifetimes there beyond the summer holidays. This *strangeness* acts as an omnirelevant device (Fitzgerald *et al.*, 2009) in their relationships with the locally resident Moroccans they might encounter: it undergirds their understandings of relationships with each other, even though those relationships might differ in many other ways between interlocutors. As such, *strangeness* is a categorization that DVs are always ready to manage in interaction, and which they learn to manage through their own embodied and linguistic resources.

The example below indicates how *strangeness* can be experienced in practice, and some of the tropes that influence it. In an interview at a home in Antwerp, Soumia and Ahlame responded to a question about their use of

Arabic by describing how that language skill works with their embodied performance.

Interview Extract 3.1 Crossed the water

Ahlame and Soumia, Antwerp, 25 March 2008, 2 min

1   **LW:** When um when you were traveling, for example, um () were you: speaking Arabic mostly? or-

2   **S:** yes

3   **LW:** yeah

4   **A:** yeah.

5   **LW:** umm did you-

6   **S:**   =wh'- and when I do- I didn't want they hear what you say, I spe- I spoke uh: Flemish, [(1.0) hehh but eh- ((smile voice)) normally in Arabic=

7   **A:**   [hehehhh .h he
=yeah

8   **LW:** what do you mean, when: when=

9   **S:**   =when you want to (.) .h to have some eh critics/ or you want to say something you don't want the other:: (1.5) for=example= you=are=in=a=restaurant and you say, look it's not good[, en- no I don't like, you are not going to say in Arabic [ah! maši məzyen ((not good)) hahahahhha

10 **LW:**   [yeah
[haha hhahha

11 **LW:** ḥayb ḥayb! ((bad bad))

12   ((all three laughing 3.8[))

13 **A:**   [ḥayb ((bad)) hehhe

14 **LW:** um (.9) d-did you ever find problems with people in terms of () like, understanding what they were saying, or:[(.)them understa[nding you,

15 **A:**   [n:o

16 **S:**   [no

17 **LW:** no?

18 **S:** no

19 **LW:** do people ever comment kind of oh, you=know where are you from, your accent is-

20 **S:** yes but y- they see that enh? you are different enh, even you want to speak very very ve- very good arabic, they are going to:: (1.5 .hhh) to say, she's not from here. (.8) becau[se you (.) you have another appearance,=

21 **A:**   [it's
like they, it's like ye- yeah
22 **S:**   =you:: ma- and maybe the **make**up
is different, maybe your, uh your **hair** is not eh dressed like
there, I-[they see it always
23 **A:**   [mmm
24 **LW:** mmm
25 **A:** mmm
26 **LW:** it's same for you? you d-[() they see it right away when you: =
27 **A:**   [mm
28 **A:** =yeah/ yeah/ you can't/ you can't deny the fact that,(.) if you
meet someone, he is going to say, ok/ you're not from here/
your-[you cr- you **crossed the water** and you came back on
holiday/[=
29 **LW:**   [mm
                        [hh
30 **A:**   =that's how they say it in: [(.) in <u>tanja</u>
((Tangier)), so () =
31 **S:**   [mm,
32 **A:**   =[[you're from over, over the:: .hhh [the
sea:
33 **LW:**   [[mm   [how-
in Arabic? how = do = they
34 **A:** <u>qtati el behar</u> ((you crossed the sea))
35 **LW:** yeah
36 **S:** that's how they:: =
37 **LW:** hhhahaha'
38 **S:**   =[[you cross
39 **A:**   [[that's how- you crossed the sea,/[so,
(.9) =
40 **S:**   [mm
41 **A:**   =you're from across the sea/ that's how they- they say,
it's like they **smell** (.6) .h [the fact that you're not **born**
there and you're not from °there so°.h =
42 **LW:**   [yeah
43 **LW:** yeah
44 **A:**   =d-d- we **do speak the**
language, I think ye- you do speak the language but there are
some certain: (.5) =
45 **S:**   [[accents mmm
46 **A:**   [[=**mentality differences** and and, **accents** and:
(.)which tell them that you're not from there, that you're not
born there, so

This discussion on the experience of strangeness encapsulates the range of modes in which it was reported, enacted and negotiated through embodimentality by Moroccan DVs in this research. Soumia and Ahlame describe their strangeness as bodily and sensory: local Moroccans can hear that they are not from there (through their use of language), they can see it on their bodies in the way they dress and do their hair, and they can even (metaphorically) 'smell' it. Soumia and Ahlame know they are *strange* because they are told: they are not out-of-Morocco; they 'crossed the sea'.

In relation to such crossings, Ahmed (2007) focuses on border policing in relation to strangeness. Through a framework of whiteness, border zones produce an imaginary of 'black' bodies processed through them, infiltrating 'white' spaces. These bodies are all the more dangerous because they belong in some way; they are attached to the 'right' passport and are permitted to pass over borders despite having the 'wrong' embodied attributes or name.

These same processes are inverted for DVs entering Morocco. Having the 'right' passport permits their physical motility to 'cross the sea', but it is the 'wrong' passport for their 'Moroccan' bodies. If the presence of strangers helps to define boundaries by defining otherness, the presence of 'strangers' who also have a claim to localness might shape these boundaries in unexpected ways. In this sense, strangeness functions as an acceptance of *descent* and but denial of *place*: DVs are allotted the right to be 'Moroccan' through having a materially 'Moroccan' body-by-*descent*, but their bodies are recognized, nevertheless, as out-of-*place*.

For Ahlame and Soumia, their situational descriptions reflect both sides of this strangeness, in how it is told to them – how they are recognized as 'not-being-Moroccan' (by unspecified others) – but also in how they produce it themselves. Ahlame cites 'mentality differences', a concept frequently repeated by DVs as a source of difference in preference and habit between DVs and resident Moroccans (see Wagner, 2011). Soumia describes how she uses her European language as a secret language in Morocco, effectively closing out others who cannot understand when she wants to criticize. Both of them, then, reflect on this strangeness through how they are 'out of place' through differences in habits and preferences, or difference in access to languages. Strangeness becomes something produced through practices by all parties, in the ways DVs maintain place-based distance, like using their European languages or feeling themselves categorized as being when they cross the sea again. Their strangeness inhabits the distance between bodies that fit the attractor 'Moroccanness' and their ambiguous bodies, which are apparently (visually) Moroccan, but also apparently (visually, audibly, 'smellably') not-Moroccan. These bodies can be situationally read as 'being-European', and other times as 'not-being-Moroccan-enough' – in any case, *strange*.

For many Moroccan diasporic visitors, being recognized as Moroccan matters – as demonstrated, in one distinct event, by Wafae's act of returning to the vendor to correct his misrecognition. If anything, the tropes of being 'neither here nor there' discussed in the previous chapters reflect the importance of being able to call oneself 'Moroccan', and of that dimension being acknowledged and reinforced by others. Not being recognized as Moroccan is a mirror of the integration problems experienced by Moroccan Europeans when in Europe. Whereas rejections of localized 'identities' in Europe are named as 'minority oppression' and 'racism', problems in being accepted as Moroccan in Morocco are not necessarily named, but are often expressed as akin to a denial of one's birthright.

The practical effects of this aspect to their strangeness are at issue in the following two extracts. In the first, cousins Naim and Otman talk about their strategies for managing their 'out of place' demeanor; in the second, Fedwa relates how certain contexts of strangeness cause her discomfort.

Interview Extract 3.2 *They know immediately*

Naim B and Otman B, Antwerp, 24 March 2008, 1 min 30 sec

1   **LW:**   a lot of people tell me about/ when- when you're negotiating something you=have=to speak Arabic or else they'll know:: they'll know where you're from. Something like that. [do you ev-

2   **N:**   [yeah b- of course, but they see it=

3   **O:**   = they see it. They see it right away. [(.) you can't hide it. Soheheh uh .h [eh

4   [mm
                                                   [so what language do you speak while you're there?

5   **O:**   Arabic,=

6   **N:**   =Arabic=

7   **O:**   =[[Arabic#

8   **LW:**   [[°Arabic yeah°

9   **N:**   =mye (.) .h but ah- but they can see it, eh: just our ehm: manner of clothing, you=know ahw: the clothes that you wear, and how we (1.1 .h)°y=know° just how we w:alk, and how we drive, and how we talk/ (.) they can- they::- they can immediately (.) kn:ow that we are not from Morocco.

10 **LW:** °yeah yeh°

11 **N:**   and that's why also the prices [(.8) [cha::nge en ah (.5) =

12 **LW:**   [hh

13 **O:**   [but it depends, it
    depends. .h w- [it just eh: it just like he said so:
14 **N:**   [=in Tangiers
15 **LW:** like Naim said/ yeah
16 **N:** they really see it yeah but we have re- [there's really a
    problem.
17 **O:**   [w- (.) it depends with
    people so: I mean eh:#: if yer- if you're gonn:e: (1.5) wear
    the **same** clothes as them then it's much #less, much less#. =
18 **LW:** really/
19 **O:** =you're gonna see just eh: #(.6 .h) en- and if you g- eh- you
    e- with eh: some guys of the neighborhood, then they'll think/
    automatically oh, (.4) th-those are all together. So
20 **LW:** kamlin ((all together)) yeah
21 **O:** families. that's it
22 **LW:** um: whad- when you mean the same clothes as them/ like what?
23 **O:** djellaba, jabador, uh:# # # šnu hadi baqe? ((what's that
    already?))
24 **N:** bəlek? šnu ((yours? what))
25 **O:** just eh::m traditional clothes of some:

Interview Extract 3.3 *They see you are not from here*

Fedwa (Mimount, Amina C), Al Hoceima, 22 July 2008, 1 min 20 sec
1 **LW:** wha- what problems did you have? when you were::
2 **F:** ah- me? (1.1) eh: men, general.
3 **LW:** yeah.
4 **F:** ahhehehehehe .h
5 **LW:** that sounds familiar
6   ((all laughing 3.3))
7 **F:** when you are traveling like women, (.) an:d they see ah- on
    your c clothes that you are not somebody from here/=
8 **LW:** yeah
9 **F:**   =eh: so they
    try to (.) say not nice things/ and you don't feel- **good** like,
    (1.1) if eh-h- every time eh: pspspss= ((imitating cat noise
    used to call women on the street))
10 **LW:** yeah
11 **F:** eh::
12 **LW:** yeah
13 **F:** like pfffhh hhhh ((slow outbreath/sigh))
14 **LW:** hehehe

15 **F:**   .h I'm not a cat, meow! hahahahh[ha
16 **LW:**   [hehah .h yeah. () no/ eh- I-I
        know that (.) problem [(.) ((laughing)) well so
17 **F:**   [yeah hahahaha
18 **LW:** [[understood
19 **F:**   [[that is the only- the only problem, ah-ah- ah:: for me, like-
        like a: woman traveling, I don't have any- any problem with the
        police, but it's (.) cause I speak the language and I know, .h
        eh the mentality that I have to speak to them, so they: say- I
        never had any problems.

In these two extracts, being recognized as a body that is 'Moroccan but not from here' is attributed direct, practical and negative consequences. In the first, both Naim and Otman agree that they are recognized on sight as *strange* (Lines 2–3), and then Naim directly attributes the allegedly higher prices they received for goods to that recognition (Line 11). Fedwa in the second extract links verbal harassment on the street to being recognized as from another place (Line 7). Because of such seemingly direct, tangible consequences, DVs are constantly engaged in processes of projecting and defending their 'Moroccanness' as moments and situations arise where it becomes relevant.

These reported examples are descriptions of archetypal situations where 'local-Moroccanness' is interpreted as a pivotal entity in a course of events, becoming a category with specific consequences and significances. The negative affect of these events – for example, 'being recognized' as from another *place* linked with extortion or harassment – is common in the ways in which such moments are remembered and reported, both by Moroccan DVs and in the other examples of diasporic visitation (see King & Christou, 2009; Phillips & Potter, 2006; Potter & Phillips, 2006a, 2006b; Wagner, 2011). As negative experiences, they become relevant to DVs' rememberings of their time in Morocco as moments where affects and impressions are particularly potent and visceral. Furthermore, the negativity embedded in these rememberings is often reported as initiated by resident Moroccans, who recognize them, then exploit their strangeness in some way. They are narratives that evoke vulnerability on the part of the teller, but give little detail about the other interactant(s)' roles or positions at that moment apart from a negative generalization.

The above examples also illustrate how DVs verbalize and identify the ways they feel themselves to be recognized as 'not-being-(locally)-Moroccan' through two indexical embodied attributes: dress and language. All five interviewees above identify clothing as key to being recognized; recognition is visual ('they see') but also more instinctive ('they know'). Language is a part of these narratives, although less so for Fedwa who spent five years of her childhood in Morocco. She claims that her linguistic skills combine with her knowledge of the 'mentality', so that she avoids such problems (Interview Extract 3.3, Line 19). Otman and Naim, however, attest that they are speaking Arabic (*derija*) in Morocco, although they are still recognized (Interview Extract 3.2, Lines 4–9). For Otman, dress is a way to effectively disguise oneself, to blend in with a crowd of 'neighborhood guys' by wearing the same clothes as they do, 'traditional clothes' (Interview Extract 3.2, Lines 19–25), while Soumia maintains that 'they see it always' because of their appearance, through elements like hair and makeup (Interview Extract 3.1, Line 22). This combination of 'dress + language' becomes part of a categorially relevant embodimentality of 'being-Moroccan' that they cannot manage to manipulate in order to be perceived by others as part of that unmarked category. Consequently, according to their logic, they become marked as *strange* – as Moroccan bodies who 'crossed the sea', who may have claim to some sort of belonging in the community, but are nevertheless out-of-*place*.

Passing: Being or Becoming?

One strategy with which to address this dispreferred categorization is to attempt to pass as 'being-locally-Moroccan' – being a Moroccan from the neighborhood, rather than a Moroccan from elsewhere. This potential to pass is constantly relevant, or omnirelevant (Fitzgerald *et al.*, 2009), to the extent that DVs are implicitly 'Moroccan-by-*descent*' and those described here choose to visit Morocco as part of their annual time spent on holiday in their ancestral homeland. Yet passing here describes a different kind of 'other' than in its usages elsewhere. Examining the transformation of embodied practices DVs might attempt in order to blend in indicates how different dimensions of embodimentality come into play as both materialities that can and cannot be reshaped, and expressivities that need to coordinate with materialities in order for passing to succeed.

In relation to other elements of embodimentality, such as skin pigmentation, for example, dress and language (as described above) are relatively malleable. As stylistic or situational choices, they may appear deceptively malleable. Choice of dress can be imagined as a simple act of purchase; switching from a European language into a Moroccan language is imagined to be a frictionless transition. In practice, however, clothing style is more culturally embedded and complex, in terms of responding to subcultural aspirations (Hebdige, 1979) as much as reflecting a class habitus (Bourdieu, 1984). Clothing becomes bonded to a body in specific ways, as movements permitted or encouraged by certain garments and becoming learned through the habitual interaction between body and adornment. Bodies react in assemblage with the garments they wear by learning how to wear them in socially specific iterations (Banerjee & Miller, 2003; Barrett, 1999; Tavory, 2010).

Likewise, language is bonded with bodies as an expressive function, and different codes are not always interchangeable. Bodies become habituated into modes of communication, from gestural to semantic forms, which leave traces in communicative practices, like accent or slang. As Ahlame and Soumia identify in the initial extract, DVs are known as much because of their accents as their clothes (Interview Extract 3.1, Lines 44–46). In moments where DVs are recognized as *strange*, these two attributes are frequently cited as potential ways to mask themselves by changing the most obviously perceived and seemingly malleable aspects of 'not-Moroccanness' in order to pass.

A traditional definition of passing is the effective assumption of an identity outside what one might normally be categorized. The most common dimensions along which passing is attempted would be described as race, ethnicity or gender (Garfinkel, 1984; Kroeger, 2003; Sanchez & Schlossberg, 2001). The ontological assumption in these accounts describe individuals who pass as 'being' one thing while 'passing as' another; they tend to assume that individuals have an essential identity and adopt a superficial mask – a perspective that discounts the flexibility and ambiguity of categories, and of bodies.

Turning away from these ontological assumptions, Bucholtz argues for embracing the potential for ambiguity, and against their implicit imagined authenticities:

The assumption that an essential core, whether biological or social, determines one's race and ethnicity promotes the belief in ethnic authenticity. Authenticity – that is, the legitimacy of one's claim to ethnicity – underlies the traditional definition of passing given above, which posits a recategorization of the passing individual from her 'own' ethnic group to another that is not her 'own.' The framework of authenticity is especially difficult to sustain, however, in the case of individuals of ambiguous or mixed ethnic background, for when multiple identities are available it is not at all clear which identity takes precedence … *[p]assing is the active construction of how the self is perceived when one's ethnicity is ambiguous to others.* (Bucholtz, 1995: 352, italics in original)

Following Garfinkel (1984), she considers passing as a temporary project as opposed to a permanent pursuit, based in contextual dynamics made relevant because of an exploitable ambiguity in 'identity' (Bucholtz, 1995: 359).

Individuals who attempt to pass along a given dimension could be aligned with one side or the other, and use that ambiguity for situationally specific purposes. Bodies that are read as ambiguous, like these DVs in Morocco, struggle with feedback about where they belong, caught between one category or another (Mahtani, 2002).

Passing, then, provides a possibility for resisting or disputing categorizations, although the trajectories along which such disputes can play out are limited by embodied constraints, while simultaneously taking advantage of the perceived fixity of categorization to become-other. In the context at hand, certain bodies which can claim 'Moroccanness-by-*descent*' can often more easily adhere to visually perceived markers of materially embodied 'Moroccanness'. Approaching such visual categorizations requires accepting, but by no means endorsing as deterministic, the ways in which material aspects of bodies – like skin pigmentation – are part of the assemblage of embodimentality, and reach beyond simple materiality to become part of categorial belonging.

Discussing visible identities, Alcoff (2006) argues for the material reality of visibly perceived features, while arguing against the primacy of the visual in producing identities. Her perspective aligns with most discourses about passing, in that visual factors (like skin color, characteristic features of gender, or other tangible markers) seem to determine categorial belonging. For Moroccan DVs, this process may be inverted: although their physical features may be 'Moroccan (by *descent*)', they struggle to be 'racialized' as such in the ways that are socially significant to them. Instead, the 'Moroccanness' of their flesh becomes a factor in their strangeness – a way that they become categorically distant because they are not 'local' in a 'Moroccan' way.

While Alcoff asserts that the visibility of the material body tends to render subordinate other dimensions produced through embodiment, her context is based in experiences of majority-to-minority racialization. In contrast, Louis (2005) considers how visual cues work in the inverse in negotiations of 'African American racial identity' between African Americans born in the United States and Americans born in Africa. Arguably, 'racial identity' is not what should be at stake in this situation, but – in what Louis calls a 'paradox of racial sameness' – other dimensions beyond 'racial' become significant in determining status and political rights. 'African Americanness', as I would call it, becomes located in historical turning points and markers of socioeconomic position in relationship with foreign-born Africans in America:

> If the native-/foreign-born dispute over African American identification has its material basis in perceptions of socioeconomic competition, its symbolic foundations and justification reflect the disingenuous processes of racialization in its classical form. Within the racial paradigm,

ostensibly benign descriptions of difference and sameness are never that but placed in hierarchical order through their relationship to each other. And, as an irregular example of internal racial differentiation that ought to puncture the salience of race, the effect of the native-/foreign-born dichotomy is often the opposite. Thus, the foreign-born are not racial and demonstrate a *culture* of industry and discipline, while the native-born are taken to represent a 'culture of poverty' that is innate to their character and are therefore *racial*. (Louis, 2005: 360–361, italics in original)

Louis points out the paradox of other dimensions of difference that become subsumed in this perceived 'sameness' of race. Along the lines of Louis' subject, DV and locally resident Moroccan bodies here are ostensibly of one 'race' but nevertheless in a paradox of racial sameness. The salience of their differentiation from 'local-Moroccanness', then, comes from their distancing in *place*, such that something 'cultural' about their 'Moroccan' bodies is recognized as 'not-Moroccan' – as *strange*.

Yet, as the interviews cited in the previous section highlight, 'race' is not the only categorical marker that might be indicated through visual embodiment. Neither Alcoff nor Louis discuss how other social dimensions without material basis in physical appearance are nevertheless visible on the body and cogent to the ways these bodies are being recognized. Using Saldanha's discussions on machinic geographies of phenotype (2006) in relation to flows of capital, music, drugs and whiteness in Goa (2007), I consider materialities of bodies as more than racial. In his case, he identifies certain visually perceived attributes, such as the symbol Om worn on clothing or deeply tanned skin, as ways in which semi-resident nomads from high income nations, or 'Goa freaks', could categorize themselves and distinguish their group from other commingling groups such as package tourists and local residents. In his examples, the appropriation of Indian beliefs and the darkness of a tan marked a body as semi-resident because of the local circulation of material and expressive entities, such as religious belief and sun. By extension, they also index status along certain dimensions, like 'class' or 'vocation', that accompany Goa freaks' ability to embed themselves in the scene.

Likewise, here skin pigmentation may be one of many features observed in interaction, but it needs to be considered as assembled with other elements of embodiment – such as proximity and alignment with certain groups of people, styles of dress and the production of language. These may become *racial* (categorial) configurations through the repeated practices of masses of individuals, but they need to be recognized as composed of more complex component dimensions in embodied interactions than are allowed by a social constructionist notion of 'racial identity'.

For most DVs, 'being-Moroccan-by-*descent*' is not a problem; like 'race' for Alcoff, it is a background against which they experience the world. Occasionally it becomes relevant in encounters like Wafae's, where she was categorized as something else after the vendor's visual (and possibly audible) observation. Rather, what is ambiguous about DV bodies, and becomes relevant to passing, relates to 'being-locally-Moroccan', or belonging in a way that is not markedly 'diasporic'. What DVs would need to manipulate in their embodimentality in order to pass, or to be perceived as 'locally-Moroccan', is more closely linked to their embodied habits, or *hexis*.

Hexis may be a more malleable materiality than skin pigment, but it is not necessarily easy to manipulate. It is layered into habitual practices that 'fit' certain categorizations and interactions, including creating respectability (Skeggs, 2004) or producing socially acceptable emotion (Kawale, 2004) as means of designing bodies that adhere to social parameters of categorial behavior. It operates as a material function of how a body feels at ease in clothing, as an expressive function of many possible affiliations through style, but becomes noticeably relevant in social encounters in which, for example, a body wearing its 'normal' clothes feels problematically uncovered under the gaze of others.

While communicative practices can play a large part in how passing is ratified by others (Piller, 2002; Wagner, 2015c), these material aspects to bodies are co-occurring with them in face-to-face encounters. To accomplish rendering an ambiguous embodimentality as one category or another – as ratified by interlocutors – requires managing body and *hexis* along with communication. Of course, it is quite easy to fail at managing all of this: 'an ineffectual effort to pass is just that, a failed attempt. Passing means that other people actually see or experience the identity that the passer is projecting' (Kroeger, 2003: 7–8). A noticed attempt at passing reinforces the distance between embodimentality and the unattained category. Perceived inconsistency between material entities (like skin) and *hexis* – what might be called a discordant embodimentality – contributes to the ways DVs describe below in which they are repeatedly recognized, even when seeking not to be.

In short, participants' accounts and actions indicate how these bodies are categorized in the ways those interviewees quoted above identified their *strangeness* through clothing and appearance, but also through less malleable aspects of the body, like *hexis* or accent, that they may not be able easily to describe. These embodiments are habitual, to the point that they can be difficult to consciously manipulate, while equally instinctively read by others to index specific configurations of belonging. A definition of passing in assemblage, then, is a reorientation of embodimentality towards an alternate, accessible category – to attempt to become-Moroccan when one's 'Moroccanness' is called into question. It is by no means a permanent project, or even attempted with the end result in mind of passing completely, i.e. becoming entirely seen through a new frame. Instead, passing is used here to describe these emergent interactive relationships in which DVs attempt to be recognized as more 'Moroccan' than *strange*.

Passing Visibly: Being Recognized and Blending In

Passing emerges in my data when being recognized as 'not-being-(locally)-Moroccan' is made relevant in the course of encounters with resident Moroccans. The relevance became an explicit topic of conversation through a purposeful attempt described on the part of the DV or through feedback from others that signaled recognition. In all the instances reported,[1] DVs who attempt to pass are failing. Failure occurs when one is recognized as non-local, most often by being called by an identifying category ('hollandiya', in an example below), being asked where one is from, or simply being addressed in a non-Moroccan language. Despite being 'the same' as other interactants – or everyone being equally Moroccan in terms of *descent* – DVs practice an embedded *hexis* contributing to an embodimentality that is immediately visually recognizable as 'not-being-Moroccan'.

Fieldnote 3.1 Hello Dutch Girl

I met Rachida, a friend of Malika's from Belgium. … She recalled having been at her parents' home in Tetouan years earlier, deciding to leave the house in a long simple dress and sandals, choosing this outfit purposefully not to be recognized. Instead, as soon as she walked out the door (just to go around the corner to visit her aunt), she heard someone on the street call to her, 'Hello Dutch girl' (hollandiya). 'I didn't even open my mouth!'

Inasmuch as DVs imagine that choosing to wear certain clothing is a way to pass, it is paired, in equal or superior measure, with the idea that one should be able to pass if not given away by language. Rachida told me this story as an example of how her body (*hexis*) was recognized as 'not-being-Moroccan', despite her intentional effort to disguise herself with clothing. Although DVs are often aware that their 'Europeanness' is shown on their bodies through more than just clothing, like Rachida in this narrative, no-one I encountered was able to manipulate that aspect of *hexis* effectively. Interestingly, their attempts to pass consistently fail despite the fact that many can, to some extent, identify the elements of *hexis* that differentiate their own bodies from the bodies of resident Moroccans around them. Anissa and Shirin, below, bantered about some of the ways they themselves see differences between their bodies and 'local-Moroccan' bodies.

Interview Extract 3.4 *Can you see the difference?*

Anissa and Shirin, Den Haag, 10 April 2008, 2 min

1 **LW:** everyone tells me/ oh they know: as soon as they see you
2 **S:** ya as so- o:h yes/ they know:. I don't know how, =
3 **A:**   =you can go
   there and say you're- you're **Spanish** or hohoho=whatever=
4 **S:** yah
5 **A:**   =hehheh
   heh .h and the[y kno:w <u>nti maghrebiya</u> ((you(f) are Moroccan))
6 **S:**   [but they- (.) but they- ya <u>maghrebiya</u>
   ((Moroccan)) yah. but eh: ya. if you have a djellaba eh:: a
   djellaba and eh:: and everything and [the <u>bəlgha</u> ((sandals))
   they know
7 **A:**   [yeah they will still-
   still see that you're from Europe, that you're a Moroccan
   European
8 **S:** well, o-other women are from there they have eh: jeans, and we
   are in djellaba, but they know.[(.) they are from Morocco and
   you are he.h:he.h
                                       [(LW and A laugh 2.1)
9 **LW:** um, can you- can you see difference? [°when you go°
10 **S:**   [yeah, yeah! I see the
   diff[erence.
11 **A:**   [I can't (.) no
12 **S:** I see the differe-
13 **LW:** what do you think is like/ anything in specific? or:
14 **A:** *oh ja een beetje wel h ja* [(.)*de kleding*
   yeah a little ok [the clothes
15 **S:**   [*ja ik zie het/ ja de kleding de haar*
   ook,(.) ik we=niet de haar ook
                                       [yeah I see that/ yeah the clothes, the hair also,
   (.) I don't = know the hair also
16 **A:** they- they're always straightening their hair
17 **S:** *ja!*
   ya!

18 **A:** *toch?*
           right?
19 **S:** *ja en de shampoo, ik weet niet/ en de kleding, toch wel jo#*
           jeans but=
           the shampoo, I don't know/ and the clothing, but well yeah#
20 **LW:** yeah
21 **A:**   =old fashioned jeans hahahahahh.h=
22 **S:**   *=je zie 't ja ja*
           anders

                                           =you see it yeah
                                                    yeah
           different
23 **LW:** the- the *maquillage?* of-
24 **S:** *maquillage ook.* [ja! *maquillage!* (.) *en het zwart ja,*
           makeup also. [ya! makeup! (.) and it's black ya,
25 **A:**   [lip liner! lip liner! ahahhahha [.h ja
26 **S:**   [(.) *ja je*
           ziet `t wel (.) *ik weet niet je ziet 't, e: ook ja/* **hui:d** *denk*
           ik, en ik begrijp `t eigenlijk wel dat ze `t zien hoor gelijk
           aan ons

                                        [(.) ya you see
           it a lot (.) I don't know you see it, e: also ya/ **skin** I think, and I do
           understand actually that they see it you know immediately on us
27 **A:** *dat ze hun huid bleek maken bedoel je/*
           that they make their skin pale you mean/
28 **S:** *weet ik niet, ehm makeup of eh: ja gewoon*
           I don't know, ehm makeup or eh: ja just
29 **LW:** color, yeah
30 **S:** color, I don't know::/ *toch anders de zon en eh:*
                                but also the sun and eh:
           (1.5)
31 **A:** yeah=
32 **S:**   =ya, you see- you can see the difference
           (2.6)
33 **LW:** yeah=I=know there, um: (.) women often like to make
           themselves
           as white as possi[ble
34 **A:**   [yea[h, it's terrible
35 **S:**   [ya. and we want to make ourself eheheh
           black hehahaha .h haha
36 **A:** th- they don't do it in a good way, [they look very pale
           instead of looking white.

37 **S:**   [*nee*!(.3) yeah, (.) yeah.
                                                  [no!
       (1.5)
38 **S:**   *wij betalen hier de:: zonnebank* [ahahaha *om bruin te worden en*
             they: makes: themselves eh ya
             we pay here for the tanning salon [ahahaha to get tan and
39 **A:**   [yeah hehahaha
40 **LW:**   I don't- I don't un- I still don't understand that
41 **A:**   [[we don't even understand it
42 **S:**   [[ya hahahahha we either

Shirin and Anissa build energy in this conversation to elicit a number of ways they can 'see the difference' between their own bodies and resident Moroccan women's bodies. Much of what they elicit as different refers to style, demonstrated through clothing, hair, makeup and suntan. Their descriptions of these styles occasionally contain a value judgment, like 'old fashioned' jeans (Lines 19–22) or Shirin's negative comment on the aesthetics of skin bleaching practiced by resident Moroccan women and Anissa's agreement (Lines 36–37). Each aspect of stylistic embodiment they choose could be traced to flows of material culture and mass production of clothing like *djellaba*s and jeans (Miller, 2010), to flows of fashion and beauty that pass through Morocco (Ossman, 2002), or to global inequalities and practices of skin whitening (Glenn, 2008). Such analyses are insightful in terms of cultural categories and their seemingly fixed practices; for the purposes of this analysis, I frame these visual elements as part of embodimentality in assemblage. As much as wearing a *djellaba* or whitening one's skin can be symbolic to them of 'Moroccanness', these materialities work in concert with other entities to create 'Moroccanness', which comes into play when they try to pass.

These women recognize how others fit in a local social hierarchy, yet their recognition of these elements as salient to categorization may not be consciously traced out to broader patterns. Skin whitening, for example, is a practice with a complex relationship to post-colonialism, symbolic capital and class for women in the Global South (Glenn, 2008), but Shirin and Anissa read it as inexplicable and opposite to their own practice of tanning. The practice of tanning is also interrelated with class dynamics and a shift from sun exposure as a sign of work to a sign of leisure (Dyer, 1997: 49–50). Most saliently, however, a deeply tanned Moroccan body tends to index a DV body through classed associations with styles of beauty and leisure practices, emerging in contradictory practices between many resident Moroccan women and most DVs. Shirin and Anissa recognize these features of embodimentality in a visceral way; they know that these distinctions are part of how their bodies are visible to others as much as how others' bodies are visibly categorizable to them.

Not all visual attributes are as clearly divided between 'being-Moroccan' or 'being-European'. Veiling, for example, emerges as a marker on DVs along stylistic lines, through styles of veil that can be linked to Europe, to Morocco or to other parts of the Muslim world. Veiling has other potentially political or situationally relevant significances beyond *place*, especially in the intersection between religious and political governances of gender (Gökarıksel, 2012; Mernissi, 1991). As much as in other regions, there is potential for categorial distinctiveness in this element of embodimentality among DV participants or local residents, although it was not cited or made explicit in any systematic way during fieldwork.

All of these elements, from practices of embodimentality to the visual economic system through which it is perceived, contribute to the ability or inability to pass when attempted. When DVs target a visual element as a strategy to pass, such as wearing 'traditional' *djellaba*s or *jabador*s like Shirin or Otman previously (Interview Extract 3.2), they disregard the complex of other embodied elements that are read on their bodies simultaneously. Choosing to wear a *djellaba*, a Moroccan garment worn by both men and women, does not render the body that wears it necessarily 'Moroccan'.

Interview Extract 3.5 *Feeling covered*

Anissa and Shirin, Den Haag, 10 April 2008, 1 min

1   **LW:**   do you ever wear djellabas and things like that there? or do-
2   **S:**   there? ya eh::::::: no I can't walk with the h-djellaba-h-h, =
3   **LW:**   no?
4   **S:**   =but I la- I love to wear- wear it sometimes/ if I go to the
             hammam or something eh near,(.4) I eh wear a djellaba
5   **LW:**   you can't walk? or you can-
6   **S:**   no eh, w- ya, it's- it's- it's- **dif**ficult, I don't know, it's eh
             em (.) if you have the long djellaba, it's (.) *ja en je loopt*
             toch een beetje:, je bent niet gewend, ik weet niet
             yeah and you walk like a little: you are not used to it, I don't know
7   **A:**   *bijna nooit <aandoen>*
             I hardly <wear them>
8   **S:**   it's not that I cannot walk with it, but *ja het zit niet echt eh*
             je moet `r effe aan wennen, want hier doe je `t nooit aan dus ja
                                             yeah, it doesn't sit
             right, you have to get used to it because you don't wear them here so
             yeah
9   **LW:**   it's different feeling, you have to walk slower hehahhah

10 **S:**   ya! it's different ya. but it's **comfortable** because everything,
                (.3) you have the feeling everything is emm: (1.0)
11 **A:**   [[covered
12 **S:**   [[*bedekt/* covered
13 **S:**   yeah, but *je moet `r aan wennen*
                you have to get used to it

Shirin verbalizes a sense of *hexis* in this extract. By describing how she finds it difficult to walk while wearing the typical Moroccan clothing, she also attests to a distinction in the way she is accustomed to walking from how resident women, at least those who wear a djellaba every day, walk. This attribute is visible to others around her as a tangible, if difficult to describe, entity of *hexis* – a visually perceived attribute of embodimentality that fits into the ways DVs are 'smelled' as being from elsewhere.

Shirin refers above to the sense of being 'covered' as an internal sensation, as opposed to an expectation expressed by or produced in interaction with others. Likewise, in the extract below, Noura mentions the same embodied affect as produced by social encounter.

Interview Extract 3.6 Wear a djellaba

Noura, Arena Palace Café, Fes, 29 July 2008, 40 sec
1 **N:**   … nous, je vais dire euh: moi je vous dire eh: la journée je
                peut pas sortir en robe comme ça. la journée je-suis obligée de
                mettre un djellab- une djell[aba
                we, I'm saying euh: I'm telling you eh: during the day I can't go
                out in a dress like this, during the day I'm obligated to put on a
                djellab- a djel[laba
2 **LW:**   [ouais °ouais°
                                        [yeah °yeah°
3 **N:**   parce que: sinon c'est toute la journée eh (.4) les;; va dire
                eh/ les gens d'ici nous abordent, mais eh
                because: otherwise it's all day eh (.4) the:: let's say eh/ the people
                from here talk to us but eh
4 **LW:**   ouais
                yeah
5 **N:**   avec eh (.) sans respect quoi.
                with eh (.) without respect right.
6 **LW:**   ouais. (.) non mais pour moi ça- (.7) après- après un certain
                moment, ça: ça c'est devenu eh: [normale
                yeah. (.) no but for me it- (.7) after- after a certain point, it- it
                it's become eh: [normal

7 **N:**   [normale
                            [normal
8 **LW:** ouais/ parce que, même si je me mets eh: en djellaba ou rien du
          tout parce que avec la peau blanche c'est::
          yeah/ because, even if I put myself in a djellaba or anything at all
          because with white skin it's::
9 **N:** bah ouais
          well yeah
10 **LW:** impossible
          impossible
11 **N:** mais nous aussi, nous même- avec la djellaba, ils nous
          reconnaissent juste à notre façon de marché
          but us also, for us even- with the djellaba, they know us just by our
          way of walking
12 **LW:** ouais, ouais
          yeah, yeah
13 **N:** ils savent (.3) ils connaissent
          they know (.3) they know

Noura's experience of using a *djellaba* in many ways mirrors that of Rachida wearing a simple dress to leave her house, or Shirin wearing one to feel 'covered': in response to the visual economy of their incidental interactions in public space, they attempt to adopt styles that connote 'modesty' in *hexis* which is visually appropriate for their 'Moroccan' bodies. This 'modesty' is as much a feature of embodimentality as a consequence of being visually recognized, to the extent that wearing clothing that 'covers' their bodies in a certain way relates their instinctive sense of *hexis* to the visual perception of surrounding observers.

As these repeated descriptions show, attempts at passing visibly through clothing are an acceptable and common practice for DVs – both men and women – to negotiate a visual recognition of 'being-(locally)-Moroccan'. That said, this practice, wherein a participant dressed in a specific way with the expressed purpose of being recognized as Moroccan, was more often described than enacted in my observations – and generally reported to 'fail' in the dynamic of passing.

While they may often express the opinion that dress is a way to achieve recognition as 'being-Moroccan', the low frequency of this practice during fieldwork points to its inefficacy. Certain garments are incorporated into DV styles and form part of the vocabulary of 'Moroccan' clothes that DVs tend to wear. These items, however, are not the everyday exterior *djellabas* linked to passing, but styles of 'Moroccan' clothing that in fact embed them further in insular circuits of DV style (see Chapter 5). Attempts to pass by wearing a *djellaba* may be more common for women because of its link with a comfortable, embodied sense of modesty, as evoked in the extracts above. But *djellaba*s do not eliminate strangeness, or even necessarily reduce it. The potential to pass is maintained by the idea that wearing the right clothing might diminish strangeness, that a DV embodimentality maps onto a 'Moroccan' embodimentality closely enough that DVs could 'be-Moroccan' despite their 'not-Moroccan' *hexis*. Yet being ratified as passing would involve a plethora of practices, of *hexis*, skin coloring, and walking in the 'right' way wearing the 'right' clothing.

Passing Audibly: The Politics of Speaking *derija*

In examining linguistic and communicative practices, this section targets moments when language became relevant to the course of interaction – not necessarily as a tool for communication, but as a symbolic token relevant to being recognized as 'Moroccan'. In other words, this analysis is not focused on measuring or determining the abilities of DV participants to practice *derija*, the most prevalent spoken language in Morocco. Instead, it targets moments where being able to speak *derija* or one of the Amazigh dialects native to Morocco became part of a DV's strategy for passing audibly.

This moment seems to be a common occurrence for youth of Moroccan origin while in Morocco:

> In fact, youths say that they suffer immensely for not having the Moroccan dimension of their identity recognized there. Thus, Malika finished by accepting being considered nothing but a 'tourist' in Morocco, like a person passing through without any attachment to the place. The main reason for this stigmatization is linguistic: the linguistic practices of these youth in their ancestral language are judged qualitatively and quantitatively mediocre by people in the homeland. (Melliani, 2000: 68, translated by author)[2]

Whereas passing visibly refers to the visually perceivable factors of DVs being (mis)recognized in Morocco, passing audibly turns to the linguistic expression of prescribed codes, code choice, and ability to practice certain codes as part of 'being-Moroccan' as embodimentality. Focusing on this dynamic of code choice, Melliani makes the metalinguistic statement above in the context of her study on linguistic practices of Moroccan youth in and around

Rouen. The interviewee she refers to, Malika, recounted being ridiculed by her family in Morocco for her poor *derija*, leading to her decision to speak only French while in Morocco. Melliani characterizes this 'stigmatization' as primarily linguistic, reinforced by the way DV language skills are evaluated by the public in Morocco.

Certainly, linguistic skills are cited often in her interviews, in my interviews and in literature on migrant bilingualism as a significant source of problematized categorizations in line with ideologies of close relationships between national identity and language (Heller, 2010; Kroskrity, 2000; Portes & Rumbaut, 2001). Indeed, linguistic practices are relatively easy to single out and classify through national labels and the institutions that categorize them. Yet linguistic practices constitute one part of a multiply faceted embodimentality, in which, as Chen (2008) confirms in Hong Kong, styles of dress, gesture, embodiment and language all contribute to becoming recognized as a return migrant. While linguistic practices provide complex resources to investigate how DVs negotiate attempts to 'be-Moroccan', it is important to contextualize them more broadly through embodimentality, as communicative practices that are embodied and visual as much as audible. The agglomeration of visual, material bodies who speak these words is relevant to the way these encounters play out.

Yet something about language use seems ideologically easier to alter in order to pass. In many reports, the ability to manipulate how one is being recognized through language is considered much stronger and more accessible than the ability to manipulate visual factors. As Koven (2002) argues:

> Whereas in French, [Luso-Descendents] can use their monolingual performances effectively to distance themselves from images of migrants, in Portuguese they may be at a loss to do so. Their socialization into monolingual Portuguese has usually been more limited than into French. Although their knowledge of the boundaries between French and not-French is indisputable, they can less consistently demonstrate that they know the boundaries between Portuguese and not-Portuguese. Whereas skill and strategy defined their use of Portuguese in French, an experience of loss of control defines their use of French in Portuguese. The stakes of slipping are not small. When LDs fail to purge their Portuguese of Frantuguês, they may suddenly become 'émigrés' to listeners.
>
> Through heightened metalinguistic attention to their own and others' Frantuguês, LDs may try to protect themselves from these stereotypes and identities. At times this attention takes the form of an anti-Frantuguês purism that may not always succeed. (Koven, 2002: 280)

Koven describes a familiar scenario, populated by French nationals of Portuguese descent who return to Portugal as visitors or migrants. This displacement presents them with challenges to their habitual linguistic practices: to appear as native, local Portuguese speakers, as opposed to native, non-local Frantuguês practitioners. An enormous part of this project is 'metalinguistic attention' focused on their own and others' speech, in order to identify and manipulate audibly relevant markers of categorization. Her assertions are accurate as well to the majority of Moroccan DVs, who attain some measure of skills in their ancestral language, but still can be recognized as non-local speakers. Most importantly, she relates LDs' metalinguistic attention to their habitually and normatively codeswitched combination of French and Portuguese and the pointed efforts made to diminish that communicative practice for a 'purism that may not always succeed' (cited above). In other words, her participants could also be described as attempting to pass when in Portugal by trying to perform linguistically as local speakers of Portuguese, instead of multilingual Luso-Descendents from France.

Sociolinguistic theories related to talk-in-interaction, including Conversation Analysis (CA), Membership Categorization Analysis (MCA) and Communicative Accommodation Theory (CAT) (Giles *et al.*, 1991; Hester & Eglin, 1997; Sacks, 1992; Stokoe, 2012) are effectively separate strains that ground this analysis by sharing a basis in micro-analysis of interactive communicative encounters and a focus on how categories of speakers emerge through such encounters. They enable me to make some statements about what participants 'do' with language as opposed to what they 'say' with language. The main outlet for 'doing with language' I targeted was bargaining in Moroccan markets, as moments when DVs are negotiating 'being-Moroccan' with others in public space. That analysis will continue through the next chapters in greater interactional detail. These first examples instead reflect metalinguistic encounters, where use of different codes, along a dimension of 'national language', become a point of disjuncture or tension in DVs' efforts to pass.

Explicit practices: Policing *derija*

Pressure to speak the local 'Moroccan' code – often referred to by participants as 'Arabic' but for specificity here called *derija* – is one of the primary ways that DVs experience the distinction between themselves as non-local Moroccans and the presumably 'local', presumably resident Moroccans surrounding them in Morocco.

Fieldnote 3.2 Leave you with the police

Brahim's father makes two comments in the course of eating lunch that resonate: when Brahim is talking to his daughter, his father says in derija, you must speak Arabic to her. Later, during the fruit, he says to his grand-daughter, 'hna fi marokko. khusek tHdr bil3arabiya oula nkhullik 3and el police'. [in *derija*: we are in *Morocco* (in Dutch), you have to speak Arabic or we will leave you at the police] or something along those lines.

...

Malika and Souad are telling [daughter] as we walk that she should speak Arabic in the street or else people will know ...

Malika comments to me that her uncle told her this when she was young as well, that she shouldn't speak Dutch in the street or people would know and raise the prices.

This intergenerational example is a simple dynamic of policing code choice. Over the course of a single day, several moments of interaction with an eight-year-old daughter whose parents were both raised in Europe by their migrant parents (her grandparents) included instructions on becoming 'local' by speaking *derija*. None of these moments of 'policing' her language takes into account other aspects of embodimentality, like dress or *hexis*, framing the practice rather as the daughter's ability to choose *derija* freely as a code. In fact, they all take place in the 'wrong' code – telling her in her European language that she should speak *derija*; even her grandfather's instruction in *derija* uses the Dutch version of the placename for Morocco. Her aunt recalled to me later how as a girl she was advised to do the same by her own uncle.

The problem with this kind of encouragement to speak *derija* (or discour-agement of speaking a European language) is that communicative practice is precisely that: practiced. As discussed in Chapter 1, the circumstances under which migrants learn to use their ancestral languages usually vary distinctly from the context in which they are expected to reproduce it. That said, it is not uncommon for parents (or in this case, grandparents) to take a role in 'policing' language use when *place* shifts and a post-migrant's normal linguis-tic practice is considered too weighted towards the European language. By this time, however, the learned, habitual abilities will never match the expected ones unless particular effort is made to transform linguistic prac-tice. In fact, peer groups have a stronger influence on the continued develop-ment and use of an ancestral, migrant language, in that communication with contemporaries encourages stylistic development of hybridized practice as opposed to symbolic usage (Dabène & Moore, 1995; Koven, 2002, 2004). These evolutions, however, take place away from the soil of the homeland, and are in some ways a foreign code, rooted in another *place*. So, despite her parents and grandparents urging her, this daughter was not observed to put much effort into speaking *derija*, even immediately after her grandfather's threat, and even though she was in Morocco, the place where *derija* is spoken. These events are one example of the kind of 'policing' that was reported by other participants, and has frequently been reported in similar research (e.g. Melliani, 2000, quoted above).

If she did make such efforts, her categorial 'Moroccanness' would still likely be questioned. Whereas expectations enmeshed in approaching the category 'Moroccan' dictate that post-migrant DVs are speakers of *derija*, in actuality their practice, even when they have a relatively easy command of *derija*, exhibits markers of their 'being-European'. They might use expressions that are outdated, have accents influenced by their parents' (often rural) origins or by their European language, or use codeswitching in a way that is identifiable as non-local (cf. Koven, 2002; Chen, 2008, for parallel observation). Thinking of this in terms of embodimentality, their recognizable accents are intensively embedded in bodies, part of what is instinctively 'smelled' as 'not-quite-Moroccan'. These clues that DVs are not 'authentically' native speakers, even though *derija* may be one of their home languages, lead to situations where the complexity of language use reflects on their desires and abilities to 'be-Moroccan' by audibly masking their 'Europeanness'.

Implicit practices: Being replied to in French

As much as DVs are metalinguistically aware that they 'should' speak *derija*, doing so can be a challenge. As Koven (2002) describes in the citation above, the prospect of producing the 'wrong' code with others in public can be very stressful, as it presents the omnirelevant threat, at each interaction, that passing may be unsuccessful (Piller, 2002). One key way in which this threat is realized in DV experiences in Morocco is described through how other 'local' speakers make a conversational code choice to **not** speak *derija* with them. Many interviewees perceived this conversational move as a categorizational distancing, although, depending on individual conversational events, its motivations may index more diverse sociolinguistic factors.

Anissa and Shirin return here, describing their encounters with receiving replies in the 'wrong' language.

Interview Extract 3.7 *I'm from Morocco*

Anissa and Shirin, Den Haag, 10 April 2008, 1 min 10 sec

1   **LW:**   did you ever find that someone was () speaking **Dutch** to you?
              that- like (.) someone from Morocco would speak in Dutch? or no?

2   **A:**   ahhm::: no, just say words, like if they know you are from (.)
              Holland, you know/ *alles goed* [*alles goed*?(.) well something
              like that, but um (.3) uh: mostly people speak **French** if they
              know you're from ah: (.) Europe. (.3)
                                    everything good [everything good?

3   **S:**   [*alles goed ja-*
                                                  [everything good yes

4   **LW:**   Yeah

5   **A:**   like if they see it or they hear it, (.)=

6   **S:**   Yeah

7   **A:**   =cause you have an
              accent, they'll start talking in French to you. (.) and I'm
              always like, I don't speak **French**, I speak **Arabic**.

8   **LW:**   h h h h

9   **A:**   [[<I hate it when they speak>-

10   **S:**   [[I always speak Arabic. whn- I- and when they ask me where're
              you from I say I'm- (.) I- I s- (.) I-I-I: (.) say I'm from Morocco.

11   **LW:**   yeah.(.5) do they believe you?

12   **S:**   no he[heheheha .h hahah .h *maar ik blijf toe* xx I'm from
              Morocco! no you're not from Morocco. yes! I'm froheheh, where're
              you from then hehehehe .hhh then eh: ya I'm from eh Rabat I live
              here and here/[but they know.
                           but i stay with it

13   **A:**   [hehehh he .h he
                                  [yeah
              (1.3)

14   **LW:**   °they always know°

15   **S:**   yeah, they always know, but I don't know, I don't like to say
              it/ I'm from eh ya *ik niet* ((I'm not)).hh hhhehehe

One of the most common linguistic frustrations reported by DVs was an interaction like the one Shirin describes in this interview extract: being spoken to in French, despite having begun the interaction by speaking *derija*, or not being a French speaker. This was a practice more evident through reporting than through observation. None of the interactions I recorded in Morocco included examples of DVs initiating talk in *derija* and being replied to immediately or exclusively in French. Some included French codeswitching, but these were almost entirely in situations where DVs first initiated the codeswitching. Others were interactions where DVs prompted a switch to French by silence, indicating non-comprehension of *derija* (see Fieldnote 5.2 for an observed instance). Yet being replied to in French was a practice on the part of resident Moroccans reported by a number of participants, who linked it implicitly to their sense of belonging through linguistic *descent*.

As mentioned in Chapter 2, French is part of the sociolinguistic landscape of Morocco as an imported code that has become embedded in status structures of this triglossic (Walters, 1999) community of linguistic practice. That is, alongside standard Arabic, French exists as **a** normal code in Morocco, but not **the** normal code; it has become associated with certain kinds of elevated status that index economic power as well as access to Europe (Marley, 2004). Replying in French, even when the initial speaking turn was in *derija*, can be normal conversation between resident Moroccans under contextually appropriate conditions. Switching to French (which is not the same as normative codeswitching between *derija* and French) might result from a number of conversational or social cues, such as an addressee recognizing the initiator as elite, and therefore assuming a preference for French, or wishing to demonstrate his or her competence in a status-elevating code (Ziamari, 2008). On the other hand, in encounters between resident Moroccans and DVs, switching to French could indicate the addressee's rejection of the initiator's claim to 'being-Moroccan' through speaking the Moroccan code. All of these possibilities are part of each interaction and, as evidenced by the extracts below, DVs interpret this practice differently. However, they all, like Shirin, interpret it as a dispreferred response.

As with Anissa and Shirin's conversation above, being replied to in French becomes in many cases tantamount to contesting *descent* by rejecting one's passing as 'being-Moroccan' (as it ideologically **should** be accomplished by speaking *derija*). Anissa describes the practice as instigated by a resident Moroccan recognizing her accent in Arabic (Interview Extract 3.7, Line 7), a part of her audible embodimentality that she cannot manipulate. Her comment assumes that other aspects of her embodimentality were not equally marked as 'not-being-Moroccan', like style of dress, *hexis*, or other linguistic aspects such as grammatical usage or lexicon. Shirin adds to this discussion by describing how she resists being made *strange* by insisting that she is from Morocco (Interview Extract 3.7, Lines 10–12), despite the fact that no-one believes her. The way they describe and react to memories of this phenomenon speaks to the negotiation of passing through embodimentality that is multiple and unfixed. DVs feel themselves to be recognized as strange, and despite efforts to pass – like speaking *derija* – they are 'othered' through codeswitching.

Interviewees Said (Interview Extract 3.8) and Meryem B (Interview Extract 3.9) recounted different variations on and interpretations of being replied to in French.

Interview Extract 3.8 Everyone speaks French

Said, Paris, 9 February 2008, 40 sec

1 **S:** alors euh: non, je parle pas, j'essaie pas parler français là-bas.
   well euh: no, I don't speak, I try not to speak French there

2 **LW:** Mmm

3 **S:** quand je vais:: à la banque, euh: (.) je parle- j'essaie de parler **berbère**, j'essaie pas parler français,(.4) mais on parle <de suite> français! hhh ha! comme eux/ ils parlent le français, ils ont fait des études,
   when I go:: to the bank, euh: (.) I speak- I try to speak **berber**, I try not to speak French, (.4) but everyone speaks French <right away>! hhh ha! like they/ they speak French, they have studied

4 **LW:** oua[is
   yea[h

5 **S:** [il veulent pratiquer la langue/
   [they want to practice the language/

6 **LW:** Ouais
   Yeah

7 **S:** à l'occasion, donc=quand=ils te voient, bah e::(.) # ils essaient de parler français. # alors que, tu veux parler: eh l'arabe. (.) là=mais=ils arrivent tu sais t- t'es quand-même euh: (.6) t'es quand-même euh:: buh moi j'ai tout les ans, j'ai des expériences qui prouvent bien que tu es vu comme étranger là-bas! (1.1) tu es vu comme étranger là-bas, ça c'est certain, (.9) t'es pas- te- (.) quand tu vais là-bas on dit que t'es français.
   at the opportunity, so=when=they see you, bah e::(.) # they try to speak French. # even though, you want to speak: eh Arabic. (.) there=but=they manage you know y- you're still euh: (.6) you're still euh:: buh every year I have experiences that strongly prove that you are seen as a stranger there! (1.1) you are seen as a stranger there, that is certain, (.9) you're not- yer- (.) when you go there everyone says you are French.

In another interpretation of this practice, Said describes his memories of being replied to in French at the bank not as necessarily disaffiliative, but as frustratingly adding to his *strangeness*. He describes interlocutors as using him to practice speaking French (Line 3), honing their skill in his natively spoken elite language. He pairs this with the assertion that 'they know immediately', i.e. they know that he is *strange*, making a connection between the marked change of code and his own identity as stranger. His assumption is that part of what is accomplished when they speak French to him is recognizing him as 'European'.

Interview Extract 3.9   I don't speak French

Meryem B, Antwerp, 9 April 2008, 1 min

1   **LW:**   I hear a lot about like (.) m- m- m-Moroccans from Morocco: kind of making jokes? about (.) eh: the way the <u>kharij</u>- the way that people [from outside speak yeah

2   **M:**   [that we speak hehehhhehhyeahheh

3   **LW:**   did that ever happen to you? orz:

4   **M:**   yeah they- they can hear. sometimes I'm- I'm asking a que- I remember that I went to a store, and I asked a question, in Arab, (.) and they answered me in French. and I was=like I don't speak French and they were yes you a- you do speak French, because you are from Europe and I was=h=like, I may be from Europe, you've saw that or you have heard 't very well, but (.) I- I don't speak French hehhehhh .h so I really was/ answer me in Arab!=b(hh)ecause I don't understand you hehhh. those things happen a lot/ even in the market/ like people answer you in French or something because they- (.6) maybe they do that for(h) fun(h), or maybe they d-do that because they think they can help you better, in a- another language, but .h I really like to prefer to stay with Arab,

Finally, Meryem B's story evokes how this practice is relevant not only to 'being-Moroccan' in Morocco, but also 'being-Dutch-speaking' as a DV in Morocco. In her version, the interlocutor (or possibly more than one) defends switching to French because she is evidently from Europe, equating 'all-Europeans' with 'French-speakers' and putting her in that category instead of the *'derija*-speaker' category she asserted by asking her initial question in *derija*. In her recounting, she first considers this a disaffiliative stance which might be taken purposefully – 'for fun', at her expense – then considers it could be intended as an affiliative stance – switching to French to 'help better'. For her, the switch seems to have been felt even more disaffiliatively because, as a native Flemish speaker, French does not respond to her communicative practices or preferences. Unlike Said, a native French speaker, switching to French does not signal elite status for Meryem. Rather, it creates further exclusion.

Grouping all Europeans together as all French speakers is probably more reflective of the triglossic context of Morocco rather than any actively disaffiliative stance against non-French-speaking diasporic Moroccans. Following the discussion in Chapter 1, French persists as a language that signifies high cultural capital in Morocco, and continues to do so for Moroccans inside and outside of Morocco. In support of this claim, Sanae, the only French-speaking Belgian participant, related to me that her father made a conscious choice to move his family to a French-speaking part of Belgium, so that they would access that higher value language instead of Flemish. In these momentary interactions, switching to French could be interpreted as much a status-raising effort as a border-making act, or as an affiliative linguistic accommodation (Giles *et al.*, 1991).

In marketplace interactions, being replied to in French can have a more practical and vital consequence. Dutch DVs Mohammed and Fouzia described how they experienced French replies while they were on holiday with a group of Dutch-Moroccan students in Marrakech.

Interview Extract 3.10 So prices go up

Mohammed and Fouzia, Marrakech, 27 May 2008, 40 sec

```
1   LW:   when you walk in the souq do people speak to you in Arabic? Or
2   M:    in Arabic/ mostly in Arabic. [it's eh=
3   F:                                  [some of them also in eh French
4   M:    = in English, French, in Dutch, in::
5   F:    when you ask them the price, of something, they always re- eh
          <s>pond in French.
6   LW:   really.
7   F:    yeah [it's very odd, because (.5) you speak with them in Arabic,
          they know you speak Arabic and they-(.) they talk to you in
          French. (.4) it's very frustrating hehh
8   M:         [but also
9   M:    yes but they- they: we have eh an accent eh:::,[ the Arabic we
          speak, so they hear (.3) =
10  LW:                                                  [mmmm mmmm
11  LW:   right
12  M:                          =you are not from:- from here, so and
          then eh: (.8) the prices are ehh (.5) hh=going=h=up=hhheh
13        ((LW and F laugh))
```

Mohammed makes the interpretive move from being replied to in French, when he asks for a price, to being marked as 'non-local' by being given what he assumes is a higher price. Fouzia feels that their French response is frustrating (Line 4), but it is not clear from her description to what extent the vendor's reply is in French. In fact, it is not uncommon in normative *derija*-French codeswitching to use French for numbers (see Wagner, 2006). Fouzia may interpret this French-language price as a marked, disaffiliative codeswitch, addressed at her accent or audible embodimentality of 'non-local Moroccanness'. Mohammed, likewise, interprets changing to French as linked with a strange embodimentality through accent, and therefore with rising prices (Lines 9–12).

In all these extracts, DVs demonstrate the assumption that *derija* **is** the local code, without considering other contextual and status cues that might prompt normative, local codeswitching. Their interpretations of switching into French are colored by what Fouzia calls 'frustration' and linked with the interpretation that their audible, linguistic embodimentality of 'being-Moroccan' is rejected. Yet not being able to speak *derija* like a native, or possibly not recognizing *derija*-French codeswitching as a local unmarked code, is a conversationally relevant cue of their status. This status, in Mohammed's description, is equated with 'not-being-Moroccan' and therefore, in his estimation, not getting the right price on the market.

As explicit conversations about linguistic practices, these metalinguistic observations indicate some of the ways in which DVs encounter complex and confusing dynamics of categorization in attempting to pass audibly. Their different interpretations of what these French responses mean – whether they are being marked as 'elite', as 'European', as 'educated' or as something else unknown – likewise indicate how the repercussions of not passing create many trajectories of potential disaffiliation or 'mentality difference'. These examples all start from the same perceived linguistic action, but reverberate into many ways in which DVs might perceive themselves as categorially othered in conversation in Morocco.

Being (Mis)recognized II: Being Stopped on the Street

This final section considers some examples of embodimentalities that deviate from the patterns described above. While much of the rhetoric of 'being-Moroccan' leads towards ways DVs attempt to become 'Moroccan-in-*place*' while on holiday, there are significant ways in which they are simultaneously trying <u>not</u> to be 'Moroccan' in *place*, or becoming 'Moroccan' in ways that incorporate their 'Europeanness'. Being able to draw on these two attractors across multiple dimensions is practiced through encounters where one or the other can become instrumentally relevant.

Closing this chapter, a second example of misrecognition demonstrates the inverse effect of passing. Immediately following a discussion about clubs in Marrakech, and the 'shock' of seeing resident Moroccan women prostitutes inside these clubs, Mohammed and Fouzia offered the following stories of their last night out in Marrakech. Instead of being misrecognized as 'not-Moroccan', this group of Dutch-Moroccan students were stopped on the street for appearing, effectively, 'too Moroccan'.

Interview Extract 3.11 A lot of contradiction

Mohammed and Fouzia, Marrakech, 27 May 2008, 2 min

1   **M:**   it's a **shock**ing story yeah. (.6) but you know the-e- Morocco has two stories. we: yes- yesterday? no? (.) **last night,** we went eh with a group to: walk, it=was three o'clock in the morning like that,

2   **LW:**   mm mm

3   **M:**   so the police stopped us/ (.) they want to see the identity, and they ehf: start to talk about, eh/ you have to be married [blah blah blah =

4   **F:**   [**really**?

5   **M:**   =I thought/ what are you talking about! heheh married why?

6   **F:**   Hhhahh

7   **M:**   we're just a group from Holland, we're relaxing, so he said ya:: ok::, but eh:: next time don't walk with **girls** blah blah **blah** (.6) <said> ok: alright.

8   **LW:**   Mmm

9   **M:**   and if you go to clubs eh you see (.5)[different custom/

10   **F:**   [a lot of contradiction

((four turns excised of LW police story))

11   **F:**   I don't like it hhhahha.

12   **LW:**   hhh but um:

13   **F:**   the police stopped us also yesterday/ when=we=were (.) on our way eh to the club.

14   **LW:**   really?

15   **F:**   ya ya. (.) because we were (.) we'v- we were very remarkable/ cuz (.) we went with like (.5) =

16   **M:**   hmmm hmm

17   **F:**   =thirteen or fourteen [people (.) ya (.4) and the: and the police eh officer::, he eh stepped out of the car/ (.4) and he were ve- he was very- (.3) h-he was not **nice**. (.3) **who are you** and eh: (.) **where** are you **coming from** and where are you going to.

18   **M:**   [fourteen people ya

19 **LW:** mm-mm
20 **F:** and that- we know how to respond/ we know, you ha- you just
have to stay calm and respond in the proper way. and em (.7) and
then when we explained we are some **students**:: who are staying
at the **<name> hotel**, and we come from The Netherlands/ (.) he
was ah he was very nice then/[at the end, he said **ok**::/I just want
to say that you have to be **careful**:: blah bla=blah
21 **LW:**   [mm
22 **LW:** was he speaking in Arabic the who[le time? ah yeah, yeah/
23 **F:**   [yes yes/ [he was speaking
Arabic
24 **M:**   [ya
25 **M:** no:: a lot of words in French, *Spaans* ((Spanish))/ (.) so: I- I
didn't understand all the things, so I said (.4) please in
hh=Arabic=hhh so I of=
26 **LW:** ahehehahah
27 **M:** =I don't understand you

Mohammed and Fouzia tell very similar stories of two separate encounters
with police on the last night of their group's excursion in Marrakech. These
stories bring attention to an aspect of territorialized 'Moroccanness' which DVs
nearly always encounter with surprise: control over illicit sexual liaison between
Moroccans in Morocco. This control is institutionalized through different security measures, such as these police officers who may stop mixed-gender groups
and request proof of marriage. Hotels are also required to confirm the marital
status of a Moroccan couple at registration, but not of foreign couples.

The police may have stopped these groups to protect the honor of the
'Moroccan' girls included in it, or they could equally well have been expect-
ing bribes from the 'Moroccan' men who were breaking rules by taking out
unchaperoned women. For both Fouzia and Mohammed, however, the coun-
terargument was to explain how they are 'not-Moroccan' in that particular
circumstance – that they do not need to follow these territorializing rules.
Given the intense promotion and economic boom of Marrakech as a cosmopolitan escape for tourists, it would be difficult to imagine a Moroccan police
officer stopping a group of 13 or 14 'foreign' tourists if they were out late on
the way to a nightclub. Instead, in these cases, Mohammed, Fouzia and their
friends encountered a problem because they – their bodies, their embodimentality – were misrecognized as 'Moroccan'.

In the sequence that Fouzia describes, this incident became a negotiation
of 'being-Moroccan' but not being subject to Moroccan rules. She explains
how she and her friends justified their illicit action by 'being-European', as

Dutch students on holiday, staying at a hotel. Yet she says her interaction took place entirely in *derija*; Mohammed had to ask the police officer to use *derija* so that he would understand. In effect, both of them report explicitly asking the police to consider their groups as 'not-Moroccan' while using *derija* to do so. This encounter becomes an example of purposefully trying **not** to pass, because passing becomes problematic for their activity. For this moment, 'being-Moroccan' becomes an instrumental category: a node which DVs may attempt to use for its perceived affiliations and benefits, but may also seek to distance themselves from when 'becoming-Moroccan' means encountering barriers they wish to avoid.

Conclusion

The examples described in this chapter begin to bring shape to how 'Moroccanness' is explicitly perceived and contextually created through DV experiences and encounters while in Morocco. Specifically, these are ways in which participants explained how their bodies and language use figured into passing (or not) as 'being-Moroccan'. This shaping is multifaceted, including many different human actors – both 'local' and 'diasporic' – whose meta-categorical perceptions become part of DVs' means to interpret their status. The quoted interviews in which participants described and commented on their own experiences indicate how categories appear fixed, but are in fact shifting through situations participants encounter with different interlocutors while on holiday.

Nevertheless, the multidimensional category of 'being-(locally)-Moroccan' has here some key markers. It involves embodied aspects that are more and less stable, from skin pigmentation to *hexis*, to linguistic accents, to code use. These visual and audible markers enable instantaneous categorizations in interaction, wherein DVs can become-local-Moroccans as in the last example of being stopped by the police, or become-Others as in the opening example of Wafae and her family being addressed as Turkish. Within these instantaneous categorizations, certain entities come to have more significance, at least as perceived by DVs: speaking the right code (*derija*), in the right way (without switching to French); wearing the right clothes (traditional) that present the right type of body; but also, in a less precise realm, having the right 'mentality' to know how to 'deal with' resident Moroccans (like the police, or aggressive men), and importantly (at least for Mohammed, and for Malika's uncle) to be able to get the 'right price' at the market.

DVs' engagement with these categorial markers often manifests as an avoidance of becoming *strange* by trying to pass – but not always. Inasmuch as they can approach or distance themselves from attractors, or categorial ideal-types like 'Moroccan' or 'European', they can use their embodimentalities to respond to different situational stimuli and desires. There are moments when their (mis)recognition as 'diasporically-Moroccan' is useful or not, insulting or not, funny or not. Yet this status is not so clearly demarcated as belonging or not-belonging as their capacities to shift and refocus when desirable, to change shape in some ways, enables them to become-diasporic in different expressions and forms. Thus, the dynamics of passing are not as much about moving towards a defined 'Moroccanness' as about shaping the definition of the category through the process of defining 'Moroccanness'. The dimension of 'Moroccan' becomes less important than 'being-local' as a function of 'Moroccanness', and the potential advantages (or disadvantages) that come with being locally resident in this homeland.

Notes

(1) More female than male participants discussed passing in my data. This may indicate a gender distinction in practice, but it may also be a function of the imbalance between men and women who participated.

(2) Les jeunes, en effet, disent très massivement souffrir de ne pas voir la dimension maghrébine de leur identité là-bas reconnue. Ainsi, Malika a fini par accepter de n'être considérée au Maroc que comme une 'touriste', c'est-à-dire finalement comme une personne de passage qui n'aurait aucune attache avec le pays visité. La principale raison de cette stigmatisation est langagière : les productions des jeunes en langue des origines sont jugées par les pays concernés comme qualitativement et quantitativement médiocres.

4 Bargaining for 'Moroccanness': Categorial Work on the Market

Interaction Extract 4.1

Karima, Demnate, 5 August 2005

j'étais mort de rire.() il a dit, en fait/ il a dit ehn:
il a dit quatre-vingt:/ quatre-vingt centimes, () ehn quatre-vingt
tmenin ryal. et moi j'ai dit non səb'en parce que: mon père les a
acheté səb'en, j'ai dit non səb'en, il m'a dit non non non non
səttin səttin. (rire)

I was dying laughing. () he said, in fact/ he said uhh: he said eighty:/
eighty centimes, () uhh eighty eighty ryal. and me I said no seventy
becau:se my father bought them at seventy, I said no seventy, he said no
no no no sixty sixty

This chapter turns to marketplace interactions, where the stakes of being categorized as 'local-Moroccan' take on a tangible outcome as a price. Every diasporic visitor has stories like Interaction Extract 4.1, told to me by Karima as she was walking away from a successful transaction in the *souq* near her home in Morocco, of attempting to bargain in the ubiquitous non-fixed price Moroccan markets but doing it in some way incorrectly. In this case, in the way Karima tells the story, the vendor first offered her item at 80, and her counteroffer was 70 – her known price for this item, based on her father's experience. Instead of taking her offer, the vendor replied with a lower offer – 60 – effectively instructing her on how to counteroffer by suggesting a lower price than she had. That is, as she told me while she was dying of laughter, he was teaching her how to bargain.

This story reflects the two main aspects to bargaining that relate to categorial work that DVs regularly do on the market: knowing and getting the 'right' price for the goods they seek, and being able to do so with their varying competencies in *derija*. Both of these aspects are ideologically intertwined: according to them, one cannot achieve the 'right' price without effectively speaking *derija*, and therefore being categorized and ratified as a 'Moroccan customer' in interaction. Yet, as their interactions show, vendors are well aware of their 'non-Moroccanness', no matter what their *derija* skills, making their quest for the 'right' price – and therefore categorial 'Moroccanness' in these interactions – a never-ending negotiation.

The first section below opens with a discussion on the practices and understandings necessary to achieve a price in a non-fixed price marketplace. The section following demonstrates how the ideologies of the 'right' price – whatever it is imagined to be – are pervasive among participants in this project, and how DVs imagine, with equal ideological conviction, that the 'right' price can be obtained through specific linguistic practices.

Then, we turn to some examples of actual marketplace bargaining practice that reflect strategies for bargaining that were common across many participants. Interestingly, as was frequently the case, these examples demonstrate that vendors know, or at least suspect, that their interlocutors are 'Moroccan-from-outside', yet successful transactions happen when a price is agreed and a purchase made. Inasmuch as that price is an emergent potential – the product of interaction between vendor, client, item, supply, demand, producer, etc. – these bargaining conversations show how resident Moroccan vendors and DV clients make strategic use – successfully or unsuccessfully – of 'Moroccanness' in its categorial reference to *descent* as well as *place* to try to influence that price and make it 'right'.

Is There a 'Right' Price?

For any visitor unfamiliar with non-fixed price markets, whether in centralized sources for everyday goods or in marginal places like flea markets or car boot sales (Crewe & Gregson, 1998), deducing the 'right' price for goods can be a difficult task. Fixed-price stores and advertised brand names remove much of the uncertainty of the marketplace by ranking and regulating quality, providing satisfaction guarantees and, most of all, marking prices equally for any paying customer. There is no relationship required between vendor and client beyond the simple exchange of currency for goods. Non-fixed price markets, in contrast, involve establishing relative positionings of buyer and seller, each with the instrumental goal of getting the best price, although that best price is not necessarily the lowest or highest. Price achieved through bargaining describes a value emergent in the social relationship created as it manifests as a monetary value on the object (Khuri, 1968; Storr, 2008; Wagner, 2015b).

Discovering what that best price might be involves bargaining, which 'does not operate in purely pragmatic, utilitarian terms, but is hedged in by deeply felt rules of etiquette, tradition, and moral expectation' (Geertz et al., 1979: 222). The etiquette of bargaining involves establishing and maintaining the vendor–client relationship, to determine the best price in the present exchange and in possible future transactions. This best price will not be the same for every pair or for every interaction: myriad emergent factors are part of price, ranging from classic economics of supply and demand to more behavioral elements such as perception of quality and value of goods, time limitations, individual economic status and, of course, an affective sense of success or affiliation in the bargaining process (Flores Farfán, 2003; French, 2001; Orr, 2007). The need for an affective affiliative relationship is patent in almost any marketplace interaction, demonstrated by the extent to which vendors commonly use playful greetings, jokes and other strategies of verbal art to engage and negotiate with clients (Drivaud & Peretz-Juillard, 1984; Lindenfeld, 1990).

Importantly, non-fixed price markets are places where information is limited: consumers must choose goods and negotiate prices based on their experiences of prices and values for the goods they seek, along with whatever information they might gather *in situ* about its quality and relative value at that moment on the market. With regard to Moroccan markets, Geertz et al. (1979: 24) characterized them as the search for information, where information is 'generally poor, scarce, maldistributed, inefficiently communicated, and intensely valued'. That description may apply to many markets worldwide, but it serves as a starting point to discuss how DVs approach bargaining in this marketplace – as many flows of more or less reliable information, from vendors, past personal and reported experiences in Morocco, parents and other relatives, and their knowledge of prices abroad. In these face-to-face interactions, the affective relationship between vendor and client becomes a pragmatically crucial means to establish the trust and veracity of information about the goods at hand, in order to determine *value* – which is always fluctuating and emergent – which is then materialized as the agreed price.

In Morocco, the traditions and etiquette of establishing veracity in face-to-face market interactions engenders the use of oaths, scriptures and blessings – even when the statement is false (Kapchan, 1996: 59–60). In Kapchan's (1996: Chapter 2) example, buyer and seller use the shared category of 'Muslim' as an opening towards agreeing on a price, putting both parties in an ideal-type of 'religious co-adherents' to establish trust and progress the bargaining to an end agreement. These religious invocations become part of the strategy of bargaining that invokes affective stances and manipulates flows of information to influence the final price. However, importantly, such strategies do not lead to an economically 'right' price, in the sense of balancing supply and demand; the price achieved in successful bargaining transactions reflects that emergent situation, full of interpersonal factors along with economic ones.

This emergent agreement is perhaps better discussed as *value*, as opposed to price. Conceptually, value includes the respective perceptions and estimations of need and benefit that are emergently negotiated between parties to arrive at an exchangeable price (Alexander, 1992; Beckert & Aspers, 2011; Graeber, 2001; Gudeman, 2008). Value also reflects how these negotiations include social categorizations of the participants in bargaining transactions that relate to perceptions of value. Desforges (2001), in his research on British tourists in Peru, reflects on travelers' discourses of money and value which indicate a distance between the perceived authenticity of the experience and monetary exchange:

> Here we see travellers drawing on the idea 'that once money invades the realm of personal relations it inevitably bends those relations in the direction of instrumental rationality' (Zelizer, 1994: 11). Because monetary exchange is seen as based on pecuniary interest, it seems to mitigate against 'authentic' relationships with others. When travellers are associated with money, they perceive themselves as identified as tourists, with subsequent inability to engage 'genuinely' with place. (Desforges, 2001: 359)

This sentiment resonates with diasporic visitors, who, because of their perceived status as 'being-European', are generally seen to be more economically mobile than local residents. This impression of economic disparity follows logically from the habits of DVs, who tend to spend money, unsurprisingly, as though they are on holiday (given that they **are** on holiday). As such, vendors may not necessarily be classifying DVs as entirely 'other', but may be recognizing that they likely can access a (perceived, relative) higher economic status in Europe, making them more likely to accept a higher base level for price on merchandise. In other words, because they are from Europe, they are used to European cost-of-living levels, often making everyday goods more expensive than in Morocco. That factor is material to their categorial status as marketplace buyers.

DVs also demonstrate assumptions about economic status in Morocco that are perhaps equally as unfounded. Rabia expresses in the extract below her occasional surprise at learning that what she thought was inflated was, in fact, the 'right' price.

Interview Extract 4.1

Rabia, Marrakech, 13 June 2008, 30 sec

1 **LW:** je sais que:: (1.0) parfois c'est dur de négocier, ou bien:
I know that:: (1.0) sometimes it's hard to negotiate, or maybe:

2 **R:** mais parfois non, on a l'impression/ que:- que:/ que c'est
cher, (.5) par contre t'es avec une personne d'ici qui te
diras que c'est le prix,(.3)
but sometimes no, we have the impression/ that:- that:/ that it's
expensive, (.5) in contrast you're with a person from here who
tells you it's the price,(.3)

3 **LW:** mmm

4 **R:** donc en fait hehehfinalement, euh:/ l'inflation c'est
partout quoi hh il=n'y=pas=qu'en France/ même au Maroc
so in fact hehehfinally, uh:/ inflation is everywhere you know hh
it's=not=only=in France/ even in Morocco

Rabia was the only interviewee to state this perspective, and one of the few DVs to express awareness at all that the cost of living in Morocco might not be as cheap as it was comparatively perceived to be. Significantly, recent trends in tourism-related gentrification in Marrakech, where the conversation with Rabia took place, have increased the cost of living there generally, in response to the increase in foreign capital, property development and tourist circulation (Kurzac-Souali, 2005). Yet this disparity in price expectation is also based in differences in experiential, behavioral perspectives on value: DVs tend to retain an impression of Morocco from their occasional visits, and from their first gateway – through family – as a place where things are less expensive than in Europe. In one example I have previously analyzed (Wagner, 2006, 2015a), a DV buyer offered a low price for a handmade table, devaluing it far below what the vendor could accept to the extent that he reacted very negatively during the negotiation, indicating an indirect sense of being insulted. Again, the idea of a 'right' price is related to categorial perceptions of value, involving the quality of the good itself as well as the trustworthiness of the vendor, the economic status of the client, and the ability for both of them to develop an affiliative bargaining interaction.

Rabia's comments and other instances like her unsuccessful bargaining exchange, in which DVs significantly undercut the prices offered, seem to indicate that there may be inaccuracies in categorial assumptions and perceptions about value and economic status from both resident Moroccan vendors and DV clients. But Rabia's recollections are also reflective of the way expectation of value is a source of disparity between DVs and resident Moroccan vendors. Specifically, as elucidated below, ideologies of economic status, linguistic practices and value combine to create the illusion of a 'right', 'Moroccan', unobtainable price.

The 'Moroccan Tourist' Price: Combining *derija* and Place

Given that bargaining has waned from everyday use in Europe, it is a linguistic practice that DVs primarily learn – if they learn it at all – in Morocco. Often, they learn it 'incorrectly' (as Karima documented above), in that they are not linguistically skilled and culturally aware of the specific rhetoric, genres or valuations commonly used for bargaining in Morocco. For example, DVs may have witnessed an elder using religious sayings as Kapchan describes above (Wagner, 2006: 55–56), but in none of the examples I have recorded or witnessed have any DVs attempted to use religion as a categorial or rhetorical strategy. Instead, most often, their strategy focused on being recognized and categorized as 'Moroccan' as opposed to being a 'tourist', and in achieving the supposed 'real' price that this status should bestow upon them. That is, in nearly all of the interactions I recorded, getting the 'right' price was interactionally equated to a tangible, practical signification of 'being-Moroccan', or at least passing as 'local-Moroccan' in marketplace interactions.

The implicit assumption in this pursuit of the 'right' price is that 'Moroccans' receive it, while others (non-Moroccans) receive inflated 'incorrect' or 'unreal' prices. There are aspects to this that may be anecdotally, arguably true, to the extent that local residents – particularly those who have or can build some sort of relationship with a vendor – are able to negotiate lower prices than more fleeting clients. Yet, there is no universal 'right' price in a market, as every interaction prompts new parameters in the exchange. A repeat visitor from any background, Moroccan or otherwise, could potentially form a patronage relationship with a vendor that would result in prices more favorable to the continuance of that relationship. DVs, however, almost universally profess the conviction that getting the 'right' price is connected to simply 'being-Moroccan'.

The following examples demonstrate three versions of this ideology about how 'being-Moroccan' is connected to getting the 'right' price, each presenting a different configuration of embodimentality as it enters into the negotiations. Embodimentality may be: something that is already perceived, a precondition to the price offer; something that can be manipulated; or something that is already in-play in the interaction, but not necessarily as categorically fixed as it is often imagined.

In the first example, Said explains his perception as to how diasporic categorization works in the market, using a pen in his hand as an example.

Interview Extract 4.2

Said, Paris, 9 February 2008, 1 min

1 **S:** bah si tu vas au souq par exemple/ si je vais au souq=bah
pour achêter des petits:::/ des petits souvenirs, bah on
t'applique le prix touriste enh.
uh if you go to the souq for example/ if I go to the souq=uh to
buy litt:::le/ little souvenirs, uh you get the tourist price so.

2 **LW:** ammm

3 **S:** on te dit pas:::::ouais t'es pas-t'as pas le::- si ça coûte
euh ça, si ça coûte deux dirham, (.4) [pour un marocain
they don't say:::::yeah you aren't-you don't have::- if this costs
uh this, if this costs two dirham, (.4) [for a Moroccan

4 **LW:**   [c'est le: pour le
stylo⸮
                                                               [it's the: for the pen⸮

5 **S:** pour le touriste (.7) français ou européen/ ça va être quatre
dirham, (.3) pour le touriste, euh:: on va dire marocain, ça
va être trois ou quatre dirham (.5) donc t'es plutôt coté
touriste que coté marocain quoi
for the tourist (.7) French or European/ it will be four
dirham, (.3) for the tourist, uh:: let's say Moroccan, it will be
three or four dirham (.5) so you are more counted as tourist than
counted as Moroccan you know

6 **LW:** Ouais
Yeah

7 **S:** tu vois, parce que tu vis là-bas
you see, because you live over there

Said gave this response when I asked for an example of what makes him feel like a 'foreigner' in Morocco. He makes his thought process on the categorial distinction between 'tourist' and 'Moroccan' explicit: not receiving the 'Moroccan' price places diasporic visitors in line with 'foreign' tourists – an association he hesitates to make, evidenced through the qualifying phrase he uses to disown the category 'Moroccan tourist' (Line 5). This is a categorization that, for him, is not based on language use or any more specific element of embodimentality; it just happens, immediately, in the market.

Said's perspective partly conceptualizes 'Moroccanness' on the market as about both *place* and *descent*: to achieve the perceived 'right' price, participants have to establish themselves as of Morocco and in Morocco, and be ratified as such by the negotiating vendor. Although he hesitates to enunciate the category, 'Moroccan tourist' is an attractor in operation along these dimensions of *descent* and *place*, such that *descent* remains aligned with other interlocutors, but *place* becomes a dimension of relevant distinction. He connects his perception of this category to where he lives – his connection to one *place* and not another – as the causal logic for price differences (Line 7). That dimension seems to be always apparent to the vendor selling him this pen, who always categorizes him as being 'from-elsewhere'.

Given the way bodies play a part in these interactions, to the extent that resident Moroccans 'know' that DVs 'crossed the water' even before any intentional communication (as discussed in Chapter 3), passing as 'local-Moroccan' rather than 'Moroccan-tourist' would seem necessarily to be a project involving multiple aspects of embodiment, from dress to *hexis* to language. Yet participants often blamed language exclusively as the traitorous element that signals 'not-being-Moroccan' in these interactions. One such commentary comes from Wafae, whose encounter with a vendor in Chapter 3 involved the ways her embodied presence became relevant from afar. Immediately after having bought some decorative tassels for curtains, she made this comment about her previous unsuccessful negotiations for the same object in her ancestral hometown, citing language use as her mistake on that occasion.

Interaction Extract 4.2

Wafae, Marrakech, 7 August 2008, 35 sec

1 **W:**   it's a good price because, (.4) there was one in Agadi:r,
        (.) but ya (.7) we asked them, and we were talking Dutch at
        the time/
2 **LW:** yeah
3 **W:**   so <when> he heard us, he said um: well 25 eu- euros (.3) a
        pi[ece
4 **LW:**   [for each/ oh.
5 **W:**   for each, (.8) that was uh (.) not

Wafae makes a causal link (Line 1) between having spoken Dutch with her husband at the time of their previous shopping excursion and being given an extravagant price (25 Euros each for curtain decorations, Line 3) by that vendor. By making this direct, linear association, she disallows that he might have recognized her 'Europeanness' through any other means than Dutch-language speech. Although she spoke fluent *derija* with the vendor throughout the successful negotiation I recorded with her in Marrakech, her 'being-European' was evident from her concurrent interactions with her husband and daughter, which took place in Dutch. So even if she had made the error of revealing her linguistic otherness in Agadir, she had made the same error during her successful negotiation in Marrakech. In other words, she disproved her own assumption in practice.

The perspective she states, however, puts pressure on performing *derija* in interactions as the only way to establish oneself as belonging in *place*, by avoiding any verbal indication of being from somewhere else (even though it may be already evident). Although Wafae made this causal attribution, as did many others, she achieved her desired price in the bargaining I recorded with her, despite betraying her 'Dutchness' throughout. She, like most DVs, focuses on language as a manipulable element of embodimentality that can enable her to pass, while she may be aware, like Said, that other elements of her presentation make her immediately, visibly, 'not-from-Morocco'.

In line with Wafae, the final example comes from an interaction, and is one demonstration of how this ideology of 'being-Moroccan' through language use might play out. Latifa, a Tarifit-origin woman who was not a fluid *derija* speaker, was engaged in extended bargaining with a lampshade vendor in Marrakech. In other marketplace interactions, her Arab-origin husband had been the primary bargainer (see Hicham, below), but in this case he had walked on to another shop. This extract came from near the end of an extended and playful exchange between her and two vendors, throughout which she had been speaking primarily in French.

Interaction Extract 4.3

Latifa, Marrakech, 16 June 2008, 20 sec

1	**L:**	je vais encore t'embêter deux petit seconds
		I'm going to bother you just two seconds more
2	**V2:**	((jokingly)) ça y, prenez votre sense, <tranquilité> () les appliques s̆ad#
		that's enough, be on your way <peace> (.) the lighting fixtures closed#
3	**V:**	non non non non °ne prenez votre°
		no no no no °not take your°
4	**L:**	s̆al temen*
		'ow much ((*missing hard ḥ))
5	**V:**	laquelle? [en fer fourgé?
		which one? [in wrought iron?
6	**L:**	[c'e- oui
		[that- yes
7	**V:**	oui
		yes

8 **L:**   la bri-
         the bri-

9 **V:**   celle-là tu m'as pas dit celle-là bien <avan[t>
         that one you didn't tell me that one much <earlie[r>

10 **L:**   [celle-là là
                               [that one there

11 **V:**   celle-là elle vend à trois cent cinquante dirham
         that one she sells at three hundred fifty dirham

12 **L:**   non! le vrai prix!() mhhhh ((outbreath laugh))
         no! the real price! () mhhh ((outbreath laugh))

13 **V:**   ((playacting voice)) le vrai prix? trois cent! [(.) si t'as
         raison ehh xxx
                    the real price? three hundred! [(.) of
         course you're right ehh xxx

14 **L:**   [ha'
         ((laughing silently)) ((laughing voice)) <j'étais très
         fort> °'h'h'h'h°
         <I was too good> °'h'h'h'h°

In this very brief bargaining sequence at the end of a longer interaction, Latifa excuses herself for taking up too much of the vendor's time, and then makes a parting enquiry about the price of another lampshade. Significantly, she makes her price request (Line 4) in *derija* – a very tokenistic codeswitch, marked by her audibly non-native pronunciation – which is uncharacteristic of the rest of her talk. After a sequence identifying which object (Lines 5–10), she is given a price (Line 11), to which she makes an immediate and insistent reply, asking for the 'real' price (Line 12). The first vendor, her main bargaining partner, laughingly replies with a 'real' price, cutting 50 dirham from the original quote as though it were his mistake to give her a non-real quote initially – 'of course you're right' (Line 13). She laughs at his response, and continues laughing, mocking her own enthusiasm in bargaining – 'I was too good' (Line 14). This exchange, and others that occurred in close parallel to this structure, reflect the ideological assumption held by many DVs that there is a hidden 'real' price for each object, which vendors choose to reveal to the right ('Moroccan') customers.

It also demonstrates how the ideology about the power of speaking the 'right' language – *derija* – comes into play during bargaining. Latifa is not capable of maintaining a passing negotiation in *derija*, but she does make that code somehow relevant for asking the price in it, even if it is an utterance marked by her non-native pronunciation.[1] The vendor's playful response to her insistence on the 'real' price may be related to her playful indexing of

'Moroccanness' in her token *derija*. At the very least, their play with *place-*indexing codes and communicative practices (including in Line 2, another vendor in the shop using *derija* in playfully addressing Latifa) indicates how the categorial boundaries that Said described as relatively fixed can be more diffuse in interaction.

Being categorially 'Moroccan' is clearly more complex than simply switching to or maintaining talk in *derija*. Embedded within this categorial ideal-type as it emerges in marketplace interactions are salient distinctions of class status and wealth, alongside expectations about how much things cost, that are mixed with dimensions of *descent* and *place* and have an influence on perceptions of value. DVs can engage in strategies to be recognized as 'Moroccan' – to pass – in order to achieve this 'right', 'real', 'Moroccan' price, but getting the 'real' price is, of course, an unattainable goal in a non-fixed price market. 'Moroccanness' becomes categorially relevant in how dimensions of it interact with values for objects on the market and emerge in the process of negotiating values into prices.

The examples here range from accepting categorization as inevitable (Said), to blaming a practice for what was perceived as a disaffiliative categorization (Wafae), to strategically playing with one's capacities for categorial belonging (Latifa). The differences between these ideologies as reported by participants about their own practices (Said and Wafae) and as practiced under observation (Wafae and Latifa) indicate how what may be ideologically a very direct causality – 'local-Moroccans' get the 'right' price – becomes a much fuzzier project in practice. This fuzzy diffuseness leaves room for the interaction between Latifa and that vendor, where her 'Moroccanness-by-*descent*' is made relevant, but her 'out-of-*place*' linguistic strategies become a source of play rather than a source of negative categorization of difference.

Marketplace Encounters: Negotiating Moroccanness as Place-based Descent

More often than not, rather than passing, DVs were doing interactional communicative work, like Latifa, to smooth their *strangeness* and become-non-local-but-Moroccan. The examples in this section demonstrate different ways in which 'non-localness' becomes categorially relevant in interactions, and different interactional bargaining strategies through which DVs negotiate this dimension. These individuals do not seem to have difficulty in maintaining their 'Moroccanness-by-*descent*' through language; rather, their *place*-affiliation becomes an issue in determining price.

Figure 4.1 Diasporic visitors bargaining in Marrakech

In these sequences *derija* is the main code, as it was in the majority of the bargaining sequences I recorded. Yet, in each of these extracts, a sequence is initiated whereby the *place*-based status of 'Moroccanness' is put into question, while the *descent*-based categorial status is not. That is, these vendors continue to speak *derija* with DVs who, either explicitly or through their language use and embodimentality, are marked as being 'from outside'. The vendors are thereby ratifying their 'Moroccanness' as *'derija*-speakers' which, according to the crux of the ideologies discussed above, should be enough to get the 'right' price.

Yet other aspects of 'Moroccanness' related to *place* emerge that involve work on the part of the DV participants, either by making claims or using their *derija* competencies to establish themselves as 'Moroccan-enough' in their quest for the 'right' price. These claims and attitudes about prices and what they might signify can become a source of affective dissention in the interaction. For example, two vendors in the following interactions describe their clients' reluctance to bargain as a disaffiliative, negative affect about buying 'from here', after their clients use their *place*-based access to other markets as a strategy for bargaining. For these vendors, then, the way these DVs bargain for lower prices is not building the vendor–client relationship, but negating it by making claims about competition 'elsewhere'.

The ways in which these *place*-based categorizations emerge can vary from encounter to encounter. Yet, as these three examples demonstrate, more often than not it was the DV him- or herself who made *place* an issue during the sequence of negotiation, either explicitly as in the first two examples, or relatively implicitly through bargaining strategy and language use as in the last one. Although marketplace encounters may have begun with an initial misrecognition – like that of Wafae in the previous chapter (Interaction Extract 3.1), in which DV passersby were initiated as potential clients through calling out category guesses ranging from Algerian to Turkish to Brazilian – once *descent*-based 'Moroccanness' was established, bargaining continued in *derija* as far as that DV was capable. In other words, if 'Moroccanness' was established at the outset of the interaction, then it was generally the DV who (inadvertently) signaled that *place* might complicate that category. That signaling was either by interactionally announcing, more or less explicitly, his or her connection to the 'outside', or by claiming a strong connection to 'inside' Morocco. Looking at these interactions microanalytically demonstrates how problematically complex stances emerge when, as in the final example here, a DV's embodimentality and categorial claims did not match.

Place made explicitly relevant

The first two examples presented here are instances in which the main DV interlocutor made his or her becoming-diasporic-through-place a relevant element in the negotiation strategy. Each example is a very different context for shopping. The first is one of several recorded interactions with Karima (who opened this chapter) at the weekly regional *souq* in her familial home-town, where we were shopping for everyday items (like batteries) and clothing (like sandals and pyjamas). The second is part of a day of shopping in the central Marrakech *souq* with Hicham and his wife Latifa (cited in Interaction Extract 4.3), when they were buying various souvenirs and gifts for family on their peer-group holiday trip – the first time for both in this tourism destination. Both Hicham and Karima considered – and demonstrated – themselves to be fluent enough in *derija* to sustain bargaining interactions with various vendors. Yet, as the extracts below indicate, their bargaining strategies for getting the 'best' price involved, essentially, staking a categorial claim at being a 'Moroccan tourist'. Although they seem to be trying to position themselves as needing a lower price because of their 'outside' status, in fact that status is taken up negatively, if not hostilely, by their vendor interlocutors.

In Karima's interaction below, she is at the table of a pyjama vendor, asking about first one and then several other pyjama models and fabrics. Her younger sister Btisam interjects occasionally with other information about prices and quality, but Karima is the primary negotiator in this interaction.

Initially, Karima asks a price and nearly takes her leave (Lines 8 and 10), but the vendor convinces her to continue looking through his merchandise by offering to make a better price for her than his competitor nearby in the market (Lines 11–13). She then refreshes the potential to bargain by asking for a specific model (with shirt and trousers, Line 16) and, after some searching through the merchandise, for specific fabric ('like silk', Line 22). When she finally asks the price for her chosen model, she enters a bargaining sequence with the vendor that makes her *place*-ness explicit.

Interaction Extract 4.4

Karima, Btisam and Vendor, 5 min 3 sec
1   **K:**   yellah šḥal gulti li hadi?
      let's go how much did you say for this one?
2   **V:**   səttmya[2]
      six hundred
(1.4)
3   **K:**   səttmya? () hadək baʿa bsəttmya/ kif kif
      six hundred, this sells with six hundred/ it's the same
4   **V:**   <dihe mʿak makeyn ši muškil,[> əddəniya haniya
      <take with you no problem,[> life is peaceful
5   **B:**   [la *prend pas le* qalima *sont* [*pas douce*
                                    [no *don't take it the* material *is* [*not soft*
6   **K:**   [<xx>
      bləš
                                                [<xx>
      without
7   **V:**   bəl aḥər <xxx>
      in the last <xxx>
(1.1)
8   **K:**   barak allahu fik
      God bless you ((thanks))
9   **V:**   əddəniya haniya
      the world is peaceful
10   **K:**   smaḥəlina
      excuse us
11   **V:**   ʿəlah? (.3) əddəniya haniya. ila bġiti hadi raha gaʿ ərḥesa <wəllahila arḥesa>
      why? () the world is peaceful. if you want this one it is cheap <I swear to God it's cheap>

12 **K:** ouai/s:,
yea/h:,
13   səttmya dryel baš nḥsəbhum lək (.) =
six hundred ryal I'll calculate it for you=
14 **K:** la i-
no i-
15 **V:** =ula šəttiha ʻandu gaʻ [bʻalek lək <xxx>
=or if you see it at his place ((other vendor)) [he will sell you
16 **K:**   [ʻandu ke: eh ġir ḥədle: ġir ḥədli ṭwe
(hh) hadəkši? (.) eh: hadək eh smitu ʻandək e:lpijamat
ə:ssirwal u: l:qamija? () ki dayrin?
[he has ke: eh just
let me: just let me fold (hh) this stuff? (.) eh: that one eh
what's-it-called do you have the: pyjamas with pants and a shirt?
() how are they?
17 **B:** *on sait pas (xxx)*
we don't know (xxx)
18 **V:** <ara nšuf
<let me see>
19 **K:** ara nšuf u <ġansuwwəl w ġansuwwəl >
let me see and <I'll ask I'll ask >
20 **V:** hadu?
these here
21 **K:** ġansuwwəl
I'll ask
(2.7)
22 **K:** enh bḥal hadu be:::m:: bḥalha, bḥala m: (.) bḥal lḥrir u la
[(xxx)
yah like these li::m:: like her, likea m: (.) like silk or so
[(xxx)
23 **V:** [aj: (.) bḥal had ləḥrir? (1.0) <bḥ > al hada?
[come: (.) like this silk? (1.0) <li>ke this?
(.6)
24 **K:** eh: bḥal hada.
yeah: like this.
25 **V:** ah ha huma (xxx)
ah here they are (xxx)
26 **K:** bšḥal?
how much?
(1.3)
27 **V:** hadi tmənin dərham, (1.9) sittaš elmya
these are eighty dirham, (1.9) sixteen hundred

(1.2)
28 **K:** m:: () had ši hadi llike:na?
         m:: these are all there is?
29 **V:** ṣafi hiya llibaqat fəlḥrir. keyn tma fi (xxx)
         that's it that's left in silk (xxx)
(6.3)
30 **K:** bšḥal hadək?
         how much is this one?
(1.0)
31 **V:** səbʿen dərhəm
         seventy dirham
(1.1)
32 **K:** səbʿe[n
         sevent[y
33 **B:**   [enh enh (.) *c'est trop*
             [enh enh (.) *it's too much*
34 **K:** *cinq euro en France.* ḥəmsin dərhə[m eh fi:
         five euro in France. fifty dirha[eh in:
35 **B:**   [la la: [*non tu vas dire*
         c'était <trop> (xxx)
                      [no no: [*no you will say it was too*
         much (xxx)
36 **V:**   [(xxx) (xx[x)
                              [(xxx) (xx[x)
37 **K:**   [la wəllah
         ḥəmsin dərhəm
                                  [no I swear fifty
         dirham
38 **V:** kayna hadik bsbʿen dərham rahiya <məḥe:r/> šətiha?
         there's this one for seventy dirham it's <goo:d/> did you see it?
39 **K:** hnh:
40 **B:** uh: *je te r[amène en: souq,*
         uh: *I'll t[ake you to: a souq*
41 **K:**   [<ləḥəqqaš drok> elmuškila, (.) =
             [because now the problem (.) =
42 **B:** Karima
43 **K:** =hna hna əssuq fransa/() nəfs ʿandna muagan w ʿandna ssuq. w
         f ssuq kaydiru təmən zwi:/n bəzzaf
         =here here the souq in France/ same we have shops and we have the
         souq. and in the souq they do a reall/:y good price
44 **V:** iyyeh maši bḥal [hna daba
         yeah not like [now here

45 **K:**   [oow::mm bəl euro bəle- <bədrahəm kan-
kandiru hadak e: u ke- kaykunu nnit bhad ttəmən hada> u la
btemen <naqəs bḥal hada>
               [aaand::mm in euro in- <in dirham we- we do e: and
th- they are the same with that price or with a lower price like
that
46 **V:**   <ara nšuf l[ik>
give me I'll show y[ou
47 **B:**   [na- *les mêmes Karima* [(*xxx*)
                      [na- *the same ones Karima* [(*xxx*)
48 **K:**   [<ḥəṭa> e:: šritu b ḥəms-
bḥəmsin dərhəm.
                              [<?̣?̣> e:: I bought
them for fif- for fifty dirham.
49 **B:**   <*quand xxxxx*> euh:[: *les mêmes, t'auras- tu les auras pour
euh:* () =
<*when xxxxxxx*> uh:[: *the same ones, you'll- you will have them for
uh:* ()=
50 **K:**   [b *cinq euro*
                        [for *five euro*
51 **K:**   enh
52 **V:**   <lli bġitiha->
<whatever you what->
53 **B:**   = *pour euh:*
= *for uh:*
54 **K:**   [[yellah
[[let's go
55 **V:**   [[bġiti hadik <ow la hadi>?
[[you want that one <or this one>?
56 **K:**   yellah bla manssidʿoqš. (.3) [yellah yellahhh ehe[h
let's go without a lot of noise. (.3)[let's go let's go ((laug[h))
57 **B:**   [(*xxx*)
58 **V:**   [makayn
ḥatta muškil. bġiti dork hadi?
                                      [no
problem at all. you want this one now?
(1.7)
59 **K:**   hada bḥal haduk yəmkən nilu?
that like that one maybe nylon?
60 **V:**   <wyn keyn?

61 **K:** ela:[:/ dara bena šwiya rəṭba
  (??)a:[:/ something maybe a little soft
62 **V:** [(xxx) (.) hadək rəṭba zwina
  [(xxx) (.) that one is really soft
63 **K:** m::
(1.0)
64 **V:** ttub ərṭəb zwin
  the fabric is very soft
(2.7)
65 **K:** *il est pas mal celle-là mais*
  it's not bad that one but
(1.5)
66 **V:** <mabġitiš təqdeəš ʿandna w ṣafi >
  you don't want to buy from us and that's all
67 **K:** bəll:ati bəllati arah tṭeb rasna be::(1.5) ššəms
  sl:owly slowly wait our heads are cooking with:: (1.5) the sun

From Karima's price demand in Line 30, the sequence becomes more focused on bargaining over a specific item in relation to its quality and availability, for a price in this market or a price elsewhere. Her immediate reply, after echoing the price offer in Line 32, is to quote the price she can get for a comparable item in France (Line 34) in French, then self-translating in *derija*. Her sister Btisam is constantly interjecting: first with some simultaneous talk that the price is too high (Lines 33 and 35), then trying to get the floor to offer her own experience of a price and quality comparison from elsewhere (Lines 40, 47, 49 and 53).

As Karima continues to elaborate the price difference in comparison to France – establishing that she can obtain goods much more cheaply there, that she had in fact bought the same quality item for the equivalent of 50 dirham instead of his offered 70 (Lines 43, 45 and 48) – the vendor argues that his merchandise is different from that (Line 44), and of a good, soft quality (Lines 62 and 64). Yet Karima does not counteroffer with a price; she has only established that she can get this product elsewhere for 50 dirham, or 5 Euros, or a really 'good price' (Line 43).

From Line 46, the vendor seems to be producing different subsequent merchandise with different quality levels, in response to her continuing to search for a material that will be worthwhile for her. He offers different models (Lines 55 and 58), finally at a loss to know what she is looking for – 'where is it?' (Line 60). She is seeking a 'soft material' (Line 61) so he makes claims to softness (Lines 62 and 64), to which she responds with minimal backchannelling, and long pauses (1.0 second, then 2.7 seconds), until he finally gives up on the negotiation: 'you don't want to buy from us, and that's all' (Line 66).

Part of what Karima's interaction demonstrates is the subtle ways in which harsh confrontations can happen in bargaining. In Line 66, the vendor makes a statement about Karima's intentions – 'You don't want to buy from us and that's all' – which, in a bargaining context, acts as a severe closing. He is placing blame directly on Karima for the lack of agreement between them; further still he places this blame as lack of volition on her part, rather than on some other involuntary (e.g. religious or situational) inability to find an object to buy and agree on the price. His confrontationalness is marked by her reply, to 'slow down' (Line 67) and cool down, using an expression about getting hot-headed from being out in the sun. The transcript is stopped there, at the moment when the bargaining between these two interlocutors reached an impasse. After that moment, not transcribed here, the vendor next door intervened and closed this sale on behalf of his neighbor, asking Karima to 'give what you want' for the price. If not for his intervention, the disaffiliative stances of both parties would likely have killed this sale.

Yet, it is arguably Karima who begins this disaffiliative stance, when she explicitly extends this marketplace from this *place* in her hometown in Morocco to her other hometown in France. Her main argument about price, repeated in variation over several turns in this interaction, is that she can get the same goods cheaper in France. In short, she makes her 'being-from-elsewhere' the most relevant information in this interaction, and the most important factor for her in setting a price. While the vendor is making effort in the scope of this market – re-initiating a 'failed' sale (Line 11), repeatedly searching for merchandise that might satisfy Karima's desire, and addressing the quality and feel of the object in her hand – she insists on a lower price not related to its attributes, but to other merchandise in a distant elsewhere.

Despite her competent *derija*, which ideologically would make her able to become-Moroccan for bargaining, Karima turns to her *place*-based knowledge to construct her strategy in this negotiation. This self-categorization is not necessarily a surprise: her talk does not assume that the vendor knows that she and her sister 'crossed the water', yet her invocation of the *souq* in France is not met with surprise from the vendor. It is likely that he has already assumed this categorial status, as she and her sister are using intermittent French and may show other embodied indications that they are not locally resident. In the continuation not included in Interaction Extract 4.4 after the neighboring vendor brokers a successful end for this exchange, the main vendor asks if Karima and her sister are 'traveling'. That explicitly indicates how he might recognize them as being 'Moroccans-from-outside', yet he did not make that category relevant before she did so within the interaction, by quoting prices from outside.

Next, in a second example of *place* made explicit, the argumentation over price has a similar foundation, but a very different engagement by the vendors involved. Hicham and his wife Latifa are negotiating for a painting intended as a present for her mother, in a shop on one of the most trafficked streets in the Marrakech *souq*. They had told me earlier that day that Hicham does the negotiating because he speaks *derija* fluently. In this case, as in others, he was speaking fluently but came to a point (at Line 30) where he insisted on getting the 'Moroccan price'.

Interaction Extract 4.5

Hicham, Latifa, Vendor, Vendor2; Marrakech, 14 June 2008, 1 min 40 sec

(After about 5 minutes of already looking at paintings in the shop; H and L have asked prices on two other paintings which they found too expensive, and told V that this will be a present for L's mother.)

```
1   L:    c'est oran:ge: saumon: rouge=
          it's oran:g:e salmon: red=
2   V:                        =aš gulti ʿajbatək?
                              =what did you say you like?
3   L:    ce qui est carré là, combien il peu txx
          the square one there, how much could it xx
4   V:    huit cent
          eight hundred
(0.9)
5   H:    sowwəb mʿana temen mə[zyen afək ašrif
          deal me a good pri[ce please mister
6   V:                        [ha huwa rah fih mi[lle deux cents=
                              [this one it's one thou[sand two hundred=
/   L:                                              [j'ai mal au coeur eh
                                                    [I'm in shock
8   V:                                                        =rah le
          prix qui est affiché mille deux cent. [xx toi tu as dit le prix
          pour l'étudiant
                                                          =so the price
          that's on the tag one thousand two hundred. [xx you you said the price
          for a student
9   H:                                            [na:: ((back of throat))
10  L:    étudiant. [moi je suis plus que
          student.  [me I'm more than
```

11 **H:**   [la maši hna, hna maši étudiant(s) [hna uled bled hna
jina ḥəna bash [nfarḥ- nfarḥou bil bled
          [no not us, we're not student(s) [we're children of the
country we came here to [be hap-be happy with the country

12 **L:**   [pire qu'etudiant,
() c'est un bébé:
                                        [worse than a student, ()
it's a baby:

13 **V:**   [ḥəna étudiant ḥəssən min uled elbled yanni [ra
baqe teyqrau mʿanduš flus. [xəṣek tsaʿdu baš yəxodi elpiyasa
                              [here student is better that child of the
country because [(he who is) still studying doesn't have money. [you
have to help them so they can make purchases

14 **H:**   [hna:
                [we:

15 **H:**   [hna-
hna bġina temen məzyen ʿandna elflus li- [budget = limité hna[,
tem[en-
                                                        [we-
we want a good price, we have money li- [budget =limited we[, pri[ce-

16 **L:**   [c'est vous?
                                [it's you?

17 **V:**   [ehn?
                                                [huh?

18 **L:**   [c'est vous qui ait peigné?
                                                        [it's
you who painted it?

19 **V:** non e[h non
no e[h no

20 **L:**   [ça c'est pas beau enh, () écoute,[combien
        [that's not good enh, () listen,[how much

21 **V:**   [les jeunes artists/[les
artistes-
                                [the young artists/ [the artistes-

22 **L:**   [celui
là- celui=là pxx trois cent?
                                                [that one
there- that one there xx three hundred?

(1.2)

23 **V:** [[<doucement>
        [[<gently>

24 **L:** [[hahahahhahhhh
        [[hahahahhahhhh

25 **V:**   wa hadek *un metre/() carré/*
           and that one *one meter/() square*
26 **L:**   un metre carré
           one meter square
(11.8) ((background activity – V departs looking for change for other customer))
27 **H:**   ils sont qəṣḥeyn eh wullah, (.7) qəṣḥeyn bəzzef/
           they are hard I swear (.7) really hard/
28 **L:**   Hicham, tu préfères celui-là toi. (.5) y a aucune [couleur
           Hicham, you prefer this one you. (.5) there's no [color
29 **H:**   [*c'est pas les touristes* hna saḥa°
           [*it's not tourists* us frie°
(10.0) ((end of other negotiation in background; L discussing painting with her friend))
30 **H:**   šti, šti hna, hna ʿandna passeport maġrebi,[w ʿandna la carte
           nationale[w ʿandna kullši tʿaal maġreb/[() xəsna temen
           maġrebi, maḥəsnaš temen eh=
           look look we, we have Moroccan passports,[and we have the national
           identity card[and we have all the stuff of Morocco/[() we need a
           Moroccan price, we don't need a price=
31 **V:**   [mm
33 **V:**   [mərḥaba
                   [welcome
34 **V:**   [mərḥaba
                                       [welcome
35 **V:**   [[xxxxxxx
36 **L:**   [[il y a pas
           [there isn't
37 **H:**   [[=((loud)) smaʿ elḥədara elhamdullah/ rah keyn eh:
           [[= ((loud)) listen to the words thanks to God, there will be eh:
38 **V:**   fin gaʿa din fi-
           where are you in-
((L discussing painting with her friend; overlapping 4 turns))
39 **H:**   hna, raḥna ḥəna fi mərrakš fi:
           we, we came here to Marrakech in:
40 **V:**   la la fin fin katʿayšu
           no no where where do you live
41 **H:**   fransa
           France
42 **V:**   fransa fina blasa
           France in what place
43 **H:**   ḥəda l'allemagne ḥəda Mulhouse, tʿaref Mulhouse?
           near Germany near Mulhouse, do you know Mulhouse?

44 **V:** Mulhous[e
        Mulhous[e
45 **L:**   [très loin, Strasb[ourg
           [very far, Strasb[ourg
46 **V:**   [xxx
47 **H:** Strasbourg, Mulhouse, Besançon/ () hadi hiya el-
     Strasbourg, Mulhouse, Besançon/ () that's the-
48 **V:** mərḥaba. ari təmənalif.
     welcome. give me eight thousand.
49 **H:** la- la/   [la/ təmənalif =
     no,(.)   no[no eight thousand =
50 **L:**   [šhal temənal[if
            [how much is eight th[ousand
51 **H:**   [=*quatre cent dirham* la la walu. (.) la la
     la:.
                     [=*four hundred dirham* no no nothing. (.)
     no no no:.
52 **V:** aṭeni *trois cent*
     give me *three hundred*
53 **H:** [[gəbila gultina *trois cent cinquante/ trois cent* rah
     [[before you told us *three hundred fifty/ three hundred* that's
54 **L:** [[c'est xx::! *trois cent*!
     [[it's xx *three hundred*
55 **V:** 'aya 'aya heyt njib fiha reduction [xx
     hey hey cause I'll bring it in on discount [=xx
56 **L:**   [*trois cen*[t, xxx
                        [*three hundre*[d, xxx
57 **H:**   [šti daba xemsin
     dərhəm ma fiha walu,- šti daba ḥəna mlli kan jina ḥəna, katḥdəru
     ġir b les cents les deux cents makeyn ġir, ml[li kansəksiu šḥal
                                    [you see now
     fifty dirham there's nothing in it, you see now we since we came here,
     you speak only with the hundreds the two hundreds there's not just,
     wh[en we ask how much
58 **V2:**   [ra mabġitiš temši
     lilbled nətana sahabi
     [so you don't want to come to this country of ours
((several vendor voices overlapping))
59 **H:** šti- šti- šti- šti- (.4) šti ḥəna daba, (.4) ḥəna daba, mlli
     kan-
     look- look- look- look- (.4) look here now, (.4) here now when I-
60 **V2:** elwaqət tḥbədlat ahənaya
     times have changed here

With three principal speakers and other peripheral participants in the background, this multilayered conversation is more complex than space permits for a complete turn-by-turn analysis. For the purposes of this section, I excised some content to concentrate on Hicham's discourse with the vendor, which took place principally in *derija*. There may have been relevant activity in the background, as these vendors were negotiating with several members of this eight-person group simultaneously, but the exchange between Hicham and this particular vendor was spatially distant and orientationally separated from those. Hicham took charge of this particular negotiation on behalf of himself and his wife Latifa, both explicitly and in practice.

This extract begins as Latifa is making price demands on different tableaux displayed in this art shop. Coming to one that she and her husband have discussed, she is getting the attention of the vendor again to ask the price – beginning from 'what did you say you like؟'. When the vendor gives a price offer, both Latifa and Hicham reply incredulously, Hicham by pleading for a negotiation (Line 5) and Latifa by declaring she is in shock (Line 7). The vendor counters their objections by claiming that the price they offered is a 'student price', that is, for a buyer who is at poverty level. From this point, Hicham makes his first conversational turn emphasizing his 'Moroccanness' in Line 11 and continues these attempts to claim 'the Moroccan price' through most of the extract.

While Latifa claims that they are 'worse than students' (Lines 10 and 12), Hicham claims to not be students, but rather 'children of this country' (Line 11). The vendor replies that being a student would be better, in this case, as students need to be helped as an act of charity (Line 13). Hicham replies that they have a 'limited budget' (Line 15), at which point Latifa engages the vendor in bargaining for a lower price because he did not paint the canvas himself, and by offering another too-low price for another painting (Lines 16–26). As the vendor is drawn into another interaction, Hicham comments that they (the vendors) are very hard; not responding to his wife's question about a different painting, he continues in Line 29, calling loudly to the other side of the room, that 'it's not tourists' – in French, then with the tag 'us' in *derija*.

In Line 30, Hicham returns to bargaining, with his 'Moroccanness' as his strategy. He reasons that he is subject to all the Moroccan bureaucratic papers that signify citizenship and nationality by *descent* – with the vendor 'welcoming' him mid-utterance – then asks the vendor for a 'Moroccan price'. The vendor replies by asking where he lives (Lines 38–40), probing his answer of France to get the region and nearby cities (Lines 41–47). He then sharply inserts a 'welcome' in a new price demand ('give me', Line 48) which is still more expensive than their declared budget.

Hicham's attempts to be categorially Moroccan in this specific sequence are focused exclusively on being 'Moroccan-by-*descent*'. They do not work the way he hopes they will; the vendor does not adequately lower the price on the painting under discussion, instead introducing a dimension of *place* while Hicham is insisting on his 'Moroccanness' by *descent*. The vendor asks where he lives and, establishing that he is from France, requests a price that Hicham again finds too expensive. The immediacy of sequence between these lines (Lines 38–48) – from 'France in what place' to 'give me eight thousand' – seems to imply a connection between Hicham's place of provenance and the quoted price on the part of the vendor.

The final sequence quoted in this extract consists of particularly interesting conversational moves, as they reflect on value and categorial belonging as being in-*place* or by-*descent*. The vendor responds with a lower price offer (Line 52), but Hicham is again dissatisfied as the price compares unfavorably to another painting they had previously discussed. While the vendor insists this is a discount (Line 55), Hicham complains that there 'is nothing in' the 50 dirham (5 Euros) reduction when the prices are in the hundreds (multiples of 10 Euros) (Line 57). When in Line 57 Hicham makes the complaint that 'you' (which is not clearly these vendors or Marrakech vendors in general) only speak in large denominations, another vendor (not the one with whom he has been negotiating) interjects, questioning his desire to visit 'this country of ours' (Line 58). After Hicham responds without making any substantial claims, that vendor continues, claiming that 'times have changed' (Line 60).

This last vendor comment underlines how the different parties in this negotiation are attempting to resolve inaccurate assumptions about each other's bargaining position. Hicham's surprise at dealing with large denominations is understandable, as most daily items in Morocco cost within a single- or double-digit range; however, the object he is considering buying – an original painting – is not an everyday item, nor something that most locally resident Moroccans would normally buy. Hicham's continued rejection of prices, and his general accusation to the vendors that they 'only speak in hundreds', reflects his assumptions about the value of this painting as a piece of original art, disregarding the labor required to create it, and what value the artist's and the vendors' labor has embedded in a 'Moroccan' *place*.

Moreover, Hicham's style of bargaining does not adhere to common practice ameliorating the relationship between client and vendor through rhetoric. The tone of this negotiation is more insistent and plaintive than harmonious and affiliative, as Hicham repeatedly insists on his 'right' to 'Moroccanness' rather than demonstrating it through usage of bargaining technique that would actually create affiliation. This was not the only episode of bargaining in my recordings with Hicham that developed into an argumentative, heated conversation about value explicitly attributed to places in Europe and Morocco. After the somewhat accusatory remark by the second vendor in Line 50, the subsequent few minutes of conversation turn to a discussion on the effects of inflation felt in Morocco and in France. Like Karima's turn towards more severe differentiation of affect with her vendor, Hicham and these vendors begin to take sides and lay blame; but, unlike Karima, their further talk manages to smooth these differences and collaborate on a price.

Later in the negotiation not quoted here, Hicham makes further arguments about value. He claims that they will have to dismantle the painting to bring it on the plane, and then pay 25 Euros to have it reframed in France, adding to his total costs. These are logical arguments about this couple's budget, but do not have a distinct impact on the vendor, or his basis for negotiation. In fact, these arguments point ever more precisely at their distance in *place* and economic status, in that they can afford not only to take a vacation in Marrakech, but also to buy a painting with the intention of reframing it later for nearly the same price. Eventually, this group did find a 'right' price, by choosing a smaller painting that reflected Latifa and Hicham's 'limited budget'. As in many instances of bargaining, the price achieved is an emergent 'right' price for that vendor and client, whether or not it is the same as any other resident or diasporic Moroccan would pay.

Latifa demonstrates a counterpoint to Hicham's efforts to 'be-Moroccan' in her linguistic and bargaining abilities. According to Latifa's declared linguistic competences, as well as the placement and content of her interjections, she was likely not a comprehending listener to *derija* conversation, except in moments such as Lines 48–49, where Amazigh cognates – in this case numbers – were used. In that instance, for example, she shows that she is following the *derija* conversation well enough to know that a price has been quoted (Line 48), but she asks her husband to translate that price from *ryal* to a price she can understand (see Footnote 2; Line 50). Like her previous example, she uses *derija* for her price demand, and Hicham answers her by translating from *ryal* to dirham (Line 51). Hicham's mastery of the different currency expressions in Morocco, like *ryal*, is in fact an important part of how he is 'being-Moroccan-in-*place*' in a way that his wife is unable to practice. This localizing skill will be discussed more below. But arguably, with or without her *derija*, Latifa could have bargained this deal herself in French, as she began to do in Lines 16–24, and did elsewhere on that day with other vendors. Her husband's strategy of making their 'Moroccanness' explicit by both speaking *derija* and demanding consideration as 'children of this country' may not have achieved the 'best' price for them.

Implicitly in-*place* in contrast to embodimentality

In the next extended example, part of Yasmine A's effort to be categorially 'Moroccan' in this negotiation involves insisting on her geographic origins as being in Morocco. She does not initiate this claim explicitly, as Hicham did; rather she uses communicative resources to maintain her stance as 'Moroccan-in-*place*' even as the vendor probes this claim. This interaction also took place in the central *souq* in Marrakech, on a less trafficked street, where Yasmine, I myself and a French female friend of hers were shopping. The vendor was selling various items made of braided thread, including the napkin holders that Yasmine chose.

Interaction Extract 4.6
Yasmine, Vendor; Marrakech, 6 June 2008, 2 min

1 **V:**   bonjour
          hello
2 **Y:**   salaam u aleikum
          peace unto you
3 **V:**   salaam
          peace
(8.6)
4 **Y:**   šhal keydiru hadu?
          how much are these?
5 **V:**   hadu dyel srəbat aḥti ((passing car))
          those are for napkins my sister
6 **Y:**   yehh ʿarəft
          yeah I know
7 **V:**   ašra dərhəm. (1.5; motorcycle noise) ašra dərhəm allah yḥəllik
          ten dirham. (1.5; motorcycle noise) ten dirham God make it easy on
          you ((if you please))
((music)) (11.2)
8 **V:**   ḥodi šri ši tənaš ow la -tana ndir lik temen məzyen =
          if you buy twelve or so- I'll make you a good price =
9 **Y:**   ehh
          yeah
10 **V:**   =<xxx ḥəṣək xxxx>
          =<xxx you need xxxx>
(3.5)
11 **Y:**   sətta
          six
12 **V:**   sətta?
          six?

13 **Y:** mm
        mm ((affirmative))
14 **V:** nṣbər mʿak b ḥəmsin dərham
        I'll deal with you for fifty dirham
15 **Y:** eh?
        eh?
16 **V:** nṣbər mʿak b ḥəmsin
        I'll deal with you for fifty
(1.6)
17 **Y:** ((quiet)) la bəzzef/
        no too much/
18 **V:** bəzzef?
        too much?
19 **Y:** myateyn ryal elwaḥad?
        two hundred ryal each?
20 **V:** () eh myateyn ryal, aləf frank=
        () yeah two hundred ryal, a thousand frank=
21 **Y:**   =eh=
                                  =yeah=
22 **V:**   =hhehhhehh aləf frank
                                =hhehhhehh a
        thousand frank
23 **Y:** kanḥədr bil frank, bḥal elwalid w elwalida
        I talk with frank, like my father and mother
24 **V:** aləf frank hhehhhehh qazim[3] had elaləf frank (2.5) ašmin
        lown bġiti<hum>?
        a thousand frank hhehhhehh old that thousand frank (2.5) which
        color do you want <them>?
(1.6)
25 **Y:** emm nšuf (2.0) elḥamra zwin. ḥamra ow la elkeḥl nšuf
        emm I'm looking (2.0) the red is nice. red or the black let's see
26 **V:** li bġiti. (1.8) hata ha[jja
        whatever you want. (1.8) any[thing
27 **Y:**   [waz-
                                  [waz-
28 **LW:** ara nšuf.
        let me see.
29 **Y:** makeynaš keḥl hənaya?
        there's no black here?
30 **V:** eh keyn elmaron
        yeah there's brown
(4.8)

31 **Y:** ḥamar zwin yeki?
       red is nice yes((f))?
((to LW; nonverbal response; 7.2 looking at merchandise))
32   makeyḫəsruš?
       they don't come undone?
33 **V:** la mateyḫəsru[š <zyena:: >
       no they don't come undo[ne <well-do::ne >
34 **Y:**   [šaydin məzyen?
                 [they are well tied?
35 **V:** ana naṭek ši hajja məzyena. () mateḥafi[š
       I'll give you something good. () don't worr[y
36 **Y:**   ((smile voice)) [ntuma dima ʿandkum
       ši hajja məzyena
                 ((smile voice)) [you((pl)) always have
       something good
37 **V:** **la**! nstilək ši   haj[ja məzyena
       no! I'll select some[thing good
38 **Y:**   [((outbreath laugh))
(11.1; noise of hand movements)
39 **V:** nti šamaliya?
       are you northern?
(1.1)
40 **Y:** la səharawiya
       no I'm Saharan
41 **V:** səharawiya eh (.5) [Dakhla u la
       saharan eh (.5) [Dakhla or
42 **Y:**   [jit=
                [I came=
43 **Y:** =la, jit eh:: (.6) Errachidia,()[((town name))
       =no, I came eh:: (.6) Errachidia, () [((town name))
44 **V:**   [enh
(1.1)
45   mərḥaba
      welcome
46 **Y:** allah ybarak fik
      God bless you ((thanks))

This interaction opens in a normal pattern of a demand for a price by the buyer (Yasmine in Line 4), although the vendor replies by defining use and not giving a price (Line 5). These items are relatively unusual – produced using the same materials used for decorative embroidery on clothing and in home furnishings, in a more recently innovated design and purpose. The other items in this vendor's shop reflected other products – like curtain tassels – that are more widespread across Morocco. In Line 6 Yasmine confirms that she recognizes their purpose, and the vendor completes her price request with a price offer of 10 dirham each. After a pause during which she examines the merchandise, the vendor offers to negotiate favorably if she buys 10 units (Line 8). She chooses six (Line 11), and he offers a reduction of 10 dirham off his quoted price, for a total of 50 dirham (Line 14), which he repeats at her prompt (Lines 15–16). Her rejection of this offer is simply that it is too much (Line 17), which he echoes (Line 18) as a question. She then translates his original price (10 dirham) from dirham into *ryal* (Line 19) as a question itself. This line sets her up to bargain as 'Moroccan-in-*place*' rather than a 'Moroccan-from-outside'.

Translating to *ryal* establishes her reference currency associated with 'traditional' Morocco – profoundly in-*place* – instead of one associated with 'modern' Morocco or Europe. As she switches between currencies – indexing geographic and economic dimensions like using *derija* indexes 'Moroccanness' as a way of marking herself as 'being-Moroccan' – he responds and extends this variety of currency references. The vendor takes up her statement very quickly, replying by echoing the price in *ryal*, and adding the translated price in another alternate currency (*frank*) with a laugh (Lines 20–22). She counters by claiming '*frank*' as part of her parental *descent* (Line 23), while he continues to laugh and repeat '1,000 *frank*', marking it as 'old' (Line 24). In the same turn, he reverts to helping her select merchandise (choosing colors together in Lines 25–28), but his laughter has changed the affective tone of the interaction. It reflects that her reframing of currency from dirham to *ryal* is unusual, and possibly significant.

Yasmine was not trying to pass visibly that day – she would be recognizable to vendors immediately as *strange* from her style of dress. She would also likely be categorially marked by her shopping companions – myself and her French friend. This vendor could have no doubt that she would understand a price quoted in dirham as opposed to the 'old' *ryal* or *frank*. Yet vendors sometimes translate prices into Euros (in *derija* or in French) as much as they might translate them from *ryal* to dirham. As mentioned above in Footnote 2, and as analyzed elsewhere in more detail (Wagner, 2006, 2015b), translating currencies among the Moroccan colloquial ones and Euros is a point of difficulty for DVs. Thinking in Euros is a *place*-based habit of determining value, both as how much one can afford to spend from one's European travel money, and as comparing costs for an object between Morocco and Europe. In fact, vendors occasionally quote prices in dirham and Euros in the same turn, and sometimes undertake negotiation using the Euro quote. For example, in Interaction Extract 4.2 above, Wafae quotes prices in Euros instead of dirham, although the object she had purchased would have been paid in dirham.

The skill of translating currencies and using them effectively and correctly in bargaining practice joins into processes of becoming 'not-Moroccan' through the geographical associations of currencies, along with other bargaining skills that are *place*-based acquisitions for DVs. DVs do not often initiate using *ryal*, which involves a more complicated exchange calculation to their base currency than dirham (1 Euro is approximately 10 dirham or 200 *ryal*). Yasmine choosing *ryal* as the currency mode would be unusual for a DV, following this observation; in fact, while bargaining with him in the continuation of this interaction she uses dirham. Perhaps this ambiguity prompted his laughter, and his next initiated sequence.

After she poses a question about the workmanship, the vendor offers to 'choose something good' for her (Lines 32–38). The following audible pause (11.1 seconds) includes her activity of looking for her choice of merchandise. This pause is broken when the vendor initiates a new topic, asking if Yasmine comes from the north (Line 39).

A question like this can sometimes reflect difference in accent and vernacular expression between regions, but I would argue that in this case the vendor is trying to establish if she is resident Moroccan or not. 'From the North' spoken in Marrakech could mean almost anywhere in Morocco, but also can mean from further north – across the Mediterranean to Europe. Her answer, that she is 'saharawiya', from near Errachidia, paired with her visible embodimentality, would confirm that she is from 'outside'. His initial guess in Line 41 reflects his categorial work given her response: when she claims 'saharawiya', he suggests one of the more cosmopolitan locations of the Moroccan Sahara (Dakhla). This prompts her to reply with a specific location in Line 43, which is more peripheral, less wealthy, and deep in the Saharan south of Morocco. By claiming a local, resident home that does not match her embodimentality, she implicitly confirmed that she is resident outside Morocco. However, the vendor conversationally accepts this explanation, welcoming her (Line 45), and does not explicitly address her claims to geographic 'local Moroccanness' in the remainder of the interaction.

Neither does her 'Europeanness' enter explicitly into the remainder of the interaction. It does remain, however, underlying the entire process. As much as she might make claims to 'local Moroccanness', even her intended purchase is contradictory to that. She is buying decorative napkin holders for a table setting – implying a table set with flatware and individual plates, unlike the 'local Moroccan' style of a single central serving dish. Like the previous examples, she does not use many local bargaining methods to achieve the price. Yasmine prides herself on being *qassḥa* – a hard bargainer. Eventually she gets the price she desires by describing how regularly she visits Marrakech and promising to bring additional business to the vendor, in the form of her sister who will be arriving the next day. In the end, she achieves a 'localness' through her promise of repeat business (a promise I witnessed her keep with other Marrakchi vendors), but not explicitly through her categorial claims to being in-*place*.

Yet, Yasmine manages to defend her own sense of place and achieve a practical attachment to *place* through this interaction. Her claims to be 'saharawiya' are not questioned any further – unlike Hicham in the previous extended interaction, where the vendor questioned him specifically about where he lives. Her claim that she will return with her sister responds to the value of *place* for a vendor: even if she is not living in Morocco, he might anticipate more business by giving her a good price. *Place* then, in this example is something that can be negotiated through an attractor of 'Moroccan tourist'. While Yasmine may not be permanently resident in Morocco, she establishes her links to *place* enough to get the 'right' price.

Conclusion

As these final three examples show, the 'right' price emerges almost accidentally, no matter what bargaining strategies are used. When Karima made her *place*-distance explicit as part of her prior knowledge on price, her vendor-interlocutor did not adhere to her logic and negotiate with the European price basis for his merchandise. He focused on its quality in the local market, and took a disaffiliative stance on her intentions to cooperate. Hicham made explicit, argumentative claims to a 'Moroccan price', which was met with a *place*-referent sequence from his main vendor-interlocutor. Later, however, they did reach a price agreement that balanced the merchandise with Hicham and Latifa's spending capacity. Finally, Yasmine introduces the dimension of *place* through the more common practice of speaking with specific colloquial currencies – perhaps unintentionally setting herself up to be questioned on her *place*-origin by making regional currency denominations part of the bargaining process. The complaint about being replied to in French discussed in the last chapter (Interview Extract 3.9) was not in evidence in these recordings. Once a negotiation was initiated in *derija*, vendors generally did not resume French as the primary code, even when comprehension backchannelling was uncertain (see Wagner, 2015c).

Whether explicitly or implicitly, in all of these cases *place* becomes relevant in the interaction, and potentially relevant to the final price reached (or not reached), but place is **not** simply about speaking *derija*: it becomes a more complicated interaction between bargaining skills and strategies, individual vendors and merchandise, and DVs' spending power, access to information, established and emergent relationships, and finally the perceived value of the items they seek to purchase. Importantly, it is the DV client who initiates a sequence that makes *place* relevant in these diverse cases: Karima compares prices to France; Hicham demands a 'Moroccan price'; even, arguably, Yasmine's use of *ryal* is a move to establish that she is embedded in Morocco, using the currency of 'locals'. That initiation on the part of DVs may reflect how *place*, and their belonging in-*place* in Morocco, becomes omnirelevant for nearly all their interactions there.

Although *derija* fluency is part of these interactions, a more holistic notion of embodimentality is intrinsically relevant as well to how they play out. While DVs interpret what they assume to be higher prices as disaffiliative conversational acts by vendors – defining them as 'being-European' when they wish to be defined as 'being-Moroccan' – their efforts to pass simply by speaking *derija* are insufficient in this context to achieve the status they want. The DVs bargaining here are not having difficulty communicating in *derija*; rather, their bargaining strategies as one part of their communicative practices are frequently 'out of *place*'. By requesting or even demanding the 'real' price or the 'Moroccan' price as opposed to a 'tourist' price, instead of establishing affiliative links between themselves and the vendors – i.e. as Muslims, as Moroccans, or as potential repeat clients in Yasmine's case – DVs index a link they imagine between their communicative practices aimed at 'being-Moroccan' through *descent* and the consumption status they imagine that should bestow on them in *place*. In other words, they attribute the perceived value of goods as inherent in 'being-Moroccan', often disregarding perceptions of value being put forth by the vendor, and then – ideologically, if not in these interactions – interpreting vendors' negative responses as a rejection of their claim to 'Moroccanness'.

For the intended outcome of these interactions – that is, agreeing on a price – *place* is in fact a much more relevant dimension than *descent* because economic status operates as a function of it more than the latter. For most vendors, the value of what DVs might want to buy is governed more closely as a function of *place* – i.e. the available capital a visiting 'European' customer is presumed to have at his or her disposal and the likelihood that she or he will become a repeating client – than a function of 'Moroccanness' as *descent*. DVs often interpret this broader orientation towards value as a rejection of 'being-Moroccan' in all ways, through *descent* as much as *place*. Furthermore, several of the interactional examples and interviews in this section come from Marrakech, where each of the participant DVs were visiting on holidays taken separately from visits 'home'. They are therefore negotiating being non-local both as 'being-European' and as not being locally resident in that *place*, in the sense that Marrakech is not the site of their familial home.

'Being-European' reflects on one's economic power, but being locally resident (as few customers are in the Marrakech souq) means an increased possibility that one will return as repeat business and bring other potential buyers. Both of these aspects enter into vendors' considerations of value.

As we will see in the next chapter as well, these strategies to negotiate value through 'Moroccanness' extend beyond DVs' linguistic practices to include manipulations of embodimentality in the search for the 'right' price.

Notes

(1) French native speakers in Arabic languages often have difficulty with the pharyngeal voiceless fricative ħ, which is not a shared phoneme.

(2) The price of 600 quoted here is using *ryal*, an alternate currency measurement to the standard dirham used in Morocco. Generally, one dirham equals 20 *ryal*, so the price of 600 *ryal* equals 30 dirham. The vendor performs this currency translation in turn in Line 27. There are several alternate currencies in use in Morocco, including *ryal* as 1:20, *ryal* as 1:5, *doro* as 1:2 in the region around Al Hoceima, and *frank* as 1:10 dirham, frequently used for multiples of 10 or to express very high values, such as the price of a house. The use of *ryal* recurs in the other bargaining examples below, and will be discussed more extensively in relation to Interaction Extract 4.6.

(3) In line 24, /qazim/ is an example of dialectal variation in Marrakech, where ḍ (ض) is sometimes pronounced as /z/.

5 A New Category? Becoming 'Diasporically-Moroccan'

Interview Extract 5.1 Integrating in Morocco

Lamia, ((hometown)), 8 June 2007, 50 sec

1 **LW:** j'ai entendu par d'autres: participants, qu'il y a toujours cet
eh écart entre la communauté ici et la [communauté uh
I heard from other: participants, that there's always this distance
between the community here and the [community

2 **L:**   [la communauté mmm. (.5)
                                                  [the community mmm. (.5)

3 **LW:** [[bah tu- déjà-
[[well you- already-

4 **L:** [[moins:: (.) je le sens moins depuis que = je = suis adulte.
[[less:: (.) I feel it less since I've = become = an adult

5 **LW:** mm

6 **L:** maintenant euh: (1.1) maintenant je trouve que quand on vient
ils nous intègrent bien, alors que=c'est=vrai- tout jeune, (.5)
euh: (.3) quand on était au Maroc on n'était pas marocain, et
quand on était en France, on n'était pas français.
now uh: (1.1) now I find that when we come the integrate us well,
although=it's=true- very young, (.5) uh: (.3) when we were in Morocco
we were not Moroccan, and when we were in France, we were not French.

7 **LW:** oua/ voilà.
yes exactly

8 **L:** c'est bizarre.
it's weird

((waiter arrives with food; 9.6 sec excised))

9 **LW:** donc eh:/ (.9) tu sais exactement le::- .hh °pardon° vous savez
exacte[ment le moment hhhehheh (.) le moment où ça a changé?
c'était comme eh:

so eh:/ (.9) you know ((informal)) exactly the::- .hh °sorry° you
know ((formal)) exact[ly the moment hhhehheh (.) the moment when that
changed? it was like eh:
10 **L:**   [non on peut se tutoyer
                   [no we can use the informal
11 **L:**   bah je crois que c'est à partir du moment que je suis venu avec
             lui,
             well I think it was from the moment that I came with him,
12 **LW:**   mmm

What constitutes 'being-Moroccan-enough'? When can DVs relax from the
active pursuit of becoming categorially 'Moroccan' in everyday interactions,
into simply becoming diasporically-Moroccan as a normalized part of the
sociocultural landscape of this territorial homeland? The two previous chapters looked at their practices for making claims to 'Moroccanness', through
perceived categorizations and how they are negotiated around emergent lines
of distinction between interactants. These borders are material and expressive, relating to modes of wearing clothing and walking in the street as much
as to using *derija* to communicate with others in locally practiced genres. All
these together create an emergent embodimentality through which DVs are
often – explicitly and ideologically – pushing towards 'being-Moroccan', even
if their efforts achieve mixed results.

This chapter turns towards observed practices when DVs are *not* actively
struggling to be categorially 'Moroccan'; when they are, more or less, 'being
themselves' as 'diasporically-Moroccan' – both indelibly, vitally, genetically
related to 'being-Moroccan' and distinctively becoming-diasporic.

Such practices emerge through embodimentalities that blur lines between
bodies and communication. They arise at moments when DVs reach the limits
of their communicative capacities, and might choose to be silent or draw on
the resources of local Moroccan friends and family as proxies of 'Moroccanness'.
They also are observable when they assume themselves to be 'being-Moroccan'
in a non-diasporic way, which is not noticed, signaled or problematized by
others. Like the different agentive, active examples discussed in the previous
two chapters, these ordinary, inexplicit examples explore how embodimentalities as multiplicities can become integrated into sociocultural landscapes
where, as Lamia A describes above, she can stop dealing with being 'neither
French nor Moroccan'.

For her, that moment arrived when she started visiting her family and
returning to favorite holiday places with the 'him' mentioned in Line 11: her
French-origin husband Michel. Becoming a body that is ordinarily and inti-
mately associated with his body as a family – an example of how

embodimentality is malleable, as an assemblage that shifts in response to these two bodies forming a more durable engagement – changes the way she relates to Morocco and the way her interlocutors in Morocco engage with her. Lamia and Michel are frequent visitors to Morocco – perhaps even more frequent than her sister Yasmine, discussed in the previous chapter – but her approach towards everyday practices where she might be categorially recognized, as I will discuss in more detail later in this chapter, is starkly different from many other participants.

The examples of Lamia and others below point to how embodimentality is expressively malleable, through elements like clothing or speech, and can also be physically and materially malleable, by exceeding an individual's physical body. Individual DVs become linked with others in ways that mitigate their 'non-Moroccanness' into 'diasporic-Moroccanness'. The malleability of bodies, practices and categories combine here into something new: a category we might call 'diasporicness' that is becoming increasingly acceptable for DVs and residents alike, and increasingly embedded into Morocco as part of its future pathways.

Revisiting Embodimentality: Wearing *Gondorra*-s on the Street

To revisit it briefly, embodimentality refers to bodies as multiplicities, or assemblages, in which some aspects are seemingly permanent and others can easily be transformed. Most obviously (and often controversially), bodies are genetically linked with their ancestors through material manifestations of linear *descent*. *Descent* can be interpreted through strict, static linearity, forcing essentialist ideas and meanings onto such bodies which tend to imagine *descent* to be intrinsically linked to *place*. In fact, as is argued far and wide in relation to embodied materialities like race, ethnicity or gender, such *descent* or genetically reproduced embodiments have different forms, speeds and trajectories of malleability in expressive or in material manifestations. That is, all these seemingly intrinsic characteristics about bodies can transform physically, in interaction with technologies and other non-human agents, as much they can transform discursively in interaction with different systems of significance in different places.

Using embodimentality, I want to point to how these interactions have diverse vector trajectories, reflecting varying rates at which physical and discursive aspects to these multiplicities can change, and a spectrum of possible agents motivating change. Speech, for example, is seemingly highly malleable, as a fleeting expressivity enunciated through a body – an embodimentality that is perceived to be easily modified in interaction with specific agents. Yet speech also becomes materially fixed, in the ways in which muscles learn to operate and the vocabularies and structures become pathways in the brain.[1] Even when there is a strong agent, like the economic motivation to 'get the right price' demonstrated in the previous chapter, the malleability of speech is limited by practices of embodiment. Furthermore, as malleable as speech might be for an individual example, there are other embodied aspects to communication – especially those perceived visually – whose lower speed of malleability hinders the rate of change of the whole assemblage. By using embodimentality instead of other related terms, like habitus, performativity, body idiom or simply embodiment, I highlight this interrelation of material and expressive parts – interconnected and inseparable in assemblage, and also made relevant in different configurations in interaction with others. Beyond embodiment as a way bodies are produced or produce themselves, embodimentality is about the way bodies exceed themselves by being connected to the world around them and infuse parts of their interactions into combinations of materialities and expressivities, constantly interconnecting multidimensionally with other entities.

In fact, as we have seen in the past chapters through a variety of aspects of embodied interactions, DVs are often categorized, or at least they perceive themselves to be categorized, as something other than 'locally Moroccan'. Whether or not they exert effort to disrupt, discourage or dispute these categorizations, they recur as a consistent part of their experiences in Morocco. In some encounters, for some DVs, the negotiation of categorial belonging reaches a limit at which it is no longer a focal activity. Instead, DVs might relax into a sense of categorial acceptance in being recognized as 'diasporically-Moroccan', as belonging along certain dimensions while others remain marks of distinction. They inhabit practices with which they are comfortable – speaking the 'right' language to the extent that they are comfortable, wearing clothing that makes them feel comfortable, and choosing particular spaces of encounter where they feel comfortable.

To take into account how that 'comfort' is produced, and in contrast to the examples where DVs were using clothing to pass in Chapter 3, this chapter explores one visually recognizable example of becoming-diasporically-Moroccan through wearing *gondorra*-s. This clothing practice discursively references 'tradition', but in a diasporically mediated way. As an embodied practice of wearing comfortable yet 'traditional' clothing, it is one example of how embodimentality can become-diasporic, in the simultaneous combination of materialities that link directly to each homeland, which emerges as something new.

Traditionally diasporic

Gondorra – here referring to a general style of clothing I have also heard called *'qondorra'*, *'marrakshia'* or *'b'daya'*, depending on regional terminology and sometimes small variations in design – are a common piece of clothing found in markets anywhere in Morocco. It is a garment wearable by either gender, stylistically differentiated mostly through bright colors for women and shades of gray or tan for men. The basic shape is a long and rectangular loose-fitting sheath, made from light cotton or polyester, with arm openings but not sleeves, and sometimes pockets or holes on the hips providing access inside it. The sleeve holes, collar and seams may be embroidered, giving some stylistic variation beyond color to what is otherwise a very simple garment.

During the summer, these sheaths are more frequently visible on the street, partly because they are a hot weather style and partly because they have been adopted as a style of leisure clothing by DVs. When in Interview Extract 3.2 Otman referred me to 'traditional' clothing, on further investigation I discovered that he meant this garment. Female participants also wore it, or sought it out as something to buy during their visits. Yet, both men and women seemed to be wearing them in ways that varied from the 'traditional' manner, by using it as a covering garment over swimming clothes when going to and from the beach (Figure 5.1).

Fieldnote 5.1 Al Sabadia Beach, near Al Hoceima (22 July 2008)

> I'm noticing more and more men wearing *gondorra*-s to go to the beach: to my mind, there's a feeling of strutting in this kind of native outfit, something the same men probably would never wear in EU. Also, they all look fresh and new, the gondorras, and they are often not wearing full clothing underneath, instead wearing it as a sort of beach cover-up. Bizarre.

The manner of wearing what is physically an item of local material culture, even ideologically 'traditional', evokes how categorial differences emerge between DV and resident Moroccans in the ways in which they embody practices. Clothing practices in Morocco, in my ethnographic experience, generally include wearing two or three simple layers of fully covering clothing, like long cotton pyjamas, underneath a decorative outer layer. Changing from indoor to outdoor clothing means adding or removing the decorative outer layer, while inner layers might be worn continuously, day and night. These decorative outer layers might be *djellaba*-s, as discussed in Chapter 3, or they might be something like a *gondorra*, one variation of which is commonly worn by men attending Friday prayers. In other words, as my comment 'bizarre' indicates in Fieldnote 5.1, from my years of acclimating to what is acceptable

Figure 5.1 Participant and friend at the beach. She wears her *gondorra*; his is folded on the chair next to him

or unacceptable to wear out of the house, I was surprised to see how these men chose to wear *gondorra*-s in a distinctively 'non-local' way.

As the above fieldnote indicates, I noticed men wearing them on or near the beach, as something to cover up a bathing suit. Men did not seem to be altering the way it was worn, apart from the fact that they did not wear the combination of layers underneath, and they were not wearing it in this manner on the way to prayers (that I observed). Women were also wearing it in a non-'traditional' way, as I noticed on the streets in Al Hoceima during the summer of 2007. Girls and women I saw going to and from the local beaches wore brightly colored *gondorra*-s.

Beyond the garment itself, the repeated modification of it was remarkable to me: many women interrupted the length of the garment by tucking it in at the sides (Figure 5.2), using whatever they were wearing underneath – often a bikini that was visible through the thin material – to gather the cloth so that the fabric puffed out around the waist or hips. I interpreted, at minimum, a functional and stylistic logic to this: these garments can be difficult to walk in when allowed to hang to full length, so raising the hem by tucking them in would make walking easier. There are also potential stylistic motivations, inasmuch as breaking the length at the hips gives some distinctive shape contouring the body to the square sheath, and indicates in a visual economy something about what the wearer is wearing underneath.

Figure 5.2 Three Dutch-speaking women walking on the street in Tangier, Morocco (August 2015); the one in the pink *gondorra* on the left has tucked the left side into the underneath of her clothing

These clothing practices recall, in part, the discussion in Chapter 3 about the potential to cover one's body in 'traditional' or 'local' clothing as an effort to pass. Here, passing does not seem to be a relevant objective: DVs wearing *gondorra*-s to the beach were not seeking to become categorially 'Moroccan' for some specific interactional goal; rather, they were participating in styles and tastes relating themselves as 'diasporically-Moroccan', in the context of part of their main summertime activity – namely, beach-going. However, these garments may be imagined as 'traditional'; they take on characteristics of 'diasporicness' through these practiced embodimentalities. Embodied practices here challenge an observed categorial norm about modesty in public, in that the *gondorra* becomes commonly and repeatedly – for these 'diasporic-Moroccan' bodies – enough to cover oneself appropriately when wearing only a bathing suit.

Moreover, these practices seemed to spread diasporically. I first saw women wearing *gondorra*-s as outdoor fashion in Al Hoceima in 2007; then a Belgian DV I accompanied in a Marrakech aquatic park in 2008 wore one; then again I saw women wearing them in Liège (Belgium) in a shopping mall in 2011. It would be impossible to identify a starting point for a trend like this – it probably began long before I first saw it – but it is observable as one that spreads along socio-spatial networks that link DVs to each other, from Moroccan beaches to Belgium malls and back to Morocco. Seeing this as embodimentality – how these bodies feel comfortable wearing 'Moroccan' fashion in a 'non-local' way – enables a recognition of how DVs are becoming comfortably diasporically-Moroccan rather than being 'neither-European-nor-Moroccan' (as Lamia describes above) through a convergence of multiplicities of expressivities and materialities into a specific practice. That practice – a version of tradition-becoming-diasporic – is one assemblage that lays groundwork for a new category.

Proxy Bodies: Association and Absence

By taking embodimentality as a way in which bodies are holistically interactive, in complex combinations of materiality and expressivity that emerge in encounters, we can also recognize how bodies of individual persons become something different in combination with other persons – how collectivities are more than the sum of their parts. Figure 5.2 above is one example of how we might instinctively observe a collectivity of individuals: the three women centered in this picture are moving in concert, with nearly the same stride and at about the same speed, wearing similar clothing and carrying similar belongings. They become a cohort together so instantaneously that we may not take time to recognize how their 'groupness' is produced through various elements of their stylistic and corporeal embodiments. These women instantly stand out from others around them on the street as being 'together' with each other, and as being 'different' from others around them.

In the same way that these bodies can join together to become a collective of 'diasporicness', they can also join with resident Moroccans in an effort to become a collective of 'Moroccanness'. As an explicit strategy of some DVs, who reported how they would seek a local ally to join them on shopping trips, I describe this as using a 'proxy': the allied person was often called upon to present him- or herself as the active negotiator, or to speak in place of the person s/he accompanied. Even if this proxy person did not actively intervene, that material presence of 'Moroccanness' works associatively, changing how the DV person might be perceived from an individual who is distinctively 'from outside' to someone who is part of a 'Moroccan' collectivity.

The examples of proxies below demonstrate how this collective property of embodimentality can work through association, and also how it can work through absence. The next selections include reports and encounters where association between DVs and local Moroccans became relevant to interaction, followed by situations where the absence of some trait of 'Moroccanness' – specifically, comprehension of *derija* – is covered or masked through embodimentality of group collectivity.

Associations

The first example comes from French participant Rabia, who described how she manipulates her presentation of self when shopping.

Interview Extract 5.2 Someone from here

Rabia, Marrakech, 13 June 2008, 45 sec
1 **R:**   mais ils changent les prix quand ils voient des touristes et
        quand ils voient eh: une personne qui habite ici, (.) .h ils
        changent les prix donc toujours=mon=marie=me=dit euh (.4) tu veux
        achêter des choses euh/ qui coûtent chères, euh que t'as vraiment
        besoin, tu devrais t'habiller autrement, quoi. et montrer que
        t'es quelqu'un d'ici ou de là-bas,=je=dit=bah:: avec mon::
        accent, ils me reconnaîtront, quoi.=
        but they change the prices when they see tourists and when they see a
        person who lives here, (.) .h they change the prices so
        my=husband=always=tells=me uh (.4) you want to buy things uh/ that cost
        a lot, uh that you really need, you should dress yourself differently,
        you=know. and show that you are someone from here or from over
        there,=I=say=bah:: with my:: accent, they will recognize me, you know.=
2 **LW:** mm
3 **R:**   =que je suis pas: hhh je suis pas d'ici de toute façon,(.5) donc
        je me souviens avant quand voulais achêter des choses, eh(.3)
        euh:: mhhh j'allais avec quelqu'un d'ici (.6) <et qu' alors>
        comme ça::/ tu connaissais le prix, (1.0) xx on peux me faire
        carotte quoi=hhehe
        =that I'm not: hhh I'm not from here in any case, (.5) so I remember
        before when I wanted to buy things, eh (.3) uh:: mhhh I went with
        someone from here (.6) <and so> like that::/ you knew the price, (1.0)
        xx someone can rip me off you=know=hhehehe

As much as code choice is a part of the linguistic activity of bargaining, Rabia's narrative reflects how embodimentality is more than speech. In the context of searching for a specific purchase, her husband advises her to dress differently in order to get a better price, but she knows that because of her accent she will be (categorially) recognized. Instead, she brings 'someone from here' with her, explicitly so she will not be ripped off. That someone is trusted to have more information than her – to know the prices – but also to remedy the problem of being a 'tourist' by simply being with her. This strategy of being alongside a locally resident person when shopping in the market, usually a family member or family friend, was used even by DVs who were comfortable speaking *derija*, like Rabia. Often, the declared goal for this strategy was getting the 'real' price by having a local informer and advisor on value at hand during bargaining. Yet being alongside this locally resident person is also a strategy of embodimentality: being together with 'someone from here' engages Rabia, in this instance, tangentially into that category, shifting her position from being 'non-local' to being 'diasporically-connected' to a resident Moroccan.

This strategy was a frequently used one, both during the primary research for this project and during previous ethnographic research (Wagner, 2006). DVs called upon resident family members or friends not only to come along on shopping trips, but also to bargain for them in some cases (Wagner, 2015a). Sometimes this role as proxy-bargainer was made explicit, while at other times it became part of the interaction as the advisor about prices became engaged with the negotiation of prices directly with vendors. In the example below, the DV customer Mustafa is negotiating for a blue Saharan-style set of embroidered shirt and trousers (which he has just tried on). He is in Marrakech with a group of several male DV friends and one DV woman whose family home is in Marrakech. The cousin of one of the male friends, Simo, has accompanied them walking around the souq, and when it is time to bargain the price of this garment, he steps in (from Line 9).

Interaction Extract 5.1 Mustafa's proxy

Mustapha, Vendor and Simo, Marrakech, 10 August 2008, 1 min 21 sec

1   **M:**   bšhal hadi?
          how much is this?

2   **V:**   hadik aḫoya nsəbər mʿak, hhh ma ġadiš ngullik ši temen li huwa dyel
          smitu, ana rah bəḥəra fi rasək. rah ḥata təġədit ʿad ḥəllit elhanut.
          that one my brother I will deal with you hhh I'm not going to tell you
          some price of anyone, I'm going to do a price for you. I just ate lunch
          and reopened the shop.

3   **M:**   iyeh
          yes

4   **V:**   nšḥəsbha lik aḫoya mya u ḥəmsin dərhəm.
          I'll let it go to you for one hundred and fifty dirham.

5   **M:**   mya u ḥəmsin dərhəm?
          one hundred and fifty dirham?

6   **V:**   wullahila dirt mʿak le prix xx
        I swear to God I did the price xx for you
7   **M:**   minəheytna bəzzef
        from our side it's too much
8   **V:**   tbarakallah šuf la pièce gədda::š xx (.) adaba rah kanḥədər mʿak bḥal ši
        wəld elbled
        blessings of God look at the way it fits xx (.) now I'm going to talk to
        you like any son of the country
9   **S:**   <tanbʿe xx šri had ši>
        <to buy xx sell these things>
10 **V:**   ewa:
        so
11 **M:**   ewa rah wəld el bled ana elḥawa məši ši xx
        so being a son of the country I'm a brother not some xx
12 **V:**   wa mərḥababik aḥoya mərḥababik
        and welcome to you my brother welcome to you
        (3.4)
13 **S:**   dir mʿah ši temen zwin allah yḥəfdək asaḥabi
        do a good price with him God protect you my friend
14 **V:**   wullaha ḥoya zin <billah>
        I swear my brother it's good <I swear>
15 **S:**   ra mya u ḥemsin ra qaṣṣḥa bəzzef
        one hundred fifty it's really hard
16 **V:**   ah?
        ah?
17 **S:**   dir mʿana ši [temen zwin
        do a good price [with us
18 **V:**   [wullahila dirt mʿah tem[en zwin
                     [I swear to God I made him a goo[d price
19 **S:**   [[ahh ahh rahh
                                      [[ahh ahh well
20 **M:**   [[xx temen/
                                      [[xx price/
21 **V:**   gulliya mərḍi elwalidin ašnu had temen, ana- šti ila səwərt mʿak
        ġir ašra drihamat, rah dekši li bġit ḥətʾana. wa təqəḍi lġərəd
        nta, w tʿaud duz lʿandi tgul liya bonjour, mərḥababik! dinya hanya
        tell me bless your parents what's this price, I- look if I dealt with you
        just ten little dirham, then that's what I want too. and you could buy
        what you want you, and come back to my place to tell me hi, you are
        welcome, life is peaceful
        (5.2)
22 **S:**   aṭek mya u ašrin dirham. (.) bla mataʿud ləlkəlima safi dirha fi
        mika w la [xx
        he gives you one hundred and twenty dirham. (.) without repeating words,
        that's enough put it in a bag and don't [xx

23 **V:**   [waḥa arefti aš ġadiruʕ aṭeuni mya u tletin [w
allah ysǝhǝl ʕalik
                                    [ok do you know what we
will do? you (pl) give me one hundred thirty [and God make it easy for
you
24 **S:**   [la safi safi ari [xx
                                       [no enough enough
give me [xx
25 **V:**   [eh? c'est pas- mabaqeš ši fǝrk beynatnaš
waḥa ʕad li baš nddi-=
                      [huh? it's not- there's no more difference between us ok
return to me so I can- =
26 **M:**   =ḥaṣ nǝmši nzid naqǝṣṣ minha
                                   =must* I go still to shorten it
27 **V:** eh?
yeah?
28 **M:** wa ḥǝṣ* nǝmši nzid naqǝṣṣ minha.
and must* I go still to shorten it
29 **V:** hadek hadek tḥ- sti hadek tǝnaqeṣ, w kunkan hdaya ši ḥeyat ḥǝna,
mangullikš ana hadek elḥadara. ta:tǝlǝbsha w tǝqesha w ngullik
hada w naṭeli yduzha () laḥaqaš hadek eh hadek hadek eh naqeṣ li
bġit naqeṣ, dix dirham dyelha, faytaha bḥal lla ḥǝllǝsti elḥeyat
lǝduble
that that tḥ– you see that to shorten, were there a tailor just here, I
wouldn't say these words. you: put it on and shorten it and I tell you
what and I would take it to her (.) ((tailor)) because that eh that that
shortening that you what, ten dirham of it, more than that would be like
you paid the tailor two times as much
30 **S:** ewa ḥǝllina hadek- ḥǝllina hadek dix dirham li ġadi ndiru biha
so leave us this– leave us ten dirham so we will do that with it
31 **V:** allah ysḥǝr makeynš lmuškil mǝrḥababik aḥoya. en plaisir* ḥoya xx
tǝhna, mabġinas yǝsʕib allah yjib ġisehǝla
God help you there's no problem, you are welcome my brother. in pleasure*
my brother xx us too, we don't want to make it hard, God brings ease

In comparison to the previously analyzed marketplace interactions, this one is unique in that the vendor introduces Mustafa's 'Moroccanness-by-*descent*'. After the first demand for a price, offer and rebuttal (Lines 1–7) the vendor defends his price offer as the one he would give any 'son of the country' (Line 8). This comment immediately makes Mustafa's 'non-localness' relevant: his 'being-Moroccan' would not be made explicit unless it were categorially somehow in question. Simo enters the negotiation peripherally at that point (Line 9) but Mustafa continues in another rebuttal of the price, by reinforcing the vendor's offer of categorization as a 'son of this country' (Line 11). The vendor then welcomes him (Line 12) – again, marking him as 'non-local'.

After a relatively long pause (3.4 seconds), Simo steps in as the proxy-bargainer on Mustafa's behalf. The style of bargaining between the vendor and Simo is more reflective of other observed examples of how bargaining is performed in Morocco (Geertz *et al.*, 1979; Kapchan, 1996): they use affiliative relationship tags, addressing one another as 'friend' or 'brother'; neither says a price without embedding it in a proposition that builds on their buyer–seller relationship; and, most importantly, the vendor uses religious oaths in several formulations to swear to the correctness of his price (Line 18), to convince them that the price is justified (Line 21), and to bargain a new, lower price (Line 23), while still affirming the relationship with the buyer (Line 31).

Mustafa's communicative contribution to this portion of the conversation is relatively small. His interjection at Line 26 is clearly marked as an interruption, both in that he cuts the vendor off mid-word (not in a transition-relevant place) and that the vendor prompts him to repeat in the next turn. In his statement, Mustafa impugns the value of the item under discussion by framing it as faulty, implying that it is worth less (to him) because he will need to adjust it. This negotiation strategy, frequently used by DVs, is parallel to Hicham's argument in the previous chapter (Interaction Extract 4.5) that he would need to have the painting reframed in France. It reflects the DV customer's perceptions of value in relation to their own practical concerns, rather than the local marketplace value of the object to be purchased or the vendor–client relationship. This line of argumentation creates a logical link between a defective or lower quality object and a discount, but in the logic of fluctuating prices and vendor–client relationships, those objects are not universally 'broken' – the vendor could find a shorter buyer than Mustafa, who would not need the pants altered. Yet Simo picks up this argument as a means to continue to bargain, framing the price difference as a favor the vendor can do for them ('leave us this ten dirham', i.e. to tailor them shorter, Line 30), and the vendor acquiesces with two religious oaths (Line 31).

Although Mustafa might have been partly successful on his own, by arguing that the price was simply too high or that the garment was itself faulty, Simo provides a confident and practiced voice as a co-bargainer. His command of locally practiced codes for bargaining and competence in framing these specific forms of argumentation enables Mustafa, through his proxy, to participate in bargaining 'like a local'. After the vendor makes his '*placed*-ness' relevant early in the bargaining sequence, Simo diffuses that line of discussion by entering as Mustafa's advocate who is very much 'in-*place*'. In all likelihood, Simo does not have any so-called 'local' information about how much this particular item should cost: it is not an everyday purchase, particularly not as a garment decorated to be 'Saharan-style', frequently sold as a tourist souvenir, and located in a shop that sold many other 'touristic' Moroccan handicrafts. Being alongside Mustafa, however, enables Mustafa to approach a 'right' price on this item by becoming enmeshed with Simo as validating and complementing his 'diasporic-Moroccanness' by 'being-in-*place*'.

Absences

The relevance of embodimentality in the marketplace and other everyday interactions with strangers also appears in an inverse framing to this one: when DV communicative competences do not match the visual categorizations to which their embodimentality makes them relevant. The above case describes how a proxy enables DVs to more comfortably become-diasporically-Moroccan by associating themselves with 'local' bodies; the cases below are instances where DVs allow their own bodies to make '*derija*-speaker' a conversationally relevant category, when they cannot maintain that category through speech. That is, some DVs with extremely low linguistic competences in *derija* are faced with the challenge of being speaker-hearers. Instead of 'revealing' themselves as poor speakers, they use silences and nonverbal communicative embodiments to continue the interlocutor's categorial assumption. These are examples of using silence to pass (Wagner, 2015c), which in my data were most often connected to difficulties in speaking *derija* for DVs of Amazigh origin travelling around Morocco as diasporic-Moroccans-on-tour.

When not in their familial home towns, where their Moroccan languages are more widely spoken, Amazigh-origin DVs must negotiate an even wider distance between their actual and expected linguistic abilities to maintain categorial 'Moroccanness' than an Arabic-origin DV. As discussed in Chapter 1 about backgrounds, these DVs often do not adhere to the imagined model of resident or even of diasporic Moroccans, as competent speakers of the most common code, *derija*. While migrant bilingualism often depends on factors of access to exposure through one's household and community, Arabic-origin DVs will inevitably have more consistent exposure to *derija* as a language spoken in the home than Amazigh-origin DVs. Their skills depend on different possibilities for practice ranging from parental teaching, to watching Moroccan satellite television, to contact with relatives across several generations who may or may not speak both languages, to the predominance of

Amazigh or Arabic languages in their Moroccan hometown, to finally their peer group in Europe which also may or may not include *derija* speakers. In other words, the *derija* skills for those growing up in Amazigh migrant households are very diverse and unpredictable.

Given the premium put on being able to speak *derija* as an essential element of passing in other contexts outlined above, not speaking *derija* well, or not at all, is a significant hurdle for those who try to inhabit 'being-Moroccan' outside Amazigh-dialect dominant areas. Trying to communicate without a common code becomes part of the process of trying to pass through embodimentality. Even though they are clearly at a disadvantage, these DVs still find themselves in situations where they want to 'be-Moroccan-enough', and must use other embodied communication to reinforce their linguistic dearth.

Mounir, a DV in his mid-thirties whom I met while he and several friends were on a driving trip around Morocco, was one such example. He told me his strategy for speaking *derija* with strangers.

Interview Extract 5.3 Faking derija

Mounir, Fes, 28 July 2008, 40 sec

1   **LW:** tu parles l'arabe pas du tout* ou eh:
         you speak arabic not at all or eh:

2   **M:** non eh (.) le berbère je le parle, mais l'arabe je parle pas.
         non eh (.) I speak berber, but I don't speak Arabic

3   **LW:** ah ouais.
         oh yeah

4   **M:** <ça y>
         <that's it>

5   **LW:** tu trouves- (.4) est-ce- t'as- jamais eu des problème:s, sur ça, de:
         you find- (.4) is it- you have- ever had problem:s, on that, of:

6   **M:** bah des problèmes non, mais quand on me parle je comprends pas
         uh problems no, but when people talk to me I don't understand

7   **LW:** ouais. (.) henhenhenhenh
         yeah (.) henhenhenhenh

8   **M:** s-hheh

9   **LW:** normalement que oui! Ehenhenh
         usually yeah! Ehenhenh

10 **M:** et je fait quand mê- les gens, ils croient que je comprenne/
         and anyway I make- people, they believe that I understand/

11 **LW:**   ouais
             yeah
12 **M:**   et je leur dit ouais/ ouais/ ouais. ouais ouais. bah je
             comprends deux trois mots, mais je comprends pas ce que
             veut dire eh ce que veut dire les phrases
             and I tell them yeah/ yeah/ yeah. yeah yeah. uh I understand a
             few words, but I don't understand what sentences eh what
             sentences mean

Mounir expressed his solution to this problem quite straightforwardly. By pretending to understand, he can continue to be recognized as 'being-Moroccan' to whatever extent a given interaction allows – to pass at least as 'diasporically-Moroccan' by not admitting his lack of linguistic skills. Although he claimed to use this strategy, he did not do so while I was with him – possibly because most of his face-to-face interactions that day were with other French speakers. In another example from my fieldnotes, on a visit to a salon with Sanae, a French-speaking Belgian of Rifi origin, this kind of embodied action was happening among different DVs, with different linguistic competences.

This sequence of observed interactions demonstrates aspects of both modes of embodimentality under discussion here: while Sanae was using her limited communicative competences in *derija* mixed with silences to try to maintain her linguistic participation, other DV women in the salon were using a variety of bodies and competences as they were being coiffed for a wedding.

Fieldnote 5.2 Sanae at the salon (Marrakech, 7 August 2008)

straight to beauty salon (de Paris) and brushing/epilation. There's a bit of a wait, and Sanae goes out to look for water while I watch the NL bride.

she looks like a chinese doll, which is what threw me in the 1st place, with lots of eye makeup, scarlet red lips and rhinestones glued around her eye. She seems unhappy, which I guess is normal for a bride, and has 2 friends (cousins?) with her helping and also waiting to be done. One speaks arabic, but maybe stumbles over words for 'curls' and 'volume'. I wasn't sure they were Dutch, hearing only hints like mooi and ook, but then i heard a few full sentences and it was done.

one in short djellaba (also unexpected) and one other with a beautiful face at the ready. Mother in an aqua blue djellaba with sparkly gold bead trim, speaking in arabic/nl to the daughter-bride, who still looks unhappy (some dispute with stylist?)

shortly after they call S for shampoo, I am gone for my epilation. when i come back, bride's hair is still in the works but the pretty friend is finished with lots of big soft curls, and my epilateuse starts working on the other's nails. she got her bangs either cut or blown out...

Pretty friend asked djellaba friend to approach when it was her turn to be brushed – to translate her desires to stylist.

Sanae also has moments of not-understanding: I think she does a lot of pretending to understand arabic – has asked me about 'baqae' and it's varying significances a couple of times.

the stylist remarks something like keyn Sod (it's hot), and [Sanae] gets that look of non-understanding until it's repeated in French.

when I come down, Sanae's hair looks almost as complicated as the bridefriend's – lots of pins and curls. She tells me later the stylist insisted on doing curly, straight is no good. she characterizes this as a moroccan sensibility, telling me alternately that she looks like a poodle or Suellen from Dynasty.

The three women, as I interpreted in my fieldnotes, were using multiple embodimentalities and practices, including translation, gesture and silence, to communicate what they were having difficulty saying verbally in *derija*. The bridal party demonstrated the practice of using proxies in communication to achieve desired goals: instead of remaining silent, the bride and others in her party drew on allies who could translate their desires, as well as the embodied conversational space of gesture to expand their limited verbal skills. Importantly, the bride and the stylist did not have the resource (as evidenced by their observed practices) of an alternate common language – i.e. French. They were creating this becoming-diasporically-Moroccan context through which the bride was decorated for her 'Moroccan' wedding in this 'Moroccan' location with the help of proxies and translators that compensated for her diasporic linguistic competences.

Sanae, on the other hand, was using a strategy of silence she used elsewhere to a similar purpose (see Wagner, 2015c). As a member of a Tarifit-speaking family, she had never learned *derija* at home and had that summer taken a course in standard Arabic in order to augment her Moroccan linguistic competences. She had progressed by this time to the point where she could hold short, introductory conversations in *derija*, but was still learning and her vocabulary and comprehension skills had gaps. In this situation, Sanae was unable to recognize a relatively simple sentence – keyn ṣahd, literally 'there is heat', a phrase used to describe intensely hot weather – and her silence in a turn-relevant place prompted the stylist to repeat herself in French. This reply demonstrates how she failed to pick up the conversational opening (to complete the adjacency pair on the weather) of a fairly basic utterance, which impacted on whatever attempt she may have been making to be seen as a *'derija*-speaker' in that interaction.

In the time I spent with Sanae in Marrakech, she was trying to hone her *derija* skills in various interactions, like this one with the hairstylist. Through the way she negotiated the moment mentioned above, in which the stylist talks about the weather and Sanae remains mute, she avoided being the conversant to choose another language (usually French) as the code of communication. Indeed, later in that conversation (from what I witnessed) the stylist continued to use some *derija* phrases, although Sanae most often answered in French. Choosing silence instead of her best alternative – answering in French – becomes a way for her to maintain the potential that she is a native speaker, by not forcing a change of code and therefore revealing that she cannot speak *derija* very well.

Her example points to how embodimentality is immediately relevant for DVs in these everyday interactions: she cannot *not* attempt to speak *derija*, although she knows that her ability to maintain that conversation is limited. Like Mounir, she can use her embodimentality to become 'diasporically-Moroccan' by approximating *derija* competencies, at least temporarily. Or, as the bride and her friends did, she can harness the skills of others around her to be 'diasporically-Moroccan' through association with other variations on 'Moroccan' bodies.

These examples of proxy bodies both in association and in absence of embodimentality demonstrate how DVs make use of their immediate surroundings – of their allies, both diasporic and locally resident – to become categorically 'Moroccan'. In this sense, the bodies I described as 'proxies' are not necessarily acting in replacement of DVs. Rather, they become part of a collective embodimentality that contributes to that particular encounter. While some DVs may think of these associations as situationally strategic instances, like the way Rabia described her bargaining strategy above, each repetition makes this associative embodimentality more ordinary, and more a part of how becoming diasporically-Moroccan in Morocco involves residents in and out of Morocco.

Lamia: Not Trying to Pass

The proliferation of these strategies for embodimentality is made most evident by the exception to these practices. Although many DVs observed and recorded for this research used multiple resources, like style of clothing or communicative practice, to try to pass despite being aware of the futility of their efforts, for only one participant – Lamia A, whose interview extract opened this chapter – did passing seem to be unimportant. Unlike her peers, she was not questioning her 'Moroccanness' as she visited both her family in her ancestral hometown and frequently returned to Marrakech with her French-origin husband and their daughter. Rather, in seeming to assume that her 'Moroccanness' was not in question – even though at times it was made explicitly relevant in her interactions with residents – Lamia becomes a counterexample that helps illuminate the pattern. She is a DV who simply becomes ordinarily diasporically-Moroccan without making ideological or explicit efforts to pass.

This is not to say that she is immediately recognized everywhere as Moroccan. In fact, several of her stories and encounters demonstrate how she was often initially misrecognized and categorically labeled as 'not-Moroccan' until she demonstrated some 'Moroccan' form of embodimentality at a later point in the interaction, or even in later interactions with repeat interlocutors. Rather, while she was having similar encounters with locally resident Moroccans (in service work or on the market) to other DVs, she was not regularly doing the same kind of interactional, conversational and embodied work as others did, as described previously, to manipulate her categorial stance.

Lamia's relatively unique approach to these encounters may relate to her biography as a DV with difficult family relationships but a strong connection to territorial Morocco. First, her marriage to a *'français de souche'* man – French at the root, or not of migrant origin – caused a deep rift with her parents and some of her siblings. Lamia and Michel have been married a number of years, and have one daughter who was six at the time of the fieldwork. They only had limited contact with some of her French-resident family (despite living around the same city in France), but more frequent contact with certain siblings (like Yasmine) and were welcomed by family resident in Morocco. Other participants recounted stories about mixed-origin Moroccan and European couples that usually resulted in similar distancing from parents, whose rejection might be related to perceived religious (non-Muslim), nationalist (Algerian, Tunisian, French, etc.) or ethnic distinctions (Arab or Amazigh).

These other mixed-marriage stories were often linked to potential ways in which such a marriage might reduce familial connections, such as a reduced likelihood of visiting Morocco (Wagner, 2011). Visiting 'home' in Morocco was portrayed as an arduous task for the non-linguistically competent spouse, who might feel isolated among resident Moroccan family, in addition to the fact that the non-Moroccan origin spouse's immediate relatives might live closer to their normal residence than the Moroccan family – i.e. it is easier to visit extended family in the same country than to travel far away and feel more isolated. Yet Lamia and her husband Michel visited Morocco as much or more often than any of her siblings, nearly all of whom were married to individuals of Moroccan or North African origin.

I first met Lamia with Michel and their young daughter at a hotel near Lamia's hometown in the south of Morocco, where we all were staying over a week in the summer of 2007. I was intrigued by this family because I saw them continuously over a few days, in contrast to the brief normal occupancy at this hotel, which served more as a gateway for desert excursions than as a resort. I approached Lamia for an interview, then subsequently joined the family as they visited with her extended family in town during the days. I realized later that it was significant that their trip was timed separately from her migrant parents' occupancy of their (empty) house in town: she found her extended, resident Moroccan family accepting of her marriage whereas her father was not.

Even though their days were spent visiting family homes, they chose not to stay with family. Lamia later explained to me that the choice was mostly about comfort: the hotel where they stayed, which was at the expensive end of the available hotels with a large pool and air conditioning, was 'comfortable'. Her daughter enjoyed swimming in the pool every day, and having a separate resting place enabled an escape from family when they wanted it. In that sense, although the effort to visit this town was clearly motivated by visiting family, it also required measures of privacy and autonomy that were not possible for her in a Moroccan house: she was becoming diasporically-Moroccan, by exercising both attachment and distance.

Their frequency of return was particularly noticeable in relation to other family members. Lamia stated in her interview that she saw these visits as important in order for her daughter to know her (Lamia's) home and origins. She acknowledged that she visited more often than her siblings, dependent on means and opportunity; Lamia and Michel both have professional jobs and only one child together, which permitted them to take more international vacations than the majority of her married siblings in France whose households varied between one and two incomes, with between one and four children. Most of all, Lamia's husband Michel had a uniquely positive attitude towards her family and her origins. He expressed a shared interest in Moroccan culture and pleasure in visiting, both at the family home and elsewhere. In fact, after the visit to her hometown (when I met them), their four subsequent visits to Morocco over the next two years were to Marrakech, without any travel to her hometown.

I met up with them on more than one of these subsequent visits to Marrakech. They often time their visits to coincide with Lamia's sister Yasmine, who travels to Marrakech as frequently as they do. There, I discovered that the couple visit the same hotel so often that they have acquired a 'regular' status. Yet that reputation was not dependent on Lamia being recognized as Moroccan.

Fieldnote 5.3 At the hotel (Marrakech, 2 June 2008)

first day I find Lamia and Michel,

at the pool in the [package holiday] hotel, sunbathing and eating at the hotel café with [daughter]. they leave for 2~ hrs to the medina with us, go to the leather store that she and Yasmine visit all the time and buy a bag. then we all have a juice/soda on the terrasse at Café des epices, and they leave for the hotel animation shortly thereafter.

i record Lamia going thru the medina … not much interaction but potentially something interesting between her and vendors. At the leather shop, it occurs to me that Yasmine may 'choose' to speak arabic more than Lamia – she seems to respond to more people that way than Lamia does.

Lamia tells me a story by the hotel pool, wherein one of the people at the hotel who she had come to know, after they had been there at least 5 times, told a joke in arabic and she laughed. He said, you speak arabic, and she said of course i'm moroccan, and he was surprised, as he had thought she was brazilian.

In the souq again in the afternoon we hear someone calling out brasilienne? to them (¿) whereas others recognize and address them in french or arabic.

Seeing the two sisters together provided an interesting contrast in terms of how 'being-Moroccan' can be negotiated. Yasmine knew she was categorially recognized from the way she was dressed (Interaction, 15 March 2008) but still used some of the strategies discussed here to pass, particularly in her communicative practices, as demonstrated in her bargaining interaction analyzed in Chapter 4 (Interaction Extract 4.6). She once observed that her (older) sister would speak *derija* if necessary as she did in their hometown, but not if she did not have to, like in Marrakech where most interactants can speak French. Yet, as I observe in the fieldnote, Yasmine seems to make more frequent efforts to speak *derija*, making her 'Moroccanness' strategically explicit. Lamia may not make as much effort when with her sister, who is reported as the more comfortable in speaking *derija*, or this day may reflect her normal habits. By her lack of attempt to pass audibly, through language use that she could access when situationally necessary, Lamia becomes significantly more 'non-local-Moroccan' than her sister on the street in Marrakech. In short, Lamia's negotiation of 'being-Moroccan', on that day and others, seemed to not be an active part of her visit.

Yet she does not abandon all claim to 'Moroccanness'. In the concluding part of the fieldnote, Lamia recounted her surprise that the hotel staff did not recognize her as 'Moroccan'. In her story, the joke-teller, who was familiar with her from a number of visits and days spent by the pool, was not aware that she spoke and understood *derija*, implying that she had never chosen to speak it with him and to assert her 'Moroccanness'. By not speaking, and not even attempting to pass, she had been categorized as 'Brazilian' (by them and by others outside the hotel), incorporating something about her embodimentality with an apparent lack of 'Moroccanness'.

Yet, Lamia's 'Moroccanness' can still be called upon in strategic moments. She and her husband were in search of *tadelakt* pottery, colorfully plastered using a method created in the region of Marrakech. Since they were looking for something specific, they were asking friends and other contacts for references to trusted vendors. When visiting the hotel where I was staying, they had the following interaction with the manager.

Fieldnote 5.4 You have a Moroccan (5 June 2008)

meet the 3 and go to the hotel to drop things. everyone takes a tour, and the manager comments when we are asking about tadelakt:

Michel:	Tu as qqn pr tadelakt? [you have someone for tadelakt?]
Manager:	(gesture, flat hand palm up, moving away) au souq … [in the souq]
Yasmine:	mais pour le prix [but for the price]
Manager:	tu as une marocaine avec toi…. deja… (gesture indicating Lamia) [you have a Moroccan(f) with you… already]

This was the first time that Lamia and Michel met this hotel manager, and she had been introduced by Yasmine as her sister, also 'Moroccan'. My notes reflect what I considered a striking associative move he made between Lamia's presumed 'Moroccanness' and her ability to find a 'good price' in the market. When Michel's request for 'someone' (i.e. a recommended vendor) is followed by Yasmine's specification on 'price' – seeking a vendor who would give them a 'right' price – the hotel manager invokes Lamia's presumed 'Moroccanness' as a reason why Michel does not need his help. Even though she does not work to establish her 'Moroccanness', he implies that it will operate automatically.

In the subsequent negotiation for tadelakt, Lamia took no active role in 'being-Moroccan' in order to achieve a lower price. In fact, when her

'Moroccanness' was made explicit, it became incidental and unessential to the negotiation.

Fieldnote 5.5 But born in France (Marrakech, 6 June 2008)

Buying tadelakt (with Lamia and Michel and daughter) (which L calls 'tadelak'[2] at least once)

I meet them around 5:30 at the shop which caught L's eye last time they were here for a particular color of turquoise for their house. They are looking for a lamp, i think.

...

A very long process of getting out merchandise: looking thru everything on display in the right color (1 pied de lampe each of small round, small square and medium square); also plates and other decoration. Asking repeatedly for the vendor to see if he has a 2nd one of X style/size, if he has that kind of plate without the metal corners (M doesn't like); asking prices 1 by 1 and then asking me what I think as soon as the vendor leaves to look for a different object.

...

L is not speaking much with the vendor – M is doing more go-between/ negotiation, asking prices and models. They discuss some between themselves as well, daughter is getting really bored.

after models are brought down from above, when they are ready to start nego, L says something small in arabic, replied with nti maghrebiya? iyeh. mineen? min [hometown], etc. [you are moroccan(f)? yes. from where? from [hometown], etc.]

** mais nee en france? [but born in france?]

oui

that is the extent of the derija conversation: nearly all negotiation in French, with maybe light CS in derija, but not much from L's side.

At a conversation pause, she says to me something like, he doesn't even take into account that i'm arabic

- I hear this in a linguistic sense, i.e. speak to me in arabic; not necessarily in a price sense, i.e. lower the price for a fellow countryman

To me, the french-ness of the conversation makes sense: M is generally positioned closer to V, he's the one who is doing the price-asking and most of the conversation. L is tending to hang back and watch daughter.

V asks 1300 for 2 plates, 2 medium lamps and candle holder/photoflor¿, L says 900 is her last price. a period of nonmovement on price, V to 1200, L sticks at 900. V pushes for movement, I say 950, and L laughs repeating the 950 to M. V says il faut faire un effort, on tous fait un effort [it's necessary to make an effort, we all make an effort] (implicating me in this too – all four of us faisons un effort [(we) make an effort]) V down to 1150, then to 1050, then 1000 with the deuil¿/light sockets included (M wants to look at them)

All of this, as I remember, was in French. No particular arabic phrases/passages come to mind, from V or from L, but I think V was using some CS.

Remembering L repeating price neuf cent neuf cent c'est ca que j'ai dit [nine hundred nine hundred, that's what I said]. It's M who finally agrees/ finalizes the price.

Although it was not recorded, this interaction clearly transpired very differently from the previous DV attempts at negotiation. First of all, the *derija*-speaking spouse did not take the role of primary negotiator. Lamia did not conversationally choose *derija* as the code for interaction, as all other DVs who could, did. The vendor was apparently unaware of her 'being-Moroccan' until well into their interaction, after exhaustively choosing the items they wanted, at the point when they were ready to begin negotiation. Following the establishment of Lamia as 'being-Moroccan' and her specific region, the vendor filled in the distance between her categorial 'Moroccanness' and Lamia's visible and audible embodimentality: 'but born in France?' If this were not the case, her mode of interaction – letting her French-speaking husband do all the talking instead of being the local language speaker and primary interlocutor – would not make sense.

Lamia's 'Moroccanness' did come in to play when the negotiations became more active. Lamia commented to me that her 'Arabness' was not being acknowledged, despite the fact that the vendor explicitly acknowledged it, by questioning her birthplace, and implicitly acknowledged it, with 'light CS [codeswitching] in *derija*' for the rest of the negotiation. Her claim to 'Arabness' was not supported through her actions in that she was not using her resources of embodimentality to make it relevant. While Hicham or her sister Yasmine made concerted efforts to speak *derija* and to be categorially 'Moroccan' through their communicative practices, Lamia's efforts were minor. Despite what the manager of my hotel had suggested, her 'being-Moroccan' was not in and of itself a help to negotiation, inasmuch as she did not attempt to pass as Moroccan. Instead, her 'Moroccanness' becomes a 'diasporic-Moroccanness': simply a statement of fact, that she is Moroccan but born in France. Instead of pushing through her embodimentality for this 'diasporic' qualifier to be minimized, she negotiated the prices as 'diasporically', using French and conferring with her *français de souche* husband to find the best price.

As she claimed in her statement from the beginning of this chapter, Lamia has come to experience Morocco on different terms between her childhood and her marriage. Where she once was challenged about 'being-Moroccan', she recounted that this tension had diminished since she had been visiting with her French husband. Instead of resolving the problem of 'not-being-Moroccan enough' by trying to present herself as 'Moroccan', she passively understands 'Moroccanness' as part of her embodiment – part of what should be read on her body by others, whether or not she puts effort into it.

This dynamic implicitly intersects with her familial relationships. Her resident family has accepted her marriage, and welcome her husband and daughter. Unlike others in the same position – with a non-Moroccan spouse – she continues to maintain a presence in Morocco. In some ways, embodying her version of 'Moroccanness' has allowed her to be physically closer to Morocco than she might otherwise have been – to be more firmly 'diasporic' in her 'Moroccanness', in that she enacts the return repeatedly and frequently. In her everyday interactions with others in Morocco, she does not seem to struggle with embodimentality and trying to pass – neither visibly nor audibly. Her 'diasporic-Moroccanness' exists and is part of her life choices whether she actively pursues it in interaction or not, and whether others recognize and respond to it or not.

Conclusion

The empirical examples discussed in this chapter all demonstrate different intentional and unintentional strategies to mitigate the negative categorial effects of 'not-being-Moroccan-enough' into becoming-diasporically-Moroccan. These DVs use a gamut of embodied and communicative resources to orient themselves towards a kind of 'Moroccanness', but not, as in previous chapters, with as much of a measurable outcome to their being categorially recognized as 'being-Moroccan'. Instead, their 'Moroccanness' is not subject to argument; it simply emerges as part of their diasporic embodimentalities, with specific interlocutors or with multiple publics on the street during their summer holidays in Morocco.

The question of 'being-Moroccan-enough' is then a problem that only becomes relevant in certain circumstances, in specific moments of challenge. That is, if we take this categorial 'diasporic-Moroccanness' as an emergent ideal-type, the struggle to transform it into 'being-Moroccan' becomes the problematic recategorization. As Lamia describes in the first extract of this chapter – the same sentiment that is described almost universally in research on post-migrant generations visiting a homeland (cf. King & Christou, 2009; Potter & Phillips, 2006a, 2006b; Stephenson, 2002) – her sense during childhood was repeatedly being 'not-enough', neither in France nor in Morocco. However, her sense now is one where she simply is. 'Not-being-Moroccan-enough', as she shows in her attitudes and actions in comparison to others like her sister, is not an interactional concern of hers any more – it is no longer made relevant.

The other examples described here also show how that sense of 'not-being-Moroccan-enough' can dissipate: with a proxy body/advocate who acts 'Moroccan' on one's behalf; by being silent so that one's embodied 'Moroccanness' becomes enough, without linguistic support; by dressing in 'Moroccan' fashion in a 'diasporic' manner, among other DVs who are engaged in similar daily activities. It is, in fact, an interactional distinction that emerges between 'not-being-Moroccan-enough' and 'being-diasporic', wherein assemblages of context, actors and agents make these categories relevant in positive and negative valences.

Interactionally, then, these are not just communicative problems – a problem of not speaking *derija* with the right accent or register. Becoming-diasporically-Moroccan is embodimentality, in which certain embodied materialities and expressivities, ranging from skin to clothing to voice to activity choices, are part of an expanding and contracting assemblage that becomes much more noticeable and pervasive throughout Morocco during the summer holidays. Most importantly, these examples enable us to recognize how this categorial 'diasporic-Moroccanness' can be practiced as the unmarked, accepted category – how all the DVs here can, in many moments of their daily lives in Europe or in Morocco, simply become diasporically Moroccan along with whatever else they might become.

Notes

(1) The research in this area is overwhelmingly vast. Whalen and Lindblom (2006) provide a short introduction on biological aspects of speech production and perception.

(2) The word origin of tadelakt is Amazigh (tədəlaġt), and follows Amazigh language rules marking feminine with /t/ at word initial and word end positions. 'Tadelak' is morphologically incorrect.

Conclusion: Assembling Diasporicness

From the examples in these chapters, we can start to imagine the breadth of encounters with the locally resident public that make up the experience of 'going home' for post-migrant generation diasporic visitors. The encounters described here, by my observations and by participants' reports, demonstrate how the negotiation of belonging is a constant, and sometimes Sisyphean, process. Yet, the notion of belonging is made relevant only because these individuals are perceived, in at least some key respects, to be simultaneously 'Moroccan' and 'not-Moroccan'. This perception leads into categorial practices that attempt to resolve that confusion. These everyday categorizations render ordinary encounters rife with significance as to what it means to become 'Moroccan' or, more importantly, what it means to be unable to become 'Moroccan' when it is expected and desired.

In many instances, the processes that impugn these participants' 'Moroccanness' in Morocco mirror the processes of integration and assimilation they may face in Europe as 'immigrants' (Bos & Fristchy, 2006; Guénif Souilamas, 2000; Manço, 1999; Ouali, 2004; Tribalat, 1995). Both of these contexts make relevant an instinct to categorize between in-group and out-group through ethno-national boundary making (Brubaker et al., 2004; Wimmer, 2009), but each has different social consequences. In their European homes, 'becoming-Moroccan' has been associated with recognizable minority-group struggles like antisocial behavior, religious conservativism, and gender divisions in education and successful insertion (Buitelaar, 2007; Lesthaeghe, 2000; Maréchal et al., 2003). In Morocco, this group boundary has not had such significant attention in the same terms, but it is implicitly a key part of state initiatives to engage and maintain relationships with the diaspora – both as part of the citizenry and part of the economic future of Morocco (Brand, 2006; Fondation Hassan II & IOM, 2003). For those purposes, it is very important that the diaspora continues to feel welcomed and to feel as though they belong in Morocco. So, these everyday encounters, where categorial belonging happens or does not happen, cumulatively contribute to how this diasporic population will possibly conceive of their future interactions with Morocco as a territorial homeland: as a struggle to belong, or a feeling of being incorporated and accepted, diasporically.

What the examples of this book indicate, then, is how these categories of belonging are at work, creating different overlaps, intersections and conflicts that are manifest on how these bodies become-Moroccan, become-not-Moroccan-enough, and perhaps recognizably become-diasporically-Moroccan. While the categorial distinction they face in Europe is relevant to *descent* (not coming from the right lineage to belong), in Morocco it is relevant to *place* (not being embedded in the right environment), where *place*-based knowledges, practices and forms of embodiment are immediately recognizable and categorizable in interaction. In those moments, the materiality of these bodies as perceivable and communicating *hexis* is implicitly and immediately cogent to the flow of interaction and to the ways in which interactants categorize and respond to one another – whether or not they are acknowledged to be 'Moroccan', and however that acknowledgment happens. While their genetically and ancestrally material bodies – their *descent* – makes this category relevant, something about *how* they are embodied troubles it.

I contend that this trouble is about the imagined combination of *descent* and *place* as mapping onto each other without any division. For individuals in such diasporically oriented communities, *place* and *descent* are inevitably askew to normalized assumptions. For the participants here, the circumstances of their parents' mobilities led to their residence outside Morocco, just as the circumstances of others of their generation led to residence within Morocco. Each circumstance, through many interacting parts, leaves traces on their bodies and in their practices that are made relevant when coming face to face, in encounters where the rupture of migration, sending *descent* and *place* into different vector trajectories, is a pivot for categorial belonging.

In order to explore the trajectories and interactions of *descent* and *place* as they occur with these individual embodied participants, I introduced embodimentality as a reframing of how to think of their bodies as emergent. To reiterate, this notion approximates Grosz's idea of 'embodied subjectivity' or 'psychical corporeality', as a 'materialism beyond physicalism' (Grosz, 1994: 22), provoking an imagination of bodies as material assemblages and in assemblage in collectivities. It highlights how bodies are intensive and nonmetric, incorporating parts and characteristics through infusion – in other words, made up of indivisible parts, yet able to absorb new characteristics as older ones are sedimented and dispelled, but not wholly subtracted. This notion draws on Merleau-Ponty (2002) in making the body central to the production of knowledge, but also Bourdieu (1984) in conceiving of the body as being collectively socialized into certain dispositions. Through it, I recognize that bodies are not biologically fixed, following Butler (1993). However, they have physically manifested, material properties that become cogent in interaction, following Goffman (1966). The utility of this term should be to focus on how we are always becoming, in interaction with other entities – human, non-human and discursive – through practices that are not inherently divisible between 'communicative', 'social', 'economic' or 'pragmatic', but are all collectively part of the enactment and practicing of bodies.

Embodimentality is useful in order to explore how *descent* and *place* happen on and through bodies, occupying the same space simultaneously and indivisibly but becoming relevant in starkly different ways. It is also a methodological effort to incorporate the effects of the visual recognition and observations we make about one another's bodies – and about how bodies are collectively moving and acting together – becoming part of the flow of an encounter. In interaction, visual perception is a major source of information for participants to simultaneously interpret multiple aspects of embodimentality, in ways that often exceed our social scientific ability to record them. The examples of categorial interpretations based on visual perception of embodimentality range from assumptions about linguistic skills (being able or not able to speak *derija*), to developing embodied modes of 'being-Moroccan' (wearing specific clothing), or creating a body through association with, or the absence of, others (being with 'Moroccans' in the market, not 'tourists').

Metaphors of other senses, like smell, become part of its discussion and interpretation by DVs and resident Moroccans not because of their literal sense, but because visual perception leads to instinctive categorization – to a process of seeing and interpreting that is so automatic that it is metaphorically sensory. These instinctive categorizations are part of almost every interaction reported here, whether DVs are recognized (or misrecognized) from afar as being 'Turkish' or 'Brazilian', or whether they are recognized as 'Moroccan-from-outside' in marketplace negotiations. Thinking through these categorizations as 'embodimentality' allows us to imagine how the different interlocking parts of bodies – from appearance to dress to speech to companions – are all engaged in the moment-to-moment reorientation from categorically other to 'becoming-diasporically-Moroccan'.

Even though DVs' goal seems often to 'be-locally-Moroccan', I argue that what is more frequently accomplished, whatever the intention, is becoming-diasporically-Moroccan. The DV participants in this ethnography negotiate ongoing processes of categorization to the best of their individual capacities while practicing, for the most part, linguistic and embodied 'Moroccanness'. These practices go hand in hand with their desires to participate in certain categorial configurations – to belong. The different examples show how similar encounters recur, with variations every time, through which DVs are engaging their materially and expressively embodied selves to become-Moroccan, while they are continuously being categorized as 'diasporically-Moroccan' in spite of themselves. In some cases, becoming-diasporically-Moroccan was unproblematic, such as when DVs were taking aspects of 'Moroccanness' – like specific clothing – to wear as part of their summertime embodimentality of being in Morocco. In other cases, becoming-diasporically-Moroccan was the outcome of strategies to be recognized as 'Moroccan', like moments when DVs claimed provenance from Morocco, even when being questioned on that very marker of *place*. In all cases, negotiating belonging was a process of pushing the limits of embodimentality along axes of *place* and *descent*, to find a balance between the material and expressive capacities of their bodies and the material and expressive demands of categorial 'Moroccanness', an attractor or ideal-type exerting force on them as their ideological model of how to 'be-Moroccan'.

But further than that, embodimentality shows how the human agents involved are not single entities unto themselves, although they may move through the world as a relatively coherent unit. Bodies, as well as embodied capacities and practices, are agentive. Bodies are multiplicities, with parts that are both relatively durable and relatively malleable, all of which combine in different configurations in each moment of expressive or material interaction. They are inextricable from the materialities and expressivities of becoming-diasporically-Moroccan that are inescapable for these individuals as sentient bodies. As much as their practices are made relevant as problematic in certain situations by uncontrollably betraying the fact that they did not grow up in-*place* in Morocco, their embodied connection through *descent* – simply through the genetics of birth – makes them inevitably implicated in omnirelevant processes of belonging.

Assembling Categorization

The way I present this discussion also gives categories, and modes of belonging to them, a certain amount of agency or force: they are attractors or ideal-types working on people, evoking certain behaviors and being made relevant as specific practices. Following methods in MCA and ethnomethodology (Hester & Eglin, 1997; Stokoe, 2012), I used micro-analysis of interactions – to the extent that I was able to record and document these interactions for sequential analysis – to demonstrate how participants responded moment by moment in relation to categories that were made interactionally relevant by their practices. Over repeated iterations of similar activities, patterns emerge of a certain range of practices that are accepted by interlocutors, juxtaposed against unacceptable ones, creating the fuzzy and shifting boundary of categorial belonging. Through micro-analyses, we can see how, as people do things with categories, categories are also shaping the scope of what people can do – up to and including how new categories might emerge as a social collective of individuals are continuously pushing at the edges of current ones.

Parallel perspectives are part of many theories of interactional social life, from Sacks (1992) to Butler (1993), to Bourdieu (1984) to Goffman (1966). All these thinkers recognized pressures to conform to expectations of norms, and how those norms are often unspoken but very actively practiced as though the norms themselves have power. They told stories of bodies and practices that fit expectations, and then demonstrated how those expectations are defined by examining practices at the margins – exploring the rule by analyzing exceptions. In this book, I explore similar processes, but reframe the analysis through assemblage theory of bodies and of social life (DeLanda, 2006; Grosz, 1994). This reframes categories as attractors, working in the same realm of actors as the human agents: as they shift and realign, categories are also agents exerting centripetal and centrifugal forces, pulling some actors into them while simultaneously pushing others out. Categories, humans and places implicated in this assemblage are transforming together in ways that, moment to moment, reinvent what 'being-Moroccan' might be. The social collective, in this sense, has a kind of agency as an actor in this assemblage: a whole that is more than the sum of its parts, through which 'Moroccanness' becomes defined in in-group and out-group markers during interaction.

Yet, the potential ways in which 'Moroccanness' can be reshaped through this social collective agency open up the possibility for something like 'diasporic-Moroccanness' to solidify. As different elements in these interactions ebb and flow – like the cycle of Moroccan migrant families moving back and forth between Europe and Morocco, year after year – potential evolutionary trajectories emerge and take hold, or are forgotten. The examples recounted in this volume demonstrate how this social collective of 'Moroccan visitors from Europe' are shaped in this historical moment along a trajectory. But instead of framing this collective activity as a 'being-doing' – adhering to a relatively static category which will probably not be 'true' by the time this book is read – I try here to show how these interactions are 'becomings' which, at each moment, are both enacting established category ideal-types and creating possible trajectories for new categorial attractors. Repeated iterations of contact, if DVs continue to visit Morocco through further generations, continue to create the possibility for an emergent 'diasporic-Moroccanness' to become a norm.

This process is not quick, easy or painless, but these examples show how it is feasible to become 'diasporically-Moroccan' in a coherent way. Even though, as many stated in interviews, they know they will recurrently negotiate their sense of 'Moroccanness' in their interactions in Morocco, the participants in this research are diasporic visitors. That is, they are Europeans of Moroccan origin who continue to visit Morocco as independent adults, of their own volition and at times with their own families. Some will continue to engage in similar bargaining strategies to get the 'right' price, and they will continue to achieve a 'diasporic-Moroccanness' in those interactions. Some will continue to unproblematically become-diasporically-Moroccan as they move around Morocco and come into contact with other co-nationals who recognize them as 'Moroccans from outside' – with more emphasis on the inclusion of 'Moroccan' than exclusion of 'from outside'. The question remains, however, as to if, or how, these categorial formations will become more fixed into the Moroccan and European landscapes of diasporic belonging – how the state of Morocco will draw upon the resources of its valuable national population, or how states in Europe will be able to understand and support (or not) this tenuous categorial belonging to multiple places. A beginning, demonstrated in these examples, is the everyday understanding of the human capacity to be multiple: to belong both to Europe and to Morocco, to be categorially accepted as unproblematically emerging from both places in both places, and to be able to move freely between the two, maintaining the capacity for ordinary, everyday interactions that iteratively make this categorial diasporicness possible.

Bibliography

Agoumy, T. (2007) The transformative impact of transfer originating from migration on local socio-economic dynamics. In S. Gupta and T. Omoniyi (eds) *The Cultures of Economic Migration: International Perspectives* (pp. 77–85). London: Ashgate.

Ahmed, S. (2002) Racialized bodies. In M. Evans and E. Lee (eds) *Real Bodies* (pp. 46–60). Basingstoke: Palgrave Macmillan.

Ahmed, S. (2007) A phenomenology of whiteness. *Feminist Theory* 8 (2), 149–168. doi:10.1177/1464700107078139.

Alcoff, L.M. (2006) *Visible Identities*. Oxford: Oxford University Press. See http://www.oxfordscholarship.com/oso/public/content/philosophy/9780195137347/toc.html.

Alexander, P. (1992) What's in a price?: Trading practices in peasant (and other) markets. In R. Dilley (ed.) *Contesting Markets: Analyses of Ideology, Discourse and Practice* (pp. 79–96). Edinburgh: Edinburgh University Press.

Ali, N. and Holden, A. (2006) Post-colonial Pakistani mobilities: The embodiment of the 'myth of return' in tourism. *Mobilities* 1 (2), 217–242.

Alscher, S. (2005) Knocking at the doors of 'Fortress Europe': Migration and border control in southern Spain and eastern Poland. Working Paper No. 126. San Diego, CA: Center for Comparative Immigration Studies, University of California at San Diego.

Ameur, M., Bouhjar, A., Boukhris, F., Boukous, A., Boumalk, A., Elmedlaoui, M. and Iazzi, E.M. (2006) *Graphie et Orthographe de l'Amazighe* (Vol. 5). Rabat: L'Institut Royal de la Culture Amazighe.

Ang, I. (2001) *On Not Speaking Chinese*. London and New York: Routledge.

Anthias, F. (1998) Evaluating 'diaspora': Beyond ethnicity? *Sociology* 32 (3), 557–580.

Auer, P. (ed.) (1998) *Code-switching in Conversation: Language, Interaction and Identity*. London and New York: Routledge.

Austin, J.L. (1962) *How to Do Things with Words (The William James Lectures)*. Cambridge, MA: Harvard University Press.

Back, L. and Solomos, J. (eds) (2000) *Theories of Race and Racism: A Reader*. London: Routledge.

Baldwin-Edwards, M. (2005) *Migration in the Middle East and Mediterranean. Study for the Global Commission on International Migration*. Athens: Mediterranean Migration Observatory Panteion University.

Banerjee, M. and Miller, D. (2003) *The Sari*. Oxford: Berg.

Barbour, N. (1965) *Morocco*. London: Thames & Hudson.

Barrett, R. (1999) Indexing polyphonous identity in the speech of African American drag queens. In M. Bucholtz, A.C. Liang and L.A. Sutton (eds) *Reinventing Identities: The Gendered Self in Discourse* (pp. 313–331). New York: Oxford University Press.

Barth, F. (ed.) (1969) *Ethnic Groups and Boundaries: The Social Organization of Culture Difference.* London: Allen & Unwin.

Basu, P. (2004) Route metaphors of 'roots-tourism' in the Scottish Highland diaspora. In S. Coleman and J. Eade (eds) *Reframing Pilgrimage: Cultures in Motion* (pp. 150–174). London: Routledge.

Bauman, R. (2001) The ethnography of genre in a Mexican market: Form, function, variation. In P. Eckert and J.R. Rickford (eds) *Style and Sociolinguistic Variation* (pp. 57–77). Cambridge and New York: Cambridge University Press.

Beckert, J. and Aspers, P. (2011) *The Worth of Goods: Valuation and Pricing in the Economy.* Oxford: Oxford University Press.

Bekkar, R., Boumaza, N. and Pinson, D. (1999) *Familles Maghrébines En France, l'Épreuve de La Ville.* Paris: Presses Universitaires de France.

Bekouchi, M.H. (2003) *La Diaspora Marocaine: Une Chance ou un Handicap.* Casablanca: Editions la Croisée des Chemins.

Belguendouz, A. (1999) *Les Marocains à l'Étranger: Citoyens et Partinaires.* Kenitra: Boukili Impression.

Belguendouz, A. (2002) Moroccan border with Spain: Member or policeman of Europe in North Africa. In M. Pimental Siles (ed.) *Migratory Processes, Economy and People* (pp. 33–74). Mediterráneo Económico No. 1. Almeria: Caja Rural Intermediterránea.

Bell, A. (1999) Styling the other to define the self: A study in New Zealand identity making. *Journal of Sociolinguistics* 3 (4), 523–541.

Bennett, J. (2010) *Vibrant Matter: A Political Ecology of Things.* Durham, NC: Duke University Press.

Bentahila, A. (1983) *Language Attitudes Among Arabic-French Bilinguals in Morocco.* Clevedon: Multilingual Matters.

Berger, J. and Mohr, J. (1989) *A Seventh Man: The Story of a Migrant Worker in Europe.* London: Granta Books, in association with Cambridge: Penguin Books.

Bidet, J. and Wagner, L. (2012) Vacances au bled et appartenances diasporiques des descendants d'immigrés Algériens et Marocains en France. *Tracés* 12 (23). doi:10.4000/traces.5554.

Bistolfi, R. and Zabbal, F. (eds) (1995) *Islams d'Europe: Intégration ou Insertion Communautaire?* La Tour d'Aigues: Editions de l'Aube.

Bloch, M. (1991) Language, anthropology and cognitive science. *Man* 26 (2), 183–198.

Blom, J.-P. and Gumperz, J.J. (1972) Social meaning in linguistic structure: Code-switching in Norway. In J.J. Gumperz and D.H. Hymes (eds) *Directions in Sociolinguistics; the Ethnography of Communication* (pp. 407–434). New York: Holt, Rinehart & Winston.

Blommaert, J. (2007) Sociolinguistics and discourse analysis: Orders of indexicality and polycentricity. *Journal of Multicultural Discourses* 2 (2), 115–130. doi:10.2167/md089.0.

Blommaert, J. (2013a) Complexity, accent, and conviviality: Concluding comments. *Applied Linguistics* 34 (5), 613–622. doi:10.1093/applin/amt028.

Blommaert, J. (2013b) *Ethnography, Superdiversity and Linguistic Landscapes: Chronicles of Complexity.* Bristol: Multilingual Matters.

Blommaert, J. and Rampton, B. (2011) Language and superdiversity. *Diversities* 13 (2), 1–21.

Bodega, I., Cebrian, J.A., Franchini, T., Lora-Tamayo, G., and Martin-Lou, A. (1995) Recent migrations from Morocco to Spain. *International Migration Review* 29 (3), 800–819.

Bos, P. and Fritschy, W. (eds) (2006) *Morocco and the Netherlands: Society, Economy, Culture.* Amsterdam: VU University Press.

Bourdieu, P. (1977) *Outline of a Theory of Practice.* Cambridge and New York: Cambridge University Press.

Bourdieu, P. (1984) *Distinction: A Social Critique of the Judgement of Taste*. Cambridge, MA: Harvard University Press.

Bourdieu, P. (1990) *The Logic of Practice*. Stanford, CA: Stanford University Press.

Bourdieu, P. (1991) *Language and Symbolic Power*. Cambridge, MA: Harvard University Press.

Bourdieu, P. and Wacquant, L.J.D. (1992) *An Invitation to Reflexive Sociology*. Cambridge: Polity.

Brand, L.A. (2002) States and their expatriates: Explaining the development of Tunisian and Moroccan emigration-related institutions. Working Paper No. 52, University of Southern California.

Brand, L.A. (2006) *Citizens Abroad: Emigration and the State in the Middle East and North Africa*. Cambridge: Cambridge University Press.

Brown, J.M. (2006) *Global South Asians: Introducing the Modern Diaspora*. Cambridge University Press.

Brubaker, R. (ed.) (1989) *Immigration and the Politics of Citizenship in Europe and North America*. Washington, DC: German Marshall Fund of the United States, University Press of America.

Brubaker, R. (1992) *Citizenship and Nationhood in France and Germany*. Cambridge, MA: Harvard University Press.

Brubaker, R., Loveman, M. and Stamatov, P. (2004) Ethnicity as cognition. *Theory and Society* 33 (1), 31–64. doi:10.1023/B:RYSO.0000021405.18890.63.

Bryceson, D.F. and Vuorela, U. (eds) (2002) *The Transnational Family: New European Frontiers and Global Networks*. Oxford: Berg.

Bucholtz, M. (1995) From Mulatta to Mestiza: Passing and the linguistic reshaping of ethnic identity. In K. Hall and M. Bucholtz (eds) *Gender Articulated: Language and the Socially Constructed Self* (pp. 351–373). New York and London: Routledge.

Buitelaar, M. (2007) Staying close by moving out. The contextual meanings of personal autonomy in the life stories of women of Moroccan descent in The Netherlands. *Contemporary Islam* 1 (1), 259–276. doi:10.1007/s11562-007-0003-1.

Butler, J. (1993) *Bodies That Matter: On the Discursive Limits of Sex*. New York: Routledge.

Butler, R. (2003) Relationships between tourism and diasporas: Influences and patterns. *Espace-Populations-Societes* (2), 317–326.

Cameron, D. (1995) *Verbal Hygiene*. New York: Routledge.

Castles, S., de Haas, H. and Miller, M.J. (2013) *The Age of Migration: International Population Movements in the Modern World* (5th edn). New York: Guilford Press.

Césari, J. (1994) *Etre Musulman en France: Associations, Militants et Mosquées*. Paris: Éditions Karthala et RÉMAM.

Césari, J. (2003) Être Maghrébin en France. *Les Cahiers de l'Orient* 71.

Césari, J. and McLoughlin, S. (eds) (2005) *European Muslims and the Secular State*. Aldershot: Ashgate.

Césari, J., Moreau, A. and Schleyer-Lindenmann, A. (2001) *Plus Marseillais Que Moi, Tu Meurs!: Migrations, Identités et Territoires à Marseille*. Paris: L'Harmattan.

Chaker, S. (1998) *Berbères Aujourd'hui: Berbères dans le Maghreb Contemporain*. Paris: L'Harmattan.

Charrad, M. (2001) *States and Women's Rights: The Making of Postcolonial Tunisia, Algeria, and Morocco*. Berkeley, CA: University of California Press.

Chen, K.H.Y. (2008) Positioning and repositioning: Linguistic practices and identity negotiation of overseas returning bilinguals in Hong Kong. *Multilingua – Journal of Cross-Cultural and Interlanguage Communication* 27 (1–2), 57–75. doi:10.1515/MULTI.2008.004.

Cisneros, S. (2002) *Caramelo*. New York: Alfred A. Knopf.

Clifford, J. (1997) *Routes: Travel and Translation in the Late Twentieth Century.* Cambridge, MA: Harvard University Press.

Cohen, M.I. and Hahn, L. (1966) *Morocco: Old Land, New Nation.* London: Pall Mall Press.

Cohen, R. (1995) *The Cambridge Survey of World Migration.* Cambridge: Cambridge University Press.

Cohen, R. (1997) *Global Diasporas.* London: UCL Press.

Coles, T. and Timothy, D.J. (eds) (2004) *Tourism, Diasporas and Space.* London and New York: Routledge.

Collins, J. and Slembrouck, S. (2005) Editorial. Multilingualism and diasporic populations: Spatializing practices, institutional processes, and social hierarchies. *Language & Communication* 25, 189–195.

Collins, J. and Slembrouck, S. (2006) Goffman and globalisation: Participation frames and the spatial and temporal scaling of migration-connected multilingualism. *Working Papers in Urban Language & Literacies* 46, 1–24.

Collyer, M. (2004) The development impact of temporary international labour migration on southern Mediterranean sending countries: Contrasting examples of Morocco and Egypt. Working Paper No. T6, Sussex Centre for Migration Research. See http://www.migrationdrc.org.

Conway, D. and Potter, R.B. (eds) (2009) *Return Migration of the Next Generations: 21st-Century Transnational Mobility.* Aldershot: Ashgate.

Conway, D., Potter, R.B. and St. Bernard, G. (2009) Repetitive visiting as a pre-return transnational strategy among youthful Trinidadian returnees. *Mobilities* 4 (2), 249. doi:10.1080/17450100902906707.

Coupland, N. (2007) *Style: Language Variation and Identity.* Cambridge: Cambridge University Press.

Cresswell, T. (2002) Bourdieu's geographies: In memoriam. *Environment and Planning D* 20 (4), 379–382.

Crewe, L. and Gregson, N. (1998) Tales of the unexpected: Exploring car boot sales as marginal spaces of contemporary consumption. *Transaction of the Institute of British Geographers* 23, 39–53.

Crul, M. and Vermeulen, H. (2003) The future of the second generation: The integration of migrant youth in six European countries. *International Migration Review* 37 (4), 965–1371.

Cutler, C.A. (1999) Yorkville crossing: White teens, hip hop and African American English. *Journal of Sociolinguistics* 3 (1), 428–442. doi:10.1111/1467-9481.00089.

Dabène, L. and Billiez, J. (1984) *Recherches sur la Situation Sociolinguistique des Jeunes Issus de l'Immigration.* Vol. I. Grenoble: Université des Langues et Lettres – Grenoble III; Centre de Didactique des Langes.

Dabène, L. and Moore, D. (1995) Bilingual speech of migrant people. In L. Milroy and P. Muysken (eds) *One Speaker, Two Languages* (pp. 17–44). London: Cambridge University Press.

Dalle, I. (2004) *Les Trois Rois la Monarchie Marocaine, de l'Indépendance à nos Jours.* Paris: Fayard.

D'Andrade, R.G. (1995) *The Development of Cognitive Anthropology.* Cambridge: Cambridge University Press.

de Haas, H. (2005a) Morocco's migration transition: Trends, determinants and future scenarios. *Global Migration Perspectives* 28, 1–38.

de Haas, H. (2005b) Migrants change the appearance of Morocco. Working Paper No. 5, Migration and Development Revisited, WOTRO/NOW, Nijmegen.

de Haas, H. (2006) Engaging diasporas: How governments and development agencies can support diaspora involvement in the development of origin countries. Study for Oxfam Novib, International Migration Institute, University of Oxford.

de Haas, H. (2007) Morocco's migration experience: A transitional perspective. *International Migration* 45 (4), 39–70.

de Haas, H. (2009) International migration and regional development in Morocco: A review. *Journal of Ethnic and Migration Studies* 35 (10), 1571–1593. doi:10.1080/13691 830903165808.

de Haas, H. and Plug, R. (2006) Cherishing the goose with the golden eggs: Trends in migrant remittances from Europe to Morocco, 1970–2004. *International Migration Review* 40 (3), 603–634.

de Haas, H. and Vezzoli, S. (2010) Migration and development: Lessons from the Mexico-US and Morocco-EU experiences. Working Paper No. 22, International Migration Institute, Oxford.

DeLanda, M. (2002) *Intensive Science and Virtual Philosophy*. London: Continuum. See http://www.protevi.com/john/Postmodernity/IntensiveScienceOutline.html.

DeLanda, M. (2006) *A New Philosophy of Society: Assemblage Theory and Social Complexity*. London: Continuum.

Deleuze, G. and Guattari, F. (1987) *A Thousand Plateaus* (Trans. B. Massumi). Minneapolis, MN: University of Minnesota Press.

Deprez, C. (1994) *Les Enfants Bilingues: Langues et Familles*. Paris: Didier.

Desforges, L. (2001) Tourism consumption and the imagination of money. *Transactions of the Institute of British Geographers* 26, 353–364.

DiMaggio, P. (1997) Culture and cognition. *Annual Review of Sociology* 23 (1), 263–287. doi:10.1146/annurev.soc.23.1.263.

Doerr, N.M. (ed.) (2009) *The Native Speaker Concept: Ethnographic Investigations of Native Speaker Effects*. Berlin: Walter de Gruyter.

Driessen, H. (1998) The 'new immigration' and the transformation of the European–African frontier. In T.M. Wilson and H. Donnan (eds) *Border Identities: Nation and State at International Frontiers* (pp. 96–116). Cambridge: Cambridge University Press.

Drivaud, M.-H. and Peretz-Juillard, C. (1984) Les usages et leurs représentations sur un marché plurilingue à Paris: Belleville. *Langage et Société* 30, 29–59.

Duranti, A. and Goodwin, C. (eds) (1992) *Rethinking Context: Language as an Interactive Phenomenon*. New York: Cambridge University Press.

Duval, D.T. (2003) When hosts become guests: Return visits and diasporic identities in a Commonwealth Eastern Caribbean community. *Current Issues in Tourism* 6 (4), 267–308.

Duval, D.T. (2004a) Conceptualizing return visits: A transnational perspective. In T. Coles and D.J. Timothy (eds) *Tourism, Diasporas and Space* (pp. 50–61). London and New York: Routledge.

Duval, D.T. (2004b) Linking return visits and return migration among Commonwealth Eastern Caribbean migrants in Toronto. *Global Networks* 4 (1), 51–67.

Dyer, R. (1997) *White*. London: Routledge.

Eckert, P. (2000) *Linguistic Variation as Social Practice: The Linguistic Construction of Identity in Belten High*. Malden, MA: Wiley-Blackwell.

Eckert, P. and Rickford, J.R. (2001) *Style and Sociolinguistic Variation*. Cambridge and New York: Cambridge University Press.

Edwards, D. (1991) Categories are for talking: On the cognitive and discursive bases of categorization. *Theory and Psychology* 1 (4), 515–542. doi:10.1177/0959354391014007.

El Aissati, A. and Bos, P. (1998) Arabic and Berber in the Netherlands and France. In G. Extra and J. Maartens (eds) *Multilingualism in a Multicultural Context. Case Studies on South Africa and Western Europe* (pp. 179–194). Tilburg: Tilburg University Press.

El-Haj, N.A. (2007) The genetic reinscription of race. *Annual Review of Anthropology* 36 (1), 283–300. doi:10.1146/annurev.anthro.34.081804.120522.

Enfield, N.J. (2009) *The Anatomy of Meaning: Speech, Gesture, and Composite Utterances.* Cambridge and New York: Cambridge University Press.

Ennaji, M. (1991) Aspects of multilingualism in the Maghreb. *International Journal of the Sociology of Language* 87, 7–25.

Ennaji, M. (2002) Language contact, Arabization policy, and education in Morocco. In A. Rouchdy (ed.) *Language Contact and Language Conflict in Arabic: Variations on a Sociolinguistic Theme* (pp. 70–88). Curzon Arabic Linguistics. London: Routledge Curzon.

Erickson, F. (2004) *Talk and Social Theory: Ecologies of Speaking and Listening in Everyday Life.* Cambridge: Polity.

Étiemble, A. (2003) Filles de migrants, entre modernité et endogamie. *Hommes et Migrations* 1242, 32–42.

Extra, G. and Gorter, D. (2001) *The Other Languages of Europe: Demographic, Sociolinguistic, and Educational Perspectives.* Clevedon: Multilingual Matters.

Falzon, M.-A. (ed.) (2009) *Multi-sited Ethnography: Theory, Praxis and Locality in Contemporary Social Research.* Farnham: Ashgate.

Farnell, B. (2000) Getting out of the habitus: An alternative model of dynamically embodied social action. *The Journal of the Royal Anthropological Institute* 6 (3), 397–418.

Feng, K. and Page, S.J. (2000) An exploratory study of the tourism migration–immigration nexus: Travel experiences of Chinese residents in New Zealand. *Current Issues in Tourism* 3 (3), 246–281.

Ferguson, C.A. (1971) Diglossia. In A.S. Dil (ed.) *Language Structure and Language Use: Essays by Charles A. Ferguson* (pp. 1–26). Stanford, CA: Stanford University Press.

Fishman, J.A. (1985) *The Rise and Fall of the Ethnic Revival: Perspectives on Language and Ethnicity.* New York: Mouton de Gruyter.

Fitzgerald, R. and William, H. (2015) *Advances in Membership Categorisation Analysis.* London: Sage.

Fitzgerald, R., William, H. and Carly W.B. (2009) Omnirelevance and interactional context. *Australian Journal of Communication* 36 (3), 45.

Flores Farfán, J.A. (2003) 'Al fin que ya los cueros no van a correr': Pragmatics of power in Hñahñu (Otomi) markets. *Language in Society* 32 (5), 629–658. doi:10.1017/S004 7404503325023.

Fondation Hassan II and IOM (eds) (2003) *Marocains de l'Extérieur.* Rabat: International Organization of Migration and Fondation Hassan II pour les Marocains Résidant à l'Etranger.

Franklin, S. (2003) Re-thinking nature-culture: Anthropology and the new genetics. *Anthropological Theory* 3 (1), 65–85. doi:10.1177/1463499603003001752.

French, B.M. (2001) The symbolic capital of social identities: The genre of bargaining in an urban Guatemalan market. *Journal of Linguistic Anthropology* 10 (2), 155–189.

Gal, S. (1987) Codeswitching and consciousness in the European periphery. *American Ethnologist* 14 (4), 637–653.

Gal, S. (1989) Language and political economy. *Annual Review of Anthropology* 18, 345–367.

Gardner-Chloros, P. (1985) Language selection and switching among Strasbourg shoppers. *International Journal of the Sociology of Language* 54, 117–136. doi:10.1515/ijsl.1985.54.117.

Gardner-Chloros, P. (2008) *Code-Switching: An Introduction*. Cambridge: Cambridge University Press.

Garfinkel, H. (1984) *Studies in Ethnomethodology* (2nd edn). Cambridge: Polity Press.

Geertz, C., Geertz, H. and Rosen, L. (1979) *Meaning and Order in Moroccan Society: Three Essays in Cultural Analysis*. Cambridge: Cambridge University Press.

Giles, H., Coupland, N. and Coupland, J. (eds) (1991) *Contexts of Accommodation*. Cambridge and Paris: Cambridge University Press and Maison des Sciences de l'Homme.

Gilroy, P. (1993) *The Black Atlantic: Modernity and Double Consciousness*. Cambridge, MA: Harvard University Press.

Gil-White, F.J. (2001) Are ethnic groups biological 'species' to the human brain? Essentialism in our cognition of some social categories. *Current Anthropology* 42 (4), 515–553. doi:10.1086/321802.

Gil-White, F.J. (2005) The study of ethnicity and nationalism needs better categories: Clearing up the confusions that result from blurring analytic and lay concepts. *Journal of Bioeconomics* 7 (3), 239–270. doi:10.1007/s10818-005-3007-z.

Glenn, E.N. (2008) Yearning for lightness. *Gender & Society* 22 (3), 281–302. doi:10.1177/0891243208316089.

Glick Schiller, N. (2005) Blood and belonging: Long distance nationalism and the world beyond. In S. McKinnon and S. Silverman (eds) *Complexities Beyond Nature & Nurture* (pp. 289–312). Chicago, IL: University of Chicago Press.

Glick Schiller, N. and Fouron, G.E. (2001) *Georges Woke Up Laughing: Long-distance Nationalism and the Search for Home*. Durham, NC: Duke University Press.

Goffman, E. (1963) *Stigma: Notes on the Management of Spoiled Identity*. New York: Simon & Schuster.

Goffman, E. (1966) *Behavior in Public Places*. New York: Free Press.

Goffman, E. (1971) *The Presentation of Self in Everyday Life*. Harmondsworth: Penguin.

Goffman, E. (1974) *Frame Analysis: An Essay on the Organization of Experience*. New York: Harper & Row.

Gökarıksel, B. (2012) The intimate politics of secularism and the headscarf: The mall, the neighborhood, and the public square in Istanbul. *Gender, Place & Culture* 19 (1), 1–20. doi:10.1080/0966369X.2011.633428.

Goodwin, C. (2000) Action and embodiment within situated human interaction. *Journal of Pragmatics* 32 (10), 1489–1522. doi:10.1016/S0378-2166(99)00096-X.

Graeber, D. (2001) *Toward an Anthropological Theory of Value: The False Coin of Our Own Dreams*. New York: Palgrave Macmillan.

Grosz, E. (1994) *Volatile Bodies*. Bloomington, IN: Indiana University Press.

Gudeman, S. (2008) *Economy's Tension: The Dialectics of Community and Market*. New York: Berghahn Books.

Guénif Souilamas, N. (2000) *Des Beurettes aux Descendantes d'Immigrants Nord-Africains*. Paris: Bernard Grasset.

Gumperz, J. (1982) *Discourse Strategies*. New York: Cambridge University Press.

Hage, G. (2005) A not so multi-sited ethnography of a not so imagined community. *Anthropological Theory* 5 (4), 463–475. doi:10.1177/1463499605059232.

Hall, K. and Bucholtz, M. (1995) *Gender Articulated: Language and the Socially Constructed Self*. New York: Routledge.

Hannam, K., Sheller, M. and Urry, J. (2006) Editorial: Mobilities, immobilities, and moorings. *Mobilities* 1 (1), 1–22.

Hannerz, U. (1987) The world in creolisation. *Africa: Journal of the International African Institute* 57 (4), 546–559.

Hannerz, U. (2003) Being there ... and there ... and there!: Reflections on multi-site ethnography. *Ethnography* 4 (2), 201–216. doi:10.1177/14661381030042003.

Harwood, J. and Giles, H. (2005) *Intergroup Communication: Multiple Perspectives.* New York: Peter Lang.

Haslam, N., Rothschild, L. and Ernst, D. (2000) Essentialist beliefs about social categories. *British Journal of Social Psychology* 39 (1), 113–127.

Hatton, T.J. and Williamson, J.G. (eds) (1994) *Migration and the International Labor Market, 1850–1939.* London: Routledge.

Heath, J. (1989) *From Code-switching to Borrowing: Foreign and Diglossic Mixing in Moroccan Arabic.* New York: Kegan Paul International.

Hebdige, D. (1979) *Subculture: The Meaning of Style.* London: Meuthen & Co.

Heller, M. (2002) *Éléments d'une Sociolinguistique Critique.* Paris: Didier.

Heller, M. (2010) *Paths to Post-Nationalism: A Critical Ethnography of Language and Identity.* Oxford and Cambridge, MA: Oxford University Press.

Héran, F., Filhon, A. and Deprez, C. (2002) La dynamique des langues en France au fil du XXe siècle. *Population Sociétés* 376, 1–4.

Herskovits, M.J. (1990) *The Myth of the Negro Past* (3rd edn). Boston, MA: Beacon Press.

Hester, S. and Eglin, P. (eds) (1997) *Culture in Action: Studies in Membership Categorization Analysis.* Lanham, MD and London: International Institute for Ethnomethodology and University Press of America.

Hirschfeld, L.A. (1998) *Race in the Making.* Cambridge, MA: MIT Press.

Holes, C. (1995) *Modern Arabic: Structure, Functions, and Varieties.* London: Longman.

Hollinshead, K. (2004) Tourism and third space populations: The restless motion of diaspora peoples. In T. Coles and D.J. Timothy (eds) *Tourism, Diasporas and Space* (pp. 50–61). London and New York: Routledge.

Housley, W. and Hester, S.K. (eds) (2002) *Language, Interaction, and National Identity: Studies in the Social Organisation of National Identity in Talk-in-interaction.* Aldershot: Ashgate.

Howe, M. (2005) *Morocco: The Islamist Awakening and Other Challenges.* Oxford: Oxford University Press.

Hutnyk, J. (2005) Hybridity. *Ethnic and Racial Studies* 28 (1), 79–102. doi:10.1080/014198 7042000280021.

Hymes, D. (1972) The scope of sociolinguistics. In D.M. Smith and R.W. Shuy (eds) *23rd Annual Round Table Sociolinguistics: Current Trends and Prospects* (pp. 313–331). Washington: Georgetown University Press.

Irvine, J. (1989) When talk isn't cheap: Language and political economy. *American Ethnologist* 16 (2), 248–267.

Jones, R. (2009) Categories, borders and boundaries. *Progress in Human Geography* 33 (2), 174–189. doi:10.1177/0309132508089828.

Joppke, C. (1998) *Challenge to the Nation-State: Immigration in Western Europe and the United States.* Oxford and New York: Oxford University Press.

Joppke, C. (1999) *Immigration and the Nation-state: The United States, Germany, and Great Britain.* Oxford and New York: Oxford University Press.

Joppke, C. and Morawska, E.T. (eds) (2003) *Toward Assimilation and Citizenship: Immigrants in Liberal Nation-states.* New York: Palgrave Macmillan.

Juillard, C. (1990) L'expansion du wolof à Zinguinchor. Les interactions à caractere commerciale. *Plurilinguismes* 2, 103–154.

Kalra, V.S., Kaur, R. and Hutnyk, J. (2005) *Diaspora and Hybridity. Theory, Culture & Society.* London: Sage.

Kapchan, D. (1996) *Gender on the Market: Moroccan Women and the Revoicing of Tradition*. Philadelphia, PA: University of Pennsylvania Press.

Kapchan, D.A. and Strong, P.T. (1999) Theorizing the hybrid. *Journal of American Folklore* 112 (445), 239–253. doi:10.2307/541360.

Katz, J. (1999) *How Emotions Work*. Chicago, IL and London: University of Chicago Press.

Kawale, R. (2004) Inequalities of the heart: The performance of emotion work by lesbian and bisexual women in London, England. *Social & Cultural Geography* 5 (4), 565. doi: 10.1080/1464936042000317703.

Kendon, A. (2004) *Gesture: Visible Action as Utterance*. Cambridge: Cambridge University Press.

Kharraki, A. (2001) Moroccan sex-based linguistic difference in bargaining. *Discourse & Society* 12 (5), 615–632. doi:10.1177/0957926501012005003.

Khuri, F.I. (1968) The etiquette of bargaining in the Middle East. *American Anthropologist* 70 (4), 698–706.

King, B.E.M. and Gamage, M.A. (1994) Measuring the value of the ethnic connection: Expatriate travelers from Australia to Sri Lanka. *Journal of Travel Research* 33 (2), 46–50.

King, R. and Christou, A. (2009) Cultural geographies of counter-diasporic migration: Perspectives from the study of second-generation 'returnees' to Greece. *Population, Space and Place* 15 (2), 103–119.

Koven, M. (2002) Comparing bilinguals' quoted performances of self and others in tellings of the same experience in two languages. *Language in Society* 30 (4), 513–558.

Koven, M. (2004) Transnational perspectives on sociolinguistic capital among Luso-descendants in France and Portugal. *American Ethnologist* 31 (2), 270–290.

Koven, M. (2007) *Selves in Two Languages: Bilinguals' Verbal Enactments of Identity in French and Portuguese*. Amsterdam and Philadelphia, PA: John Benjamins.

Kroeger, B. (2003) *Passing: When People Can't Be Who They Are*. New York: Public Affairs.

Kroskrity, P. (ed.) (2000) *Regimes of Language: Ideologies, Polities, and Identities*. Santa Fe, NM: School of American Research Press.

Kurzac-Souali, A.-C. (2005) La revalorisation de la médina dans l'espace urbain au Maroc, un espace urbain revisité par les élites et le tourisme. In N. Boumaza (ed.) *Villes réelles, villes projetées. La Fabrication urbaine au Maghreb* (pp. 377–390). Rabat and Paris: Centre Jacques Berque and Maisonneuve & Larose.

Kymlicka, W. (1995) *Multicultural Citizenship: A Liberal Theory of Minority Rights*. Oxford and New York: Clarendon Press and Oxford University Press.

Kymlicka, W. (2007) *Multicultural Odysseys: Navigating the New International Politics of Diversity*. New York: Oxford University Press.

Labov, W. (1966) *The Social Stratification of English in New York City*. Washington, DC: Center for Applied Linguistics.

Lacoste-Dujardin, C. (1992) *Yasmina et les Autres de Nanterre et d'Ailleurs: Filles de Parents Maghrébins en France*. Paris: La Découverte.

Lakoff, G. (1990) *Women, Fire, and Dangerous Things: What Categories Reveal About the Mind*. Chicago, IL: University of Chicago Press.

Lamont, M. and Molnár, V. (2002) The study of boundaries in the social sciences. *Annual Review of Sociology* 28, 167–195. doi:10.1146/annurev.soc.28.110601.141107.

Leichtman, M.A. (2002) Transforming brain drain into capital gain: Morocco's changing relationship with migration and remittances. *Journal of North African Studies* 7 (1), 109–137.

Leiken, R.S. (2005) Europe's angry Muslims. *Foreign Affairs* 84 (4), 120. doi:10.2307/2003 4425.

Le Page, R.B. and Tabouret-Keller, A. (1985) *Acts of Identity: Creole-based Approaches to Language and Ethnicity*. Cambridge and New York: Cambridge University Press.

Lepoutre, D. (1997) *Coeur de Banlieue: Codes, Rites et Langages*. Paris: O. Jacob.

Lesthaeghe, R. (ed.) (2000) *Communities and Generations: Turkish and Moroccan Populations in Belgium*. Brussels: NIDI/CBGS Publications.

Lévi-Strauss, C. (1966) *The Savage Mind*. Chicago, IL and London: University of Chicago Press.

Levitt, P. (2002) The ties that change: Relations to the ancestral home over the life cycle. In P. Levitt and M.C. Waters (eds) *The Changing Face of Home: The Transnational Lives of the Second Generation* (pp. 123–144). New York: Russell Sage Foundation.

Levitt, P. (2009) Roots and routes: Understanding the lives of the second generation transnationally. *Journal of Ethnic and Migration Studies* 35 (7), 1225–1242. doi:10.1080/13691 830903006309.

Levitt, P. and Waters, M.C. (eds) (2002) *The Changing Face of Home: The Transnational Lives of the Second Generation*. New York: Russell Sage Foundation.

Lindenfeld, J. (1990) *Speech and Sociability at French Urban Marketplaces*. Amsterdam & Philadelphia, PA: John Benjamins.

Li Wei (ed.) (2010) *Bilingualism and Multilingualism*. London: Routledge.

Louis, B. (2005) The difference sameness makes: Racial recognition and the 'narcissism of minor differences'. *Ethnicities* 5 (3), 343–364. doi:10.1177/1468796805054960.

Mahtani, M. (2002) Tricking the border guards: Performing race. *Environment and Planning D: Society and Space* 20 (4), 425–440. doi:10.1068/d261t.

Manço, A. (1999) *Intégration et Identités: Stratégies et Positions Des Jeunes Issus de l'Immigration*. Paris and Brussels: DeBoeck Université.

Marcus, G.E. (1995) Ethnography in/of the world system: The emergence of multi-sited ethnography. *Annual Review of Anthropology* 24, 95–117.

Maréchal, B., Allievi, S., Dassetto, F. and Nielsen, J. (eds) (2003) *Muslims in the Enlarged Europe: Religion and Society. Muslim Minorities*. Leiden: Brill.

Marley, D. (2004) Language attitudes in Morocco following recent changes in language policy. *Language Policy* 3 (1), 25–46. doi:10.1023/B:LPOL.0000017724.16833.66.

Massey, D.B. (2005) *For Space*. London: Sage.

Mauss, M. (1950) Les techniques du corps. In *Sociologie et Anthropologie* (pp. 363–386). Paris: PUF.

Mavroudi, E. (2007) Diaspora as process: (De)constructing boundaries. *Geography Compass* 1 (3), 467–479.

McDowell, L. (1999) *Gender, Identity, and Place: Understanding Feminist Geographies*. Minneapolis, MN: University of Minnesota Press.

Melliani, F. (2000) *La Langue du Quartier: Appropriation de l'Espace et Identités Urbaines chez des Jeunes Issus de l'Immigration Maghrébine en Banlieue Rouennaise*. Paris: L'Harmattan.

Melliani, F. and Laroussi, F. (1998) Comportements langagiers des Maghrébin-Francos à Saint-Etienne-du-Rouvray: La construction d'une identité mixte. *Etudes Normandes* 1, 72–83.

Merleau-Ponty, M. (2002) *Phenomenology of Perception* (Trans. Colin Smith). Routledge.

Mernissi, F. (1991) *The Veil and the Male Elite: A Feminist Interpretation of Women's Rights in Islam*. Reading, MA: Addison-Wesley.

Miller, D. (2010) Anthropology in blue jeans. *American Ethnologist* 37 (3), 415–428. doi:10.1111/j.1548-1425.2010.01263.x.

Milroy, L. (1980) *Language and Social Networks*. Oxford: Blackwell.

Minca, C. and Wagner, L. (2016) *Moroccan Dreams: Orientalist Myth, Colonial Legacy*. London: I.B. Tauris.

Modood, T., Triandafyllidou, A. and Zapata-Barrero, R. (eds) (2006) *Multiculturalism, Muslims and Citizenship: A European Approach*. London: Routledge.

Mondada, L. (2009) Emergent focused interactions in public places: A systematic analysis of the multimodal achievement of a common interactional space. *Journal of Pragmatics* 41 (10), 1977–1997.

Montagne, R. (1973) *The Berbers: Their Social and Political Organisation*. New York: Frank Cass.

Mountz, A. and Wright, R.A. (1996) Daily life in the transnational migrant community of San Agustìn, Oaxaca and Poughkeepsie, New York. *Diaspora* 5 (3), 403–428.

Muehlmann, S. (2014) The speech community and beyond: Language and the nature of the social aggregate. In N.J. Enfield, P. Kockelman and J. Sidnell (eds) *The Cambridge Handbook of Linguistic Anthropology* (pp. 578–598). Cambridge: Cambridge University Press.

Myers-Scotton, C. (1990) Elite closure as boundary maintenance: The case of Africa. In B. Westein (ed.) *Language Policy and Political Development* (pp. 25–42). Norwood, NJ: Ablex.

Myers-Scotton, C. (1993) *Social Motivations for Codeswitching: Evidence from Africa*. Oxford: Clarendon Press.

Myers-Scotton, C. (1998) *Codes and Consequences: Choosing Linguistic Varieties*. New York: Oxford University Press.

Nash, C. (2002) Genealogical identities. *Environment and Planning D: Society and Space* 20, 27–52.

Nash, C. (2004) Genetic kinship. *Cultural Studies* 18 (1), 1–33. doi:10.1080/09502380420 00181593.

Nash, C. (2005) Geographies of relatedness. *Transactions of the Institute of British Geographers* 30 (4), 449–462.

Nash, C. (2008) *Of Irish Descent: Origin Stories, Genealogy, and the Politics of Belonging*. Syracuse, NY: Syracuse University Press.

Nguyen, T.-H. and King, B. (2004) The culture of tourism in the diaspora: The case of the Vietnamese community in Australia. In T. Coles and D.J. Timothy (eds) *Tourism, Diasporas and Space* (pp. 172–187). London: Routledge.

Noble, G. and Watkins, M. (2003) So, how did Bourdieu learn to play tennis? Habitus, consciousness and habituation. *Cultural Studies* 17 (3–4), 520–539.

Noiriel, G. (1988) *Le Creuset Français. Histoire de l'Immigration. XIXe–XXe Siècles*. Paris: Seuil.

Orr, W.W.F. (2007) The bargaining genre: A study of retail encounters in traditional Chinese local markets. *Language in Society* 36 (1), 73–103. doi:10.1017/S0047404507070042.

Ossman, S. (2002) *Three Faces of Beauty*. Durham, NC: Duke University Press.

Ouali, N. (ed.) (2004) *Trajectoires et Dynamiques Migratoires Des Marocains de Belgique*. Louvain-La Neuve, BE: Bruylant-Academia.

Pachucki, M.A., Sabrina, P. and Michèle, L. (2007) Boundary processes: Recent theoretical developments and new contributions. *Poetics* 35 (6), 331–351. doi:10.1016/j. poetic.2007.10.001.

Parkin, D. (2012) From multilingual classification to translingual ontology: Concluding commentary. *Diversities* 14 (2), 73–85.

Pennell, C.R. (2000) *Morocco Since 1830: A History*. London: C. Hurst.

Phillips, J. and Potter, R.B. (2006) Black skins–white masks: Postcolonial reflections on race, gender and second generation return migration to the Caribbean. *Singapore Journal of Tropical Geography* 27 (3), 309–325.

Piller, I. (2002) Passing for a native speaker: Identity and success in second language learning. *Journal of Sociolinguistics* 6 (2), 179–208. doi:10.1111/1467-9481.00184.

Portes, A. and Rumbaut, R.G. (2001) *Legacies: The Story of the Immigrant Second Generation*. Berkeley, CA and New York: University of California Press and Russell Sage Foundation.

Potter, R.B. and Phillips, J. (2006a) 'Mad dogs and transnational migrants?' Bajan-Brit second-generation migrants and accusations of madness. *Annals of the Association of American Geographers* 96 (3), 586–600. doi:10.1111/j.1467-8306.2006.00707.x.

Potter, R.B. and Phillips, J. (2006b) Both black and symbolically white: The 'Bajan-Brit' return migrant as post-colonial hybrid. *Ethnic and Racial Studies* 29 (5), 901–927. doi:10. 1080/01419870600813942.

Prentice, D.A. and Miller, D.T. (2007) Psychological essentialism of human categories. *Current Directions in Psychological Science* 16 (4), 202–206. doi:10.1111/j.1467-8721. 2007.00504.x.

Rachik, H. (ed.) (2006) *Usages de l'Identité Amazighe au Maroc*. Casablanca: Fondation Konrad Adenauer.

Ramirez, M., Skrbiš, Z. and Emmison, M. (2007) Transnational family reunions as lived experience: Narrating a Salvadoran autoethnography. *Identities* 14 (4), 411–431.

Rampton, B. (2006) *Language in Late Modernity*. Cambridge: Cambridge University Press.

Reynolds, T. (2008) Ties that bind: Families, social capital and Caribbean second-generation return migration. Working Paper No. 46, Sussex Centre for Migration Research, University of Sussex, Brighton.

Ritchie, J. and Lewis, J. (2003) *Qualitative Research Practice: A Guide for Social Science Students and Researchers*. London and Thousand Oaks, CA: Sage Publications.

Romaine, S. (1991) *Bilingualism*. Oxford: Basil Blackwell.

Rumbaut, R.G. and Portes, A. (eds) (2001) *Ethnicities: Children of Immigrants in America*. Berkeley, CA and New York: University of California Press and Russell Sage Foundation.

Sacks, H. (1992) *Lectures on Conversation. Vol I & II* (ed. G. Jefferson). Oxford and Cambridge, MA: Blackwell.

Saldanha, A. (2006) Reontologising race: The machinic geography of phenotype. *Environment and Planning D* 24 (1), 9–24.

Saldanha, A. (2007) *Psychedelic White*. Minneapolis, MN: University of Minnesota Press.

Samuels, D. (1999) The whole and the sum of the parts, or, how Cookie and the Cupcakes told the story of Apache history in San Carlos. *Journal of American Folklore* 112 (445), 464–474. doi:10.2307/541373.

Sánchez, M.C. and Schlossberg, L. (eds) (2001) *Passing: Identity and Interpretation in Sexuality, Race, and Religion*. New York: New York University Press.

Sayad, A. (2004) *The Suffering of the Immigrant* (trans. D. Macey). Cambridge: Polity.

Sayyid, S. (2000) Beyond Westphalia: Nations and diasporas – the case of the Muslim Umma. In B. Hesse (ed.) *Un/settled Multiculturalisms: Diasporas, Entanglements, Trans-ruptions* (pp. 51–72). London: Zed Books.

Schegloff, E.A. (2007) A tutorial on membership categorization. *Journal of Pragmatics* 39, 462–482.

Schieffelin, B.B., Woolard, K.A. and Kroskrity, P.V. (1998) *Language Ideologies: Practice and Theory*. New York: Oxford University Press.

Schnapper, D. (1999) From nation-state to the transnational world: On the meaning and usefulness of diaspora as a concept. *Diaspora* 8 (3), 225–255.

Sefrioui, F. (2005) *Marocains de l'Exterieur et Developpement. Pour une Nouvelle Dynamique de l'Investissement*. Rabat: Fondation Hassan II Pour les Marocains Residents a l'Etranger.

Semin, G.R. and Smith, E.R. (eds) (2008) *Embodied Grounding: Social, Cognitive, Affective, and Neuroscientific Approaches*. Cambridge: Cambridge University Press.

Shilling, C. (2003) *The Body and Social Theory*. London: SAGE.

Shilling, C. (2004) Physical capital and situated action: A new direction for corporeal sociology. *British Journal of Sociology of Education* 25 (4), 473. doi:10.1080/0142569042 000236961.

Shuval, J.T. (2000) Diaspora migration: Definitonal ambiguities and a theoretical paradigm. *International Migration* 38 (5), 41–57.

Silverstein, P.A. (2004) *Algeria in France: Transpolitics, Race, and Nation*. Bloomington, IN: Indiana University Press.

Simon, P. (1999) L'immigration et L'intégration Dans Les Sciences Sociales En France Depuis 1945. In P. DeWitte (ed.) *Immigration et Intégration : L'état Des Savoirs*. Paris: Éditions la Découverte.

Skeggs, B. (1997) *Formations of Class and Gender: Becoming Respectable*. London: Sage.

Skeggs, B. (1999) Matter out of place: Visibility and sexualities in leisure spaces. *Leisure Studies* 18 (3), 213–232.

Skeggs, B. (2004) *Class, Self, Culture*. London: Routledge.

Smith, A. (2003) Place replaced: Colonial nostalgia and pied-noir pilgrimages to Malta. *Cultural Anthropology* 18 (3), 329–364.

Smith, L.B. (2005) Emerging ideas about categories. In L. Gershkoff-Stowe and D.H. Rakison (eds) *Building Object Categories in Developmental Time* (pp. 159–173). Mahwah, NJ: Lawrence Erlbaum.

Sniper, B.B., Selmi, R. and Appela, K. (2003) *Entre Deux. mp3*. Paris: Desh Music.

Sollors, W. (1986) *Beyond Ethnicity: Consent and Descent in American Culture*. New York: Oxford University Press.

Sorensen, N.N. (2004) *Migrant Remittances as a Development Tool: The Case of Morocco*. Copenhagen: Danish Institute for Development Studies.

Stephen, L. (2007) *Transborder Lives: Indigenous Oaxacans in Mexico, California, and Oregon*. Durham, NC: Duke University Press.

Stephenson, M.L. (2002) Travelling to the ancestral homelands: The aspirations and experiences of a UK Caribbean community. *Current Issues in Tourism* 5 (5), 378–425.

Stokoe, E. (2012) Moving forward with membership categorization analysis: Methods for systematic analysis. *Discourse Studies* 14 (3), 277–303. doi:10.1177/1461445612 441534.

Storr, V.H. (2008) The market as a social space: On the meaningful extraeconomic conversations that can occur in markets. *Review of Austrian Economics* 21 (2–3), 135–150. doi:10.1007/s11138-007-0034-0.

Tavory, I. (2010) Of yarmulkes and categories: Delegating boundaries and the phenomenology of interactional expectation. *Theory and Society* 39 (1), 49–68. doi:10.1007/ s11186-009-9100-x.

Tetreault, C. (2004) Communicative performances of social identity in an Algerian-French neighborhood in Paris. Austin, TX: University of Texas at Austin.

The Economist (2015) Jihad at the heart of Europe, 21 November. See http://www.economist.com/news/briefing/21678840-brussels-not-just-europes-political-and-military -capitalit-also-centre-its.

Tilly, C. (2004) Social boundary mechanisms. *Philosophy of the Social Sciences* 34 (2), 211–236. doi:10.1177/0048393103262551.

Tilmatine, M. (ed.) (1997) *Enseignement des Langues d'Origine et Immigration Nord-Africaine en Europe: Langue Maternelle ou Langue d'Etat?* Paris: INALCO/CEDREA-CRB.

Tölölyan, K. (1996) Rethinking diaspora(s): Stateless power in the transnational moment. *Diaspora* 5 (1), 3–37.

Tribalat, M. (1995) *Faire France: Une Grande Enquête sur les Immigrés et Leurs Enfants.* Essais. Paris: Editions La Découverte.

Tribalat, M. (1996) *De l'Immigration à l'Assimilation: Enquête sur les Populations d'Origine Étrangère en France.* Paris: Éditions la Découverte/INED.

Twine, F.W. (1998) Brown skinned white girls: Class, culture and the construction of white identity in suburban communities. *Gender, Place and Culture* 3 (2), 205–224.

Urciuoli, B. (1996) *Exposing Prejudice: Puerto Rican Experiences of Language, Race, and Class. Institutional Structures of Feeling.* Boulder: Westview Press.

van Amersfoort, H. and van Heelsum, A. (2007) Moroccan Berber immigrants in The Netherlands, their associations and transnational ties: A quest for identity and recognition. *Immigrants & Minorities* 25 (3), 234. doi:10.1080/02619280802407343.

Van den Berg, M.E. (1986) Language planning and language use in Taiwan: Social identity, language accommodation and language choice behavior. *International Journal of the Sociology of Language* 1986 (59), 97–115. doi:10.1515/ijsl.1986.59.97.

van Wolputte, S. (2004) Hang on to your self: Of bodies, embodiment, and selves. *Annual Review of Anthropology* 33 (1), 251–269. doi:10.1146/annurev.anthro.33.070203.143749.

Verdery, K. (1993) Whither 'nation' and 'nationalism'? *Daedalus* 122 (3), 37–46.

Vermeulen, H. and Govers, C. (eds) (1994) *The Anthropology of Ethnicity: Beyond Ethnic Groups and Boundaries.* Amsterdam: Het Spinhuis.

Vigouroux, C. (2005) 'There are no whites in Africa': Territoriality, language, and identity. *Language & Communication* 25 (3), 237–255.

Wagner, L. (2006) Les pratiques langagières des jeunes d'origine Marocaine au Maroc. Enquête sur les compétences linguistiques aux marchés. Mémoire de Masters 2 Recherche, Paris: Université René Descartes – Paris V.

Wagner, L. (2008) Pratiquer la langue pendant les vacances: Les compétences communicatives el la catégorisation de Françaises d'origine parentale Marocaine. *Cahier de l'Observatoire des pratiques linguistiques 2. Migrations et plurilinguisme en France* (September), 80–86.

Wagner, L. (2011) Negotiating diasporic mobilities and becomings: Interactions and practices of Europeans of Moroccan descent on holiday in Morocco. Doctoral thesis, University College London. See http://discovery.ucl.ac.uk/1317815/.

Wagner, L. (2012) Feeling diasporic. Tilburg Papers in Cultural Studies No. 21. Babylon Center for Studies of the Multicultural Society, Tilburg University. See http://www.tilburguniversity.edu/research/institutes-and-research-groups/babylon/tpcs/download-tpcs-paper-21.pdf/.

Wagner, L. (2015a) Shopping for diasporic belonging: Being 'local' or being 'mobile' as a VFR visitor in the ancestral homeland. *Population, Space and Place* (March, online). doi:10.1002/psp.1919.

Wagner, L. (2015b) 'Tourist price' and diasporic visitors: Negotiating the value of descent. *Valuation Studies* 3 (2), 119–148. doi:10.3384/VS.2001-5992.1532119.

Wagner, L. (2015c) Using silence to 'pass': Embodiment and interactional categorization in a diasporic context. *Multilingua – Journal of Cross-Cultural and Interlanguage Communication* 34 (5). doi:10.1515/multi-2014-1039.

Walters, K. (1999) 'Opening the Door of Paradise a Cubit': Educated tunisian women, embodied linguistic practice, and theories of language and gender. In M. Bucholtz, A.C. Liang and L.A. Sutton (eds) *Reinventing Identities: The Gendered Self in Discourse* (pp. 200–216). New York: Oxford University Press.

Walters, K. (2003) Fergie's prescience: The changing nature of diglossia in Tunisia. *International Journal of the Sociology of Language* 163, 77–109.

Weinreich, U. (1953) *Languages in Contact: Findings and Problems*. The Hague: Walter de Gruyter.

Werbner, P. (2002) The place which is diaspora: Citizenship, religion and gender in the making of chaordic transnationalism. *Journal of Ethnic and Migration Studies* 28 (1), 119–133.

Whalen, D.H. and Lindblom, B. (2006) Speech: Biological basis. In K. Brown (ed.) *Encyclopedia of Language & Linguistics*. Oxford: Elsevier. See http://www.sciencedirect.com/science/article/B7T84-4M3C3K0-328/2/02440d64aa93ca6f86478987e5751148.

Willis, P.E. (1977) *Learning to Labour: How Working Class Kids Get Working Class Jobs*. Farnborough: Saxon House.

Wimmer, A. (2008) The making and unmaking of ethnic boundaries: A multilevel process theory. *American Journal of Sociology* 113 (4), 970–1022. doi: 10.1086/522803.

Wimmer, A. (2009) Herder's heritage and the boundary-making approach: Studying ethnicity in immigrant societies. *Sociological Theory* 27 (3), 244–270. doi:10.1111/j.1467-9558.2009.01347.x.

Woolard, K. 1985. Language variation and cultural hegemony: Toward an integration of sociolinguistic and social theory. *American Ethnologist* 12 (4), 738–748.

Woolard, K. (1999) Simultaneity and bivalency as strategies in bilingualism. *Journal of Linguistic Anthropology* 8 (1), 3–29.

Ylänne-McEwan, V. and Coupland, N. (2004) Accommodation theory: A conceptual resource for intercultural sociolinguistics. In H. Spencer-Oatey (ed.) *Culturally Speaking: Managing Rapport through Talk Across Cultures* (pp. 191–214). London: Continuum International.

Zentella, A.C. (1997) *Growing up Bilingual*. Malden, MA: Blackwell.

Ziamari, K. (2008) *Le Code Switching au Maroc: L'Arabe Marocain au Contact du Français*. Paris: L'Harmattan.

Index